CYCLICAL GROWTH
IN MARKET AND
PLANNED ECONOMIES

CYCLICAL GROWTH
in Market and
Planned Economies

Edited by Claude Hillinger

OXFORD · CLARENDON PRESS
1992

Oxford University Press, Walton Street, Oxford OX2 6DP

Oxford New York Toronto
Delhi Bombay Calcutta Madras Karachi
Petaling Jaya Singapore Hong Kong Tokyo
Nairobi Dar es Salaam Cape Town
Melbourne Auckland
and associated companies in
Berlin Ibadan

Oxford is a trade mark of Oxford University Press

Published in the United States
by Oxford University Press, New York

British Library Cataloguing in Publication Data
Data available

Library of Congress Cataloging in Publication Data
Cyclical growth in market and planned economies / edited by Claude Hillinger.
p.   cm.
Includes bibliographical references.
1. Business cycles. I. Hillinger, Claude, 1930–
HB3714.C93   1992   338.5'42—dc20   92–16083
ISBN 0–19–828314–8

Typeset by Pure Tech Corporation, Pondicherry, India
Printed in Great Britain by
Bookcraft (Bath) Ltd,
Midsomer Norton, Avon

Preface

The papers assembled in this volume reflect two streams of research. One evolved in the context of the project on economic fluctuations at the Seminar for Mathematical Economics (SEMECON) in the Economics Department of the University of Munich. The other tradition is that of a more loosely associated group of economists at various academic and research institutes in Hungary who have been studying the growth cycles of planned economies. As will be seen from the contributions, the two streams of research dealing with distinct economic systems arrived at remarkably similar descriptions and explanations of economic fluctuations. The explanations focus on technology and on adjustment lags in investment and production. These appear to be more alike across ecomomic systems than has been assumed.

Research at SEMECON is a continuing team effort, and the papers published here build on earlier published and unpublished contributions. Much has been available only in the form of diploma theses and dissertations.

This book could not have been realized without the support of several individuals. Significant contributions to the early phases of the research at SEMECON were made by Klaus Schueler and Gerhard Wehner. Utz P. Reich had the idea for the first workshop. He also did much of the planning and organizational work which allowed the workshop to convene in Starnberg, near Munich, in 1985. Attila Chikan proposed and organized the two subsequent workshops at Lake Balaton, Hungary, in 1986 and 1988. Giancarlo Gandolfo donated generously of his time and expertise to read an early version of the manuscript; he provided many valuable comments which are reflected in the final version. Birgit Edener (at the time a student of economics) and Souila Puffarth (at the time a student of statistics) efficiently handled the word processing despite the pressure of academic deadlines.

The research at SEMECON was also supported by institutional grants from Stiftung Volkswagenwerk (Grant no. II 2354, 34 668) and from Deutsche Forschungsgemeinschaft (Grant no. Hi 332/1–3).

I sincerely thank all of the above for their encouragement and support.

May 1991   C. H.

Contents

Contents

List of Contributors

ANDRAS BRÓDY is Scientific Adviser with the Institute of Economics of the Hungarian Academy of Sciences, and Chairman of its Council of Economic Science. He is also a Professor at Budapest University.

He is a Fellow of the Econometric Society, a member of the Council of the Input-Output Association and editor of its journal *Economic Systems Research*. His main research interest has been in the area of multisectoral growth processes. He is the author of a well-known work on the socialist economy: *Proportions, Prices and Planning* (1970). More recently, he wrote *Slowdown: Global Economic Maladies* (1985).

ATTILA CHIKAN is Professor and Chairman of the Department of Business Economics of the Budapest University of Economics.

After postgraduate studies at Stanford University, he had an international career with over 200 publications in Hungarian, English, Russian, and German. He is especially interested in the economics of inventories and in logistics. Professor Chikan has prominent positions in many national and international institutions and organizations.

CLAUDE HILLINGER is Professor of Economics at the University of Munich, and Director of the Seminar for Mathematical Economics—SEMECON.

Beginning with his dissertation at the University of Chicago, his main research focus has been on economic fluctuations. A related interest concerns the use of the methodology of the natural sciences in applied econometrics. He has published articles on economic cycles and various other topics in micro- and macroeconomics.

MICHAEL REITER joined the SEMECON research team on economic fluctuations after studying economics and philosophy.

He has written or co-authored articles in economics and philosophy and is now completing his dissertation on econometric models of cyclical growth.

MONIKA SEBOLD-BENDER is a management consultant with Mummert & Partner.

After studying statistics she joined the SEMECON research team. Her research has focused on the time-series analysis of economic fluctuations and on the application of maximum entropy methods in this context. This has also been the theme of her publications and dissertation.

TAMAS G. TARJAN is Senior Research Fellow at the Institute of Economics of the Hungarian Academy of Sciences.

Before turning to economics, he had obtained a Ph.D. in information theory. Dr Tarjan has published articles on mathematical and economic topics. He is especially interested in economic cycles and the investment process.

THILO WESER is a management consultant with McKinsey & Co.

After obtaining a Ph.D. in experimental physics, he joined the research on economic fluctuations at SEMECON, University of Munich, and obtained a second Ph.D. in economics. Dr Weser has published papers in physics and economics.

List of Abbreviations

AIC	Akaike Information Criterion
ARIMA	autoregressive integrated moving average
CAT	Criterion for Autoregressive Transfer Functions
DECG	disequilibrium econometrics of cyclical growth
EECM	early econometric cycle models
FOA	first-order accelerator
FPE	final prediction error
GDP	gross domestic product
GFCF	gross fixed capital formation
GT	*General Theory of Employment, Interest and Money* (Keynes 1936)
HEA	*History of Economic Analysis* (Schumpeter 1954)
ICT	investment cycle theory
II	inventory investment
ML	maximum likelihood
MSE	mean squared error
NCM	New Classical macroeconomics
NKE	New Keynesian economics
NLS	nonlinear least squares
OLS	ordinary least squares
RBCT	real business cycle theory
RD	residual demand
RE	rational expectations
SNR	signal–noise ratio
SOA	second-order accelerator
VAR	vector autoregression

Introduction

Macroeconomics has been through half a century of paradigm changes at an accelerating pace: Keynesianism, monetarism, equilibrium business cycle theory, first with monetary, then with technology shocks, and New Keynesian theory are only the most prominent movements to rise and fall (at least in the eyes of all but their most devoted adherents) during this period.

Equally dramatic have been the alternations of fashionable macroeconometric methodologies: large-scale econometric models, VAR and ARIMA models, unit roots, and stochastic trends.

At the end of these developments, macroeconomics is fragmented and has been largely discredited. At many universities it is no longer a basic required subject, and few economists list it as their primary field of research.

This book reports on a strand of research that has evolved apart from the spectacular battles of macroeconomics. This strand goes back at least to the work of Juglar and others in the nineteenth century, and incorporates the work of the Accelerationists in the early twentieth century and the pioneering economometricians in the late 1920s and early 1930s. In the 1950s this tradition was merged with Keynesian dynamics by W. A. Phillips and A. R. Bergstrom. Broadly the same approach is currently being employed by G. Gandolfo and associates in Rome and by myself and associates at SEMECON at the University of Munich.

Part I, 'Evolution of Doctrine and Methodology', contains two chapters by myself, which place the following ones in a broader context. In Chapter 1 I do this in relation to the evolution of macroeconomic doctrines. In Chapter 2 I explain the view of the methodology of empirical science, which has decisively influenced the work of SEMECON. A key element in this methodology is that 'stylized facts' must be established independently of the theories designed to explain them.

Part II, 'Economic Fluctuations in Market Economies', contains two SEMECON contributions. Chapter 3, by Hillinger and Sebold-Bender, describes the stylized facts of macroeconomic fluctuations. It is revealed that 15 OECD countries typically show a three- to five-year quasi-cycle in inventory investment and a seven- to ten-year quasi-cycle in equipment investment. Together, these cycles account for a large share of the total fluctuation of output. Chapter 4, by Hillinger and Reiter, contains econometric tests of the models developed at SEMECON to explain these cycles.

Part III, 'Economic Fluctuations in Planned Economies', contains the contributions of the Hungarian economists. In Chapter 5, Chikan looks at some stylized facts concerning cyclical fluctuations in Hungary, which turn out to be remarkably similar to those found in Chapter 3 characterizing the market economies. In Chapter 6, Bródy presents a model of fluctuations, based on the concept of a gestation lag in fixed investment, which goes a long way towards explaining the investment fluctuations of socialist countries and, I suspect, of public investment in market economies as well. In Chapter 7, Tarjan extends Bródy's analysis to the case of gestation lags with more than two periods.

Part IV, 'Microeconomic Foundations', contains two papers on the theoretical underpinning of the SEMECON cycle models. In Chapter 8, Hillinger, Reiter, and Weser show that the second-order accelerator mechanism, which is basic to these models, can be derived from the intertemporal optimization of the firm, in the presence of adjustment costs. Chapter 9 by Weser makes use of the mathematical theory of parametric resonance, in order to show how cyclical behaviour on the part of some firms can be aggregated to obtain the fluctuations observed at the aggregate level.

PART I

Evolution of Doctrine and Methodology

1

Paradigm Change and Scientific Method in the Study of Economic Fluctuations

Claude Hillinger

1. Introduction

The purpose of this chapter is to place the other contributions in perspective. Those of the Hungarian economists evolved independently from the work of SEMECON, from which the remaining contributions are derived. Both approaches are quite distinct from the dominant paradigms of Western macroeconomics since Keynes. They are rather in the *investment cycle tradition*, which evolved and largely dominated the field from about 1870 to 1930 and was then pushed back, first by Keynesianism and then by monetarism. More broadly, the ICT is one of a number of *real* theories of economic fluctuations which over the course of several centuries have alternated with *monetary* theories of fluctuations.

To understand the motivation for the SEMECON approach, it must be placed in the historical context of the evolution of competing paradigms for explaining economic fluctuations. This context is today almost completely missing. The teaching of the history of economic doctrines, as part of graduate education, has been de-emphasized in recent decades. Furthermore, existing histories of thought stress the relatively straightforward evolution of equilibrium theory, rather than the convoluted history of thought regarding fluctuations.

The history of doctrines of economic fluctuations raises the issue of the lack of progress in economics as an empirical science, since, after a particular view has been the dominant orthodoxy for some time, it has regularly been replaced by the essentially opposite view. Historians of thought, seeking to explain paradigm changes in economics, emphasize general cultural influences and changing policy issues. Remarkably, the question of factual truth of the various theories, which one would suppose to be the central issue for an empirical science, is hardly discussed.

In discussing the driving forces in the evolution of economic thought, D. R. Fusfeld has the following to say:

One of the great themes in the advance of economics, then, has been the interaction of ideology and science. . . .

A second theme is the relationship between economic theories and practical problems . . .

A third theme in the development of economics is its close relationship to the climate of opinion. (Fusfeld 1966)

In discussing the failure of economists to test factual hypotheses, M. Blaug remarks:

It is not difficult to think of many good reasons why economists fail to practice the methodology that they preach: all scientists sometimes cling tenaciously to 'degenerating' research programs in the presence of 'progressive' rivals, but economists are particularly prone to this tendency . . . (Blaug 1980 : 260)

A major theme of this chapter is that the non-progressive character of economics, in this as in other areas, is due to a neglect of the standard scientific method of the natural sciences—in particular, a failure to test empirical (descriptive) and theoretical (explanatory) hypotheses. The inception of my own work on economic fluctuations, which later led to the SEMECON research programme, was a direct consequence of the effort systematically to test the two types of hypotheses in relation to economic cycles.

The bulk of the rest of this chapter is devoted to a description of paradigm changes relating to macroeconomic fluctuations. This is a neglected topic in histories of economic thought, which tend to emphasize the evolution of equilibrium analysis.

2. Key Concepts for Analysing the Paradigm Changes in Macroeconomics

This section prepares the ground for the description and analysis of paradigm changes in macroeconomics.

First, a disclaimer: I am not a historian of thought. Moreover, there are no standard histories of the subject. On the pre-Keynesian literature my principal source is Schumpeter's (1954) *History of Economic Analysis*.[1] Also relevant is Haberler's (1958) *Prosperity and Depression*, Part I. Other histories of thought, particularly Spiegel (1971), also contain some useful materials, as does *The New Palgrave* (Eatwell *et al.* 1987). The interpretations of Keynes and subsequent developments are my own. The purpose of this discussion is to bring out features of the major paradigms which are relevant for understanding the origins of current macroeconomics and consequently of the contributions in this book. No conventional history of thought is intended.

The subsequent discussion will be facilitated by defining some key concepts. They come in pairs. Usually, those listed first were associated with each other in one paradigm, while a paradigm change involved a move to the concepts listed second, or vice versa.

[1] Particularly significant passages are: Pt II: Ch. 4, Sect. 3 (*a*); Ch. 6, Sects. 1 and 6; Part III: Ch. 7, Sect. 6.

2.1. Equilibrium–disequilibrium

In economic theory, equilibrium is defined in a static context in terms of markets for which supply equals demand at the market-clearing price. Theories of economic fluctuations usually assume that in the short run quantities rather than prices adjust.

In a dynamic context, a key consideration is that adjustment is never instantaneous. Aspects of the adjustment process are discussed in microeconomics in relation to the concepts of the short, medium, and long run. Pragmatically, it seems reasonable to classify short and medium runs as states of disequilibrium and the associated adjustments as economic fluctuations.

2.2. Real–monetary

The most important paradigm changes have been between real and monetary theories of economic fluctuations. A real theory is one in which only physical quantities and relative prices play a role. Monetary theories involve *nominal* quantities. It would be more logical to speak of 'nominal' rather than 'monetary' theories, since real theories can include real balances. Since the term 'monetary' has become well established, it will be retained here.

While purely real theories of economic fluctuations have been important, it is not possible to have a purely monetary theory of fluctuations, since these are defined as involving, among other magnitudes, the volume of physical output. I will classify theories as 'real' or 'monetary' according to where the major thrust of the analysis is.

2.3. Fluctuation–cycle

An economic 'fluctuation' may be simply defined as any disequilibrium movement. Beginning in the late nineteenth century, the word 'cycle' came into use when it was seen that fluctuations contain periodic components. Only in the last decades has it become customary to refer to all fluctuations as 'cycles' while typically explicitly denying an aspect of periodicity. This usage is certainly confusing. In this book, 'cycle' denotes a periodic movement and 'fluctuation', in accordance with the classification scheme of the American Economics Association, is used as the general, unspecific, term. 'Periodic' will be interpreted as a tendency of time series, possibly after suitable adjustments, to exhibit maxima and minima at regular intervals. More precise definitions will be given in subsequent chapters as needed.

2.4. Micro–macro

Here the usual definitions present no difficulty. 'Micro' is any theory expressed in terms of individual economic units, particularly households and firms; 'macro' is any theory expressed in terms of sectoral aggregates. Traditionally, theories of fluctuations have been macro theories.

2.5. Exogenous–endogenous

Again, quite conventionally, 'exogenous' is what impinges on the economy from 'without' or which is not explained. 'Endogenous', applied to fluctuations, is a movement explained in terms of some economic mechanism. Endogenous theories may postulate exogenous shocks or other initial conditions which initiate the movement. The endogenous movement may then be thought of as the solution of a dynamic system with stochastic or other exogenous inputs.

2.6. Investment–consumption

In the context of real, endogenous theories of fluctuations, these are the sectors thought to be mainly involved in the causation of economic fluctuations. Theories having investment as the central element have traditionally been termed 'overinvestment' theories and those focusing on consumption have been called 'underconsumption' theories. The former have typically been used to explain cyclical movements, the latter secular stagnation.

2.7. Speculative–empirical

Some paradigms have been predominantly speculative in the sense of having only a slight empirical component; others have been mainly empirical, in which case the theorizing has typically been *ad hoc* and largely descriptive.

2.8. Formal–informal

Another distinction is between formal and informal styles of reasoning. In contemporary economics, formal theory has become equivalent to mathematical economics. This has not always been the case. For example, the early Marginalists were highly formal in that they took pains to elucidate all of the implications of a few basic assumptions. However, they were non-mathematical.

2.9. Central–peripheral

These terms are intended as measures of the importance and influence of a paradigm. Generally, static equilibrium theories, based on maximizing assumptions, have been the central paradigm of economics throughout most of its history. From this centre it was possible to go in different directions to the periphery, there to find theories of fluctuations. These alternately gained dominance or centrality relative to each other, sometimes also relative to the equilibrium theories.

3. From Aristoteles to Keynes

3.1. From *c.* 300 BC to *c.* AD 1600

Real and monetary theories of economic fluctuations are only particular cases of real or monetary theorizing about economics. Such theorizing was initially almost entirely real. Important writers or schools of writers who, among other subjects, also touched on economics include Aristotle and the Scholastic Philosophers.

In terms of the concepts of the previous section, this style of theorizing may be characterized as *real, microeconomic, speculative*, and *informal*. A discussion of fluctuations had not begun, so this was the *central* (and only) paradigm.

3.2. Mercantilism: *c.* 1500–1760

Mercantilism is a loose and long-lasting stream of economic writings stretching from about 1500 to 1800. It was dominated by English writers in the seventeenth century and by the French Physiocrats in the eighteenth. All were men of affairs, supporters of the rising national states, and, especially in the case of the English writers, were interested primarily in policy rather than theory.

Mercantilists were the first writers to think primarily in monetary terms and to analyse real consequences of changes in the money supply. W. R. Allen writes:

wealth was intimately associated with specie. The better mercantilist writers in their better moments did not make wealth and specie synonymous. Wealth and specie were closely associated, however, . . . excessive hoarding of money by either government or citizens would depress prices and curtail employment. With later writers, the emphasis was increasingly on the circulation of money rather than on simply the held stock of money. More bullion and its expenditure would alleviate the commonly perceived 'scarcity of money' and serve to 'quicken trade'. A persistently rising and vigorously circulating money stock somehow would conduce prosperity, facilitate exchange and encourage employment. . . . (Allen 1987 : 446)

This passage captures the essentials of the monetary point of view, not only of the Mercantilists, but also of other, later, schools.

An analytical step going beyond earlier mercantilism was taken by the Physiocrat Quesnay. He constructed what is in effect the first macroeconomic model, for which he analysed the circular flow of payments between the sectors.

If we add to the movements considered the names of Petty and Turgot (called the 'econometricians' by Schumpeter), then it seems reasonable to say of the period as a whole that speculative and empirical elements, though informal and rudimentary, were in better balance than at any time in the subsequent history of economics. With Adam Smith, the academic and speculative tradition acquired the upper hand and with minor exceptions has kept it to the present day.

This period can be characterized in terms of the following key concepts: *disequilibrium, monetary, fluctuation, macro, endogenous*, both *speculative* and *empirical, informal* and *central*.

3.3. The Dominant Tradition: 1760–1930

The year of the birth of modern economics is conventionally and justly taken to be 1776, the date of the publication of Adam Smith's *Wealth of Nations*. It also marks the end of the period of monetary disequilibrium analysis just described and the beginning of a tradition of real equilibrium analysis which has continued unbroken to the present.

Starting with Smith, the competitive model with its efficiency property became the central paradigm of economics. Smith's analysis contained a strong dynamic element. The equilibrium point was defined as that to which the economy tended in a dynamic, disequilibrium adjustment process. He argued that if it is possible, with the factors used for current production, to produce goods more desired by consumers, then there is a profit to be made in producing them. The profit motive thus guides firms to the most efficient activities, and losses eliminate inefficient firms. In this description there is a recognizable picture of an entrepreneur making decisions in real time and in disequilibrium. In principle, real analysis could have been extended to fluctuations as well as equilibrium, but this did not happen. The ideological thrust of Smith and even more of his successors was to stress the efficiency of the market mechanism and to minimize the importance of fluctuations.

Beginning with the Marginalists, especially Gossen, Menger, Jevons, and the subsequent synthesis by Marshall, the emphasis shifted to the analysis of the *equilibrium conditions*. This is equally true to the subsequent general equilibrium analysis, from Pareto and Walras to Debreu and Arrow–Hahn. To deal with disequilibrium, Walras postulated his famous auctioneer, while modern analysis postulates a response of the market price to excess demand. In neither case is there a description of the behaviour of the individual entrepreneur out of equilibrium. One reason for the focus on equilibrium was, as already mentioned, the ideological commitment to the defence of the capitalistic market economy. Another, no less important, reason is more interesting. It is the confluence of the abstract, increasingly formal, and ultimately mathematical style, that characterized academic economics with static equilibrium analysis. The reason for the confluence is simple. Relative to static equilibrium analysis, the realistic analysis of economic agents in disequilibrium involves two additional dimensions: time and uncertainty. These are joined in the concept of *expectation*. The current actions of the agents are based on their uncertain expectations of the future. By opting for static equilibrium analysis, economists simply chose that field for which they were able to obtain the required tools of analysis relatively easily from existing mathematics.

Competence in elementary calculus and algebra came to be regarded as a universal requirement for economists only after the Second World War. Calculus of variations and deterministic control theory are still regarded as specialized tools for theoreticians. Finally, stochastic control theory, the branch of mathematics that deals with dynamic optimization under uncertainty, is only about twenty years old and is a working tool for only a small number of mathematical economists.

The level of formal rigour to which academic economists aspired could until recently be carried out only with respect to static equilibrium analysis. The analysis of economic fluctuations was pushed into the 'underground' mentioned by Keynes.

It remains to characterize economic orthodoxy in terms of the key concepts. In doing so, I focus on those tendencies that became increasingly strong and culminated in general equilibrium theory. The relevant concepts are *equilibrium, real, micro, speculative, formal*, and *central*.

3.4. Fluctuations and the Underworld of Economics: 1790–1870

The analysis of fluctuations was taken up again in this period and considerable progress was made. The main contributors were Tooke and Overstone. Tooke's approach was strongly empirical, that of Overstone theoretical. This led to some antagonism and mutual criticism. In fact, they produced rather similar theories.

The outstanding achievement of Tooke and Overstone is that they produced the first endogenous theories of 'cycles' and brought this term to the analysis of economic fluctuations. They also used 'period' to denote the length of a cycle, but they did not fix a specific period. Both authors analyse how each phase of cycle leads to the next. In this connection they considered a multitude of factors, but the emphasis was on the role of credit. An overexpansion of credit in the boom phase leads to overinvestment beyond the point that is sustainable by real conditions. Overinvestment and over-extended credit ultimately lead to the collapse.

The emphasis on credit has led to the classification of these theories as monetary. There were, however, also real elements. In particular, Overstone held technical progress to be the main cause of the upswing.

Both authors, but especially Tooke, emphasized the role of fixed investment in fluctuations. Interestingly, J. S. Mill, writing about the same time, emphasized the role of stocks (inventories, in today's terminology).

Altogether, the understanding of fluctuations greatly advanced during this period and the foundations for subsequent further advances were laid. This interlude of monetary analysis of fluctuations, in contrast to the earlier one, was not able to dislodge real equilibrium analysis from its central position and thus remained marginal.

Using our key concepts, this period can be summarized as follows: *disequilibrium, monetary* with *real* elements, transitional from *fluctuation* to *cycle, macro, endogenous, investment, speculative* and *empirical, informal, peripheral*.

3.5. Marx: *c.* 1870

Marx's views on economic fluctuations will be briefly mentioned here, even though they had little influence on non-Marxian analyses. As Schumpeter notes, among Marx's interpreters there is little agreement concerning what these views were. I will stress only one very general feature:

Marx produced the first integrated theory of growth and fluctuations. He held that capitalism progresses, by its nature, with a wave-like movement, in which the depressions become more severe as time goes on, leading to the ultimate collapse. It is also clear that Marx's theory is real and has the falling rate of profit as its central element.

Marx's analysis of fluctuations is discussed rather sympathetically by Schumpeter, who, half a century later, also produced a theory of capitalist development proceeding in waves, but did not reach Marx's conclusion of an inevitable collapse.

Key concepts for the theory of Marx are: *disequilibrium, real, fluctuation* or *cycle, macro, endogenous, investment, speculative, peripheral*.

3.6. Real and Monetary Theories of Investment Cycles: 1870–1930

I now come to a long and very fruitful period in relation to both empirical and theoretical research on economic fluctuations. In contrast to the two earlier periods of analysis of fluctuations, this time there are two traditions of research. One is primarily *empirical* and *real*, the other primarily *theoretical* and *monetary*.

The empirical and real tradition

A major novel element was the discovery of *periodicity* in the sense of a characteristic length of cycles. The breakthrough occurred with Juglar (1862), who discovered a cycle of roughly ten years. This finding was based on the visual analysis of plots of large numbers of time series, an important advance in methodology, taken over by later analysts.

A further great advance, associated with the names of Tugan-Baranovsky and even more decisively A. Spiethoff, was the recognition that these fluctuations occurred almost exclusively in plant and equipment investment, whereas consumption developed relatively smoothly. Spiethoff also recognized that the ten-year cycle occurred against a background of longer swings, analogous to those identified later by Kondratieff.

As a result of these findings, the earlier view of fluctuations as isolated 'crises' disappeared and was replaced by endogenous analyses of the dynamics of investment cycles. Such analyses were given also by mainstream theoreticians such as D. Robertson and A. Pigue. Particularly relevant for the subsequent evolution was the emphasis placed by A. Aftalion, and somewhat later by J. M. Clark, on the accelerator mechanism in the explanation of fixed investment.

Ultimately, this line of development merged with the beginning econometric movement in the work of Frisch and other investigators, who employed formal mathematical and statistical methods for the analysis of fluctuations (cf. Section 5.2).

The theoretical and monetary tradition

It should be emphasized at the outset that the difference between the real and the monetary work of this period is much less than that between the work of this period as a whole and that of earlier periods. The monetary theories are also theories of the endogenous dynamics of investment cycles. Moreover, real elements are not absent from the monetary, nor monetary from the real theories. Schumpeter, whose classification I am using, states that it depends on the extent to which a given writer emphasized the various elements in his explanation. The monetary analysis of investment cycles, in this period, has as its starting point the cumulative process of Wicksell. The essential feature is the distinction between the 'real' interest rate, meaning the rate of return on physical assets, and the 'monetary' interest rate on financial assets. Credit and investment in plant and equipment expand as long as the real rate is above the monetary rate. This expansion must come to an end—when banks have exhausted their free reserves. The monetary rate rises, ending the expansion and leading to the contraction. Wicksell's analysis was elaborated, particularly with respect to the explanation of cycles, by L. von Mises and F. von Hayek.

In view of our interest in paradigm changes, it is interesting to cite Schumpeter's comment on the reaction to Hayek's theory:

On being presented to the Anglo-American community of economists, [it] met with a sweeping success that has never been equalled by any strictly theoretical book that failed to make amends for its rigours by including plans and policy recommendations or to make contact in other ways with its readers' loves or hates. A strong critical reaction followed that, at first, but served to underline the success and then the profession turned away to other leaders and other interests. The social psychology of this is interesting matter for study. (Schumpeter 1954 : 1120)

Somewhat aside from the writers just discussed is Hawtrey. He presented an almost entirely monetary theory of the cycle with the emphasis on the financing of stocks rather than plant and equipment. With the work of Kitchin and Hawtrey, we move towards the recognition of shorter inventory cycles as a distinctive form of cyclical fluctuation.

Conclusions

While this period exhibited great diversity and two broad schools with different emphasis, there was nevertheless a greater unity at a fundamental level than in contemporary macroeconomics. A basic stylized fact was recognized by all: namely, the quasi-periodic nature of fluctuations and the key role played by investment. Accordingly, it was recognized that dynamic theories of investment were called for as explanations.

In summary, it may be said that this period provided the key ideas and empirical regularities which led to the models of equipment and inventory cycles formulated by mathematical economists and econometricians from the 1930s to the 1960s.

The key concepts to characterize this period are: *disequilibrium, real* and *monetary, cycle, macro, endogenous, investment* (fixed and inventory), *empirical* and *speculative, formal* and *informal, peripheral.*

4. The Dominant Keynesian Tradition: *c.*1930–1960

4.1. Keynes and the General Theory

Introduction

The publication in 1936 of Keynes's *General Theory of Employment, Interest and Money (GT)* marks a profound and many-faceted transformation of macroeconomics and even of economics itself. My assessment of this transformation differs from others that have been given.

I begin my discussion with some relatively uncontroversial facts. The *GT* was written in response to the Great Depression. Keynes considered the Depression as marking a permanent change in the world's capitalist economies. He believed that deficient aggregate demand and hence high unemployment would characterize the world economy into the indefinite future, unless governments undertook appropriate counter-measures. In essence, Keynes believed that government expenditure would have to substitute for private expenditure, though measures to stimulate private investment and consumption could also play a role.

Keynes was an intuitive, pragmatic, policy-oriented economist. His views on how to cure the Depression were prior to, not derived from, his theory. This may in fact be the usual sequence in economics. For example, *laissez faire* was already a strong ideology before Adam Smith provided it with a theoretical rationale. Being a principal insider of the dominant neoclassical tradition, Keynes was strongly motivated to convince his peers and he realized that he could do this only by providing an alternative theory, from which his interventionist policy recommendations could be deduced. The *GT* was the result, and it was enormously successful.

Before discussing the *GT* further, it must be said that it contains two theories: the *static* theory usually associated with it, and a *dynamic* theory which has gone virtually unnoticed. I will discuss the static theory first and will be referring to this theory whenever I mention the *GT* without qualification.

The static theory of the GT

To obtain the static part of the *GT*, Keynes started from the dominant paradigm of general equilibrium theory. He modified this in two important respects. First, he formulated a *macro* model using sectors rather than individual agents. This aspect is similar to the contribution of Quesnay, only Keynes defined the sectors and variables now generally accepted as relevant for a modern economy. His definition of the sectors and the variables they control was subsequently never really questioned. In addition, he was a moving force in the establishment of the national accounts, which provide the data required for making the theory (or even competing theories) operational. The national accounts greatly contributed to the prestige and 'scientific' status of macroeconomics in the postwar period.

Secondly, Keynes focused on the possibility that the supply and demand schedules might be such that markets would not clear. For this purpose he invented a catalogue of 'pathologies'—most importantly inelasticity of the investment schedule, money illusion, price rigidity, and the liquidity trap.

That, in the short run, quantities adjust faster than prices is a basic stylized fact of economic life to which I shall refer again in Section 8. While there is little empirical evidence for the other 'pathologies' envisaged by Keynes, rigid prices and wages are enough for the derivation of the basic results.

The subsequent evolution and ultimate triumph of Keynesianism is based on the static part of the *GT*. Its ultimate success cannot be explained solely by reference to the objective merits of Keynes's thought. At least equally important were two other factors:

1. The *GT* provided the rationale for an activist government policy against depression and unemployment. Such a policy was in harmony with the ideological trend of the age.

2. The basic elements of the static theory of the *GT* could be readily formalized. This allowed Keynesianism to become a part of the rising econometric movement.

The dynamic theory of the GT

I have stressed that the *GT* was motivated by Keynes's vision of a post-De-
pression world of mature capitalism, characterized by stagnation and chronic
deficient demand. Most of the *GT* elaborates a model of such an economy.
However, in Chapter 22, 'Notes on the Trade Cycle', Keynes cast a backward
glance at a world which he thought had ceased to exist. He attempted a brief
explanation of economic cycles which he explicitly described as a 'nineteenth-
century phenomenon'.

The building blocks for Keynes's dynamic theory are contained in Chapters
5 and 12 on short- and long-run expectations. The entrepreneur is described
as making his current decisions on the basis of his expectations regarding the
future. Future expectations are based on extrapolations from the past, but these
may be strongly influenced by irrational or volatile factors of individual or
mass psychology. Keynes discusses two fundamental decisions of the firm. In
Chapter 5 it is the decision on how much to produce, which is related to
short-term expectations regarding the demand for the product and also to
current inventory levels. Chapter 12 is devoted to the firm's decision to invest
in fixed capital. Here the decisive consideration is the relationship between
the current cost of capital and its expected long-term yield. The current cost
depends on the price of capital goods and the rate of interest, on the expected
long-run evolution of market demand and on costs of producing with old or
new capital.

Keynes's attempt in Chapter 22 to construct an endogenous dynamic theory
of economic cycles, based on these building blocks, has remained rudimentary. The main reason appears to be that he devoted little effort to the task,
since he regarded the chapter as no more than an historical aside. Also relevant
is the fact that a logically tight description of the dynamics of an oscillatory
process is virtually precluded by the rather diffuse verbal style of Keynes and
earlier writers on economic cycles.

Considering the three chapters together, Keynes made a substantial contribution to the explanation of economic fluctuations, which was firmly in the
tradition of the theories of investment cycles.

4.2. Static Keynesian Economics

Hicks published '*Mr. Keynes and the "Classics"* ', his interpretation of the *GT*,
containing the *IS–LM* model, in 1937, only one year after the book appeared.
This may have been the decisive step in transforming a controversial challenge
to the old orthodoxy into a new orthodoxy.

The *IS–LM* model exhibits, in the simplest possible manner, the sectors and variables of the *GT*, as well as the 'pathologies': liquidity trap, interest-inelastic investment demand, money illusion, and rigid wages, which, singly or in combination, produce the 'Keynesian' rather than the 'classical' solution.

With the *IS–LM* model, Hicks achieved the following:

1. He provided an easily teachable canonical interpretation of the *GT*, which became the centrepiece of intermediate macroeconomic textbooks.
2. The mathematical formulation of behavioural equations and equilibrium conditions helped to dispel the confusion about *ex ante* and *ex post* relationships, which had characterized the first reactions to the *GT*.
3. The comparative-static analysis associated with the *IS–LM* model, either in diagrammatic form or by means of total differentials, was at just the right level for the beginning mathematization of economics.
4. The behavioural equations of the model could be readily operationalized. In connection with the rising econometric movement and the new availability of national income data (which owed much to Keynes's own efforts) a flood of applied and theoretical econometric work resulted. Even the large-scale macroeconometric models could be regarded as disaggregated and dynamized *IS–LM* models.

Even simpler than the *IS–LM* model was the 'Keynesian cross' diagram, in which income is measured on the horizontal, expenditure on the vertical axis. It became the standard device for explaining Keynesian ideas in introductory textbooks.

Keynes's first influential apostle in the USA was A. H. Hansen. His student Paul Samuelson accomplished the decisive popularization of Keynesianism in the USA. In his immensely popular introductory text (Samuelson 1948), he propagated the 'Neoclassical Synthesis', according to which a society in which the government stabilizes aggregate demand can have the efficiency problem solved by the market.

4.3. Popular Keynesianism

The enormous and for a long time almost unquestioned prestige that Keynesianism acquired among the lay population and in the practical sphere was only loosely connected with academic or textbook Keynesianism or even with the writing of Keynes himself. I label the set of beliefs on which this acceptance was based *popular Keynesianism*. They are:

1. that the principles of stabilization had not only been found, but had actually been put into practice, and that the result was the stable high growth era of the 1950s and 1960s;
2. that the Phillips curve exists as a stable long-run relationship exploitable by economic policy;

3. That money does not matter: (*a*) monetary policy was thought to be ineffective for stabilization purposes; (*b*) even inflation was considered to be
   due to monopoly power rather than to the too rapid expansion of the money
   supply.

At best, some of these propositions can be deduced from standard Keynesian
models when specific assumptions are made; their empirical validity was
never demonstrated.

The key concepts characterizing the most important parts of the Keynesian
tradition are: *disequilibrium, real* and *monetary, fluctuation, macro, exogenous, investment* and *consumption, speculative, formal, central.*

5. Macroeconomic Dynamics: *c.*1930–1960

5.1. Introduction

As described in the previous section, Keynes reacted to the Great Depression
by creating a static theory which came to dominate economics for the next
half-century. An immediate consequence of the success of the *GT* was that
work on dynamics, which was being done by other economists, was pushed
from centre-stage and was subsequently largely ignored. This applies to the
informal work on period analysis done by Robertson and Lundberg as well as
to the mathematically sophisticated cycle models of the pioneer econometricians Tinbergen, Frisch, and Kalecki. This work will be discussed in Section
5.2. Section 5.3 deals with economic dynamics in the Keynesian tradition
which began with the work of Harrod. In Section 5.4 the two streams are
compared and the reasons for the rejection of the one and the (at least tem-
porary) acceptance of the other are further elaborated.

5.2. Non-Keynesian Dynamics and the Rise of the Econometric Movement

Work in the disequilibrium tradition continued in the 1920s and 1930s.

Robertson (1936) and Lundberg (1937) analysed the temporal sequence of
decisions in disequilibrium. To this end they developed a verbal or arithmetic
form of period analysis, which was a precursor of the use of difference or
differential equations in economic analysis. The work of Lundberg proved
particularly significant for the understanding of inventory cycles and inspired
the later work of Metzler.

The three other authors to be discussed in this subsection—Frisch, Tinbergen, and Kalecki—had a level of mathematical sophistication far above that
of other economists of the time. Frisch began his studies in economics
and went on to obtain a Ph.D. in mathematical statistics. Tinbergen studied

mathematical physics and wrote a dissertation on minimum problems in physics and economics. Kalecki had to break off a study of civil engineering for financial reasons and went on to become a self-taught iconoclast in economics.

Frisch and Tinbergen are rightly considered to be the founders of the econometric movement. Kalecki was less interested in the development of econometric methods, but along with Frisch and Tinbergen he provided the first quantitative parameter estimates for mathematical economic models. All three may therefore be regarded as pioneers of econometrics.

The models estimated by the three authors were all intended to explain economic cycles. They have some strongly similar features which are related to their common origin in cobweb models of agricultural product cycles. Models of the type now referred to as 'cobweb' were elaborated by Tinbergen and by a number of other authors, all of whom published in German in 1930.

In that same year, Tinbergen published a model of the shipbuilding cycle which proved seminal in a number of respects. In the first place, the cobweb model was utilized for the first time to explain investment in a producer's durable goods. Secondly, the idea of a gestation lag covering the time from initiation to completion of an investment project was introduced. In the case of shipbuilding, this lag is about two years. Finally, the dependent variable was taken to be the rate of investment, regarded as a continuous variable. The consequence is that the investment process is governed by a characteristic mixed-difference differential equation which became the basic building block also of the models of Frisch and Kalecki.

Inspired by statistical evidence, Tinbergen made the following assumptions:

1. When shipping capacity is low/high, freight rates are high/low.
2. When freight rates are high/low, the rate of orders for new ships will be high/low and so will be the increase in tonnage or ship launchings θ years later, θ being the gestation lag. The fundamental equation obtained by Tinbergen is

$$f'(t) = \alpha f(t - \theta),$$

where $f(t - \theta)$ is the tonnage θ years ago and $f'(t)$ is current investment (increase in tonnage). He shows that, depending on the parameter values, a variety of cyclical and non-cyclical solutions are possible.

Both Frisch (1933) and Kalecki (1933) took the decisive next step of constructing 'business cycle' models meant to be applicable to a national economy rather than an isolated market. The key variable of their models is the volume of fixed business investment.

The basic assumptions entering Frisch's model are as follows:

1. Capital is required in fixed proportion for the production of consumer and producer goods.

2. Orders for new capital goods have two components: (*a*) a replacement component assumed proportional to total production; (*b*) an acceleration component proportional to the rate of change of the production of consumption goods.
3. Following an order, investment takes place at a constant rate over an interval ε, the gestation lag, until the completion of the capital good.
4. Consumption is a constant, modified by a relationship between the fixed money supply and the transaction demand for money.

Frisch demonstrates that for plausible parameter values his model produces two cycles, regarding which he writes:

The primary cycle of 8.57 years corresponds nearly exactly to the well-known long business cycle ... Furthermore, the secondary cycle obtained is 3.50 years, which corresponds nearly exactly to the short business cycle. (Frisch 1933 : 170)

The cyclical properties of the model are shown to depend sensitively on only one model parameter, the gestation lag ε.

In part V of his paper, entitled 'Erratic shocks as a source of energy in maintaining oscillations', he gives the first precise definition of the type of irregular cyclical movements which I refer to as 'quasi-cycles'. He gives the example of a damped (frictional) pendulum which can be modelled by differential equations with complex roots, giving the period and damping of the oscillations. If the pendulum is subject to erratic shocks, they can be added to the deterministic equation. After analysing the effect of the shocks, he concludes that:

The result of this analysis is ... a curve that is moving more or less regularly in cycles, the length of the period and also the amplitude being to some extent variable, their variations taking place, however, within such limits that it is reasonable to speak of an average period and an average amplitude. In other words, there is created just the kind of curves which we know from actual statistical observations. (Frisch 1933 : 183)

Unfortunately, much of the discussion of economic fluctuations to the present day suffers from a failure to use this clear-cut concept of a quasi-cycle.[2]

In contrast to Frisch, who made no further contribution to this subject, macroeconomics was the main interest of Kalecki throughout his professional career. Despite his many articles and books on economic cycles, his basic approach and model did not change very much. The basic formulation is contained in his 1933 paper which was published in Polish (translated in 1966). In that paper Kalecki cites no references, and it is likely that he was unaware of the cobweb models mentioned earlier. After moving to England, he published in 1935 a more elaborate paper in *Econometrica* in which he

[2] A more refined analysis is given by Sargent (1979: Ch. 3, Sect. 10): he defines a 'cycle' of a single time series either in terms of the frequency of a complex root of a stochastic difference equation describing the data, or in terms of a peak of the spectrum. As he points out, there is little difference between these definitions in practice.

cited Frisch and Tinbergen and used their solution methods to analyse a highly sophisticated and carefully specified lag structure of the investment process.

Kalecki also makes a considerable effort to obtain range estimates of the parameters. He shows that, for plausible parameter values, the model generates cycles which lie in the observed range of 8–12 years. In subsequent publications (particularly Kalecki 1954) he tested his model against different data-sets and obtained generally plausible results.

Regarding the investment process, Kalecki distinguishes between *orders* for investment goods, actual *investment*, which takes place subsequently for the duration of the gestation lag, and *additions to the capital stock*, which occur at the end of the gestation period.

The rest of Kalecki's model is rather unsatisfactory. He assumes that workers do not save and that they consume a constant amount. Capitalists base their investment decision on their gross profit without an accelerator effect or the consideration of capacity utilization. Gross profits in turn are in his model a simple accounting consequence of the level of investment.

The early econometric work on cycles, and particularly the models of Frisch and Kalecki, clearly fell within the investment cycle theory, advanced that theory substantively, and moved it methodologically in the direction of the natural sciences. The main weakness of the models of Frisch and Kalecki is that they are unsatisfactory as closed models of an economy, both in accounting for the circular flow of income and in distinguishing between *ex ante* and *ex post* variables. In this they are truly pre-Keynesian. The force of this criticism is limited because it is not clear that an economy-wide model is required to explain investment cycles. The work of SEMECON suggests that the dynamic adjustment of investment by itself explains the cycle at least to a first approximation. Similarly, the investment adjustment equations of Frisch and Kalecki are sufficient for the generation of cycles. The cyclical properties of their models are only slightly affected by the remaining equations which complete them.

The work of Frisch and Kalecki had limited influence on the further evolution of macroeconomics. This is highly unfortunate, because the early work on fluctuations in the Keynesian tradition is by comparison primitive. Several plausible reasons for the neglect of the early econometric cycle models may be given. In the first place, the models had little in common with the static explanation offered by Keynes, as enshrined in the *IS–LM* model of Hicks. Given the total triumph of Keynesianism, there was little interest in alternative approaches. Secondly, Keynes made an intensive effort to 'sell' his ideas; the *GT* may be regarded as primarily an effort in persuasion, the conclusion already being fixed in his mind before he wrote the book. There was no comparable effort made by the econometricians. Frisch wrote only one paper on fluctuations. Tinbergen changed his approach, and pioneered what became the standard style of macroeconometrics of the 1950s and 1960s. Kalecki, the only one to make a sustained effort, remained an outsider unconnected to the

mainstream of economic theorizing. Finally, the mathematical difficulty of the
mixed difference–differential equations, which might have been regarded
positively a few decades later, was an insurmountable barrier to almost all
economists at the time.

Key features of the explanations of cycles by the early econometricians,
which re-entered macroeconometrics only with a delay of decades, will be
recapitulated here.

Methodological

1. Models must explain independently established stylized facts.
2. No distinction between theoretical and empirical models is made. Explanatory models must be based on plausible assumptions.
3. Model parameters must be estimated and the quantitative features compared with those of the stylized facts.

Substantive

1. Fluctuations mainly take the form of investment cycles.
2. The principal explanation of investment cycles is the complex lag structure
   of the investment process.

5.3. Keynesian Macrodynamics

Introduction

Two strands of theorizing in the Keynesian tradition began with the work of
Harrod (1939 and later) and Domar (1946): growth theory and the theory of
accelerator/multiplier cycle models. The reason for labelling these models
'Keynesian' is that they all build on the *ex post* identity of saving and investment.

Harrod and Domar set out to correct the static nature of the *IS–LM* model,
which results from the fact that it does not take into account the change in the
capital stock resulting from positive net investment, and the change in the
labour supply resulting from population growth. Their aim was the same as that
of Keynes—to explain persistent unemployment—but the explanations they
suggested were completely different from Keynes's 'pathologies'. They discussed two basic reasons for disequilibrium and consequently unemployment:

1. the 'warranted' rate of growth, at which saving equals investment may not
   correspond to the 'natural' rate of population growth;
2. a divergence between *ex post* and *ex ante* magnitudes, which can push the
   economy off the 'knife's edge' of equilibrium growth.

They offered no remedies, and their informal analyses of reason 2 were
unsatisfactory.

Growth theory

The early postwar decades were characterized by rapid economic growth, punctuated by minor recessions. Economists were quick to attribute this performance to the success of Keynesian stabilization policies and to project relatively uninterrupted growth into the future. According to the *neoclassical synthesis* propagated by Paul Samuelson (1948) in his enormously successful textbook, the macroeconomic ship would be kept on a steady course by demand management policies, while the market systems provided efficiency and the welfare state looked after those unable to compete.

Stabilization policy was held to be capable of dealing with the knife-edge problem. This still left the first problem of a likely divergence between the natural and the warranted growth rate. The central message of equilibrium growth theory was that this is not a real problem since the economy can, by its own automatic mechanisms, harmonize the two rates. The central idea, due to Solow (1956) and Swan (1956) was to allow labour-capital substitution, thereby eliminating in one stroke the theoretical possibility of unemployment. Equilibrium growth theory flowered in the 1960s concerning itself mainly with optimality aspects.

This theory is of direct relevance for the explanation of economic fluctuations only in so far as some of the basic formulations were also taken over or adapted by later models of cyclical growth.

Cycle models based on accelerator–multiplier interaction

Simultaneously with the attempt of Harrod to analyse verbally the behaviour of an economy away from the equilibrium growth path, Samuelson (1939) published his mathematical model of cycles, based on a unit lag in the consumption as well as the investment equation. Metzler (1941), following the earlier analysis of Lundberg (1937), constructed a model of the inventory cycle also based on accelerator–multiplier interaction.

The most ambitious attempt at constructing a theory of economic cycles was that of Hicks (1950). Hicks cites Keynes, Frisch, and Harrod as his main sources of inspiration whose contributions he attempted to integrate. The book failed to have a significant impact, however. Part of the reason is that the interest of macroeconomists (including Hicks) shifted to growth theory in the 1960s.

Hicks's attempt to fuse the approach of the early econometricians with that of Keynes must be judged a failure.[3] Thereafter, concern with economic fluctuations in macroeconomics disappeared almost completely. When it returned, in the form of the New Classical macroeconomics, the break with the earlier tradition was complete.

---

[3] Hahn (1990) in his memorial essay calls the book 'perhaps his least successful'.

Starting with Phillips (1961), a small number of economists did continue work on the explanation of economic cycles with a distinctive approach incorporating Keynesian ideas as well as those of the early econometricians. I refer to this work as the *disequilibrium econometrics of cyclical growth* (DECG). It is described in Section 9 below.

5.4. The Segmentation of Macroeconomics

A central feature of natural science is the close linkage between the generation of hypotheses and of data. This linkage is provided by the process of hypothesis-testing in the course of which hypotheses are modified or new ones invented to explain the data and new data are generated to test the implications of hypotheses. This process was never as organized or systematic in economics as in natural science, but the empirical and theoretical aspects of economics were at least linked, because they corresponded to interests of one and the same person. This is particularly true of Marshall, who strongly influenced Keynes, of Keynes himself, and of the early econometricians. Particularly relevant in this connection is that Keynes had a strong interest in data and was a moving force behind the development of the national income and product accounts, which reflect the basic categories of Keynesian theory.

In the postwar era, different empirical and theoretical functions were parcelled out among different specialities and institutions with little communication between them. The task of generating data was given to statistical agencies, which substantially lost contact with academic economics, particularly economic theory. One consequence was that little progress was made in going beyond the Keynesian flow accounts to integrated accounts of stock and flows, which are needed for dynamic macroeconomics. On the academic side, economists became naïve about data and uninformed about the data-generating process, and consequently about the likely properties of the data.

The determination of what is to count as proper scientific method for economists fell into the hands of statisticians and econometricians with primary training in mathematical statistics, who lacked close acquaintance with problems of applied research, be it in economics or in natural science. This led to a general overemphasis on formal criteria. Also, most work was on asymptotic properties of estimators for static models. These are of little relevance in connection with large-scale, dynamic models being estimated with very limited data-sets. Econometric theory and the practice of macroeconometric model construction became substantially separate enterprises.

Macroeconometric model-building became a very distinct speciality with an applied orientation and little connection to ongoing theoretical research. Ultimately, the activity moved out of the universities and into the commercial arena.

The segmentation of macroeconomics does not appear to have been widely recognized as a problem, but rather as an inevitable consequence of a specialization. It should, however, be regarded as the outward manifestation of a failure to organize macroeconomics as a progressive scientific enterprise.

6. Empirical Macroeconomics: *c*.1930–1960

In this period there were some significant advances in knowledge concerning the stylized facts of macroeconomic fluctuations. Concern with stylized facts in economics tends to be casual, non-systematic, and not a theme much discussed in the professional journals. For example, when I entered graduate school around 1960, the existence of a 40-month inventory cycle was generally accepted mainstream opinion in the USA. Yet, I am unable to say either precisely how that opinion arose, or how it soon thereafter dissolved. Neither process, to my knowledge, was the result of discussion in the journals. Still another difficulty is that I do not know of the existence of any study of the empirical literature of this period, even though this would be of great interest from several points of view. Consequently, my discussion has to be limited to a few major publications and to some general impressions.[4]

A large amount of research on business cycles was conducted at the National Bureau of Economic Research (NBER) in a style and with a methodology largely determined by Wesley C. Mitchel and Arthur F. Burns. The NBER style was predominantly empirical and shied away from bold generalizations, particularly with respect to periodic components of fluctuations. This research did lead to a wealth of detailed empirical findings regarding contemporaneous and sequential patterns of many economic fluctuations. An updated account of the stylized facts that have emerged from this research tradition is given by Zarnovitz (1990).

The empirical econometric tradition, which came to the fore in the 1950s, had two prominent macroeconomic branches. One was large-scale econometric model-building, an enterprise not concerned with the establishment of stylized facts. The other was applied time-series analysis. This branch would have been predestined to establish stylized facts relevant to economic time series. Unfortunately, the methods used were inappropriate for short economic time series so that, again, little in the way of stylized facts could be established. This will be discussed further in the next chapter.

New insights into the stylized facts of macroeconomic fluctuations came from outside of these mainstreams. The first contribution is methodological rather than substantive. It is contained in Schumpeter's (1939) *Business Cycles*. While most of the book is devoted to the detailed historical study of cyclical episodes in different countries, Chapters IV and V are devoted to a (non-mathematical) study of the decomposition of economic time series.

---

[4] Stigler (1988) criticizes the editors of *The New Palgrave* (Eatwell *et al.* 1987) for excluding empirical material (in contrast to the original *Palgrave's Dictionary*). This is indicative of the low, and apparently declining, importance economists attach to the determination of stylized facts and, consequently, also the greater difficulty of documenting these.

Schumpeter states that there is typically more than one cycle in a given time series, and that in order to find any pattern these must be separated from each other and from the trend. This fundamental lesson was unfortunately not absorbed by the majority of economists who discussed the possible existence of cycles. The irregularity of observed turning points is typically taken to refute the hypothesis of cyclicity. But even the superposition of two perfect sine-waves of different periods yields a very irregular-appearing pattern. In economic time series we have a superposition of trend, one or more cycles, and a stochastic term. The irregular appearance of economic time series is no argument against the existence of quasi-cycles, and it will be shown in Chapter 3 that they actually account for a large part of the variance of most macroeconomic time series.

I am unable to describe in detail the further progress in refining the stylized facts of economic fluctuations. However, during the 1950s the following set of stylized facts become widely accepted:

1. *Inventory cycle–Kitchin cycle.* There exists a three- to four-year cycle mainly evident in inventory investment. This cycle is responsible for most of the short-run fluctuation in output.
2. *Equipment cycle.* There is a seven- to ten-year cycle concentrated in equipment investment and to some extent in all fixed investment. It accounts for most of the medium-term fluctuation in output.
3. *Building cycle.* This cycle of about 20 years in building investment is prominent mainly in data pertaining to before the Second World War.
4. *Cycle length.* The different lengths of the cycles were explained by differences in *adjustment speeds*. In disequilibrium, inventory stocks can be adjusted most rapidly out of current production, while the adjustment of the stock of building takes the most time. Equipment occupies an intermediate position.

This description of the stylized facts corresponds closely to that given, with much more detail, by Matthews (1959).

Key concepts to characterize this research are: *disequilibrium*, mainly *real*, *fluctuation* and *cycle, investment, empirical, informal, peripheral.*

7. Monetarism

7.1. The Decline of Keynesianism and the Rise of Monetarism

In Section 4.3, I described the rise of popular Keynesianism as a politico-economic ideology which incorporated the following beliefs:

1. The high-growth/low-unemployment performance of the 1950s and 1960s was due to successful Keynesian demand management.

2. The Philipps curve is a valid, exploitable, long-run relationship.
3. Money does not matter.

These beliefs implied the policies of permanent stimulation of aggregate demand which are very congenial to democratic politicians and were increasingly followed by the governments of the industrialized market economies.

During the late 1960s and early 1970s the world economy gradually changed regimes, from that of high growth, low inflation, and low unemployment which had characterized the first two postwar decades to one of lower growth, rising inflation, and substantial unemployment. The oil shock of 1973 was the dramatic event which signalled that a new economic act had started on the world stage.

Since popular Keynesianism had taken copious credit for the booming 1950s and 1960s, and since it claimed to have the instruments for perpetuating this performance, it was discredited by the subsequent poor experience.

Unfortunately, with the defeat of popular Keynesianism, significant and valid ideas of academic Keynesianism also lost their influence on macroeconomics. In particular, the analysis of the components of GNP and the emphasis on fixed and inventory investment as the most fluctuating components were replaced by the simpler view that the fluctuations of GNP can be explained in one step on the basis of exogenous disturbances.

The set of beliefs that rose to dominance in macroeconomics as Keynesianism declined is usually referred to as *monetarism*. It would have been better to speak of Friedmanianism, both because the beliefs are those that were successfully promoted by Milton Friedman[5] and because they include diverse propositions, such as the Quantity Theory, which is of course much older, and others not specifically related to money at all. In the following, however, I will abide by the established term.

I list below the principal tenets of monetarism, taking first those that are substantive and then those that are methodological.

PROPOSITION 1. The Quantity Theory is valid.

Friedman formulated the Quantity Theory, in analogy to the behavioural relationships of microeconomics, as a demand function for real balances, depending on real income, wealth, and real interest rates.[6] He and his associates and students were able to test this relationship successfully against data for many countries.

The next proposition constitutes the distinctive element in monetarism.

PROPOSITION 2. Economic fluctuations are due mainly to disturbances arising in the monetary sector. Such disturbances impact the real economy with variable lags. There is no significant endogenous dynamics of the real sector.

---

[5] A general discussion of Friedman's thought is given by Walters (1987).
[6] The basic reference is Friedman (1956); see also Walters (1987).

Monetarism is thus firmly in the tradition of the monetary theories of economic fluctuations. A major effort to establish monetarism is documented in Friedman and Schwarz (1963) and subsequent publications. The principal findings were: (*a*) that major contractions in the money stock which were due to exogenous events were followed by contractions in real output; (*b*) that changes in the growth rate of the money stock lead at cyclical turning points. These findings, in conjunction with those discussed in connection with Proposition 4 below, did much to establish monetarism.

PROPOSITION 3 (*The Natural Rate Hypothesis*). The equilibrium rate of unemployment is determined by real forces in the economy. The unemployment inflation trade-off postulated by the Philipps curve does not exist in the long run.

The Philipps curve, already discredited by the empirical fact of rising unemployment and inflation during the 1970s, was also demolished at an intellectual level by Friedman (1968) and Phelps (1968). They made the persuasive point that persistent inflation will be recognized and incorporated in the calculations of agents. Real variables will therefore take on the same values as in a non-inflationary environment.

The fourth proposition is related to the second and is partly methodological, partly substantive.

PROPOSITION 4. A sectoral analysis is unnecessary in order to understand economic fluctuations.

This assumption does away with the entire Keynesian apparatus of sectoral behavioural relationships and interaction between the sectors. Also rejected is simultaneous equation econometrics, not only in the particular form of the large-scale econometric models, but in any form whatever. Monetarist econometrics instead took the form of the 'St Louis equation', which is simply a regression of GNP on the lagged values of the growth rate of the money stock. This relationship appeared to be stable in the USA in the 1960s, a fact that was influential in popularizing monetarism. Conversely, when the relationship became unstable, in the 1970s and 1980s, it contributed to the demise of monetarism.

PROPOSITION 5. Realism is unnecessary in the assumptions of economic theories.

While this proposition was advanced by Friedman (1953) in a microeconomic context, it is also congenial to monetarism. It supports in particular the extreme simplification involved in the neglect of any structural detail of the economy. I also believe that the subsequent acceptance of the New Classical macroeconomics, involving assumptions that appear highly fanciful to a nonconvert, would have been much more difficult without the influence of Friedman's methodological stance.

In contrast to Keynesianism, which divided into a number of distinct streams, monetarism remained essentially unitary and did not deviate significantly from the characteristic cast given to it by Friedman. This is partly because Friedman, unlike Keynes, remained the dominant figure of the movement he had initiated. Another reason is the more complex structure envisioned by Keynes which invited elaboration in various directions.

It is very much to the credit of Friedman that he always considered his substantive beliefs as hypotheses to be confirmed or rejected in accordance with empirical evidence. He also refrained from excessive claims which could not be empirically supported. With respect to the Quantity Theory, his tests were highly successful. With respect to the influence of money on economic activity, however, his hypothesis proved to be too simplistic. The empirical work done with Anna Schwarz is however of the highest quality, and in some aspects—scrupulous attention to the generation of data, relevant knowledge of institutions, and the imaginative use of episodes from economic history to test hypotheses—it is a valuable corrective to the dominant style of current econometrics with its almost total preoccupation with test statistics.

Monetarism was able to escape the fate that it had provided for Keynesianism: the replacement of one set of beliefs by the diametrically opposite ones. The New Classical macroeconomics that succeeded it is in some ways a more extreme form of Friedmanian monetarism, rather than its negation.

Key concepts to characterize the monetarist view of fluctuations are: *disequilibrium, monetary, fluctuation, micro* and *macro, exogenous, speculative* and *empirical, formal* and *informal, central.*

8. The Analysis of Economic Fluctuations in Contemporary Macroeconomics

8.1. Introduction

In this section we shall consider the most influential work on macroeconomic fluctuations carried out in the last 15 years, in order to provide a basis for comparison with the recent work in the investment cycle theory (ICT) tradition and the work of SEMECON discussed in the next section. The most obvious comparison is with the New Classical macroeconomics (NCM), particularly its second incarnation, real business cycle theory (RBCT). Both RBCT and ICT have as their aim the quantitative modelling of macroeconomic fluctuations by means of small models derived from economic theory.

The principal criticism of the NCM has come from the New Keynesian economics (NKE). The NKE itself has not provided an alternative theory of macroeconomic fluctuations.[7] Instead, it has focused on the explanation of rigidities in specific markets, which generally cause short-run adjustments to occur in quantities rather than in prices and lead to persistent disequilibria. This work can be viewed as compatible with traditional Keynesianism as well as the ICT in providing rationales for the processes of quantity adjustment assumed there. The further discussion will focus on the RBCT, with some reference to Keynesian economics in connection with current perceptions of stylized facts.

Since I am dealing with prominent work in contemporary macroeconomics, a consideration of detail appears neither feasible nor desirable. Instead, I have attempted to isolate and clarify some basic features of current macroeconomic paradigms. Some of the methodological issues involved are treated more fully in Chapter 2.

8.2. The Perception of Stylized Facts

The principal stylized fact recognized in contemporary macroeconomics is that most time series show positive serial and contemporaneous correlations. Keynesian economists recognize also that fixed and inventory investments are the components of GNP that fluctuate most.

The ICT view of the stylized facts, while implying both of the preceding statements, makes a much stronger claim: the fluctuations in investment are taken to be quasi-periodic, the period of the equipment cycle being typically in the 7–12-year range, and that of the inventory cycle in the 3.5–5-year range.

This difference is crucial; it has the consequence that models in the ICT tradition are constructed so that they can explain these quasi-cycles, while other models do not. The NCM and the NKE regard the ICT view of the stylized facts as naïve, either the result of misinterpreting random movements or the inadvertent creation of the investigator himself, through the transformations to which the data were subjected.

The evidence on quasi-cycles gathered at SEMECON is reviewed in Chapter 3 and can be evaluated by readers themselves. In the remainder of this subsection I try to explain why the dominant macroeconomic schools have persistently denied the clear evidence on quasi-cycles.

1. We generally see what we expect to see in the light of our preconceptions or hypotheses about the world. In psychology this phenomenon is referred to as 'cognitive dissonance'. In the philosophy of science it is well recognized that data speak to us only when approached with the right kind of hypothesis. Macroeconomists do not find quasi-cycles because they are

---

[7] An effort to move the NKE in this direction is Malinvaud (1980). He does not attempt to explain the stylized facts of economic fluctuations as understood in the ICT. More recently, Solow (1988) in his Nobel lecture argued the need for a disequilibrium theory of economic fluctuations. In this connection he is also critical of the implausibility of the assumption of the *NCBT*.

incompatible with the largely static types of theories to which they are committed.

2. The failure to identify quasi-cycles is only an example of a general problem of establishing stylized facts in economics. This a recurring theme of this and the next chapter.

3. A static framework with an emphasis on asymptotic theory has pervaded much of econometrics, particularly in the early decades. This has been inimical to the development of realistic methods of dynamic inference in the small samples relevant for macroeconomics.

4. Time-series methods should have corrected the static bias of econometrics, but for a variety of reasons (cf. Chapter 2, Section 3 and Chapter 3) they have not been successful in econometric applications.

A cardinal example of the inability to find evidence on quasi-cycles is the use of spectral and cospectral analysis, which, in principle, is the proper method for establishing the stylized facts of time series. As is more fully described in Chapter 3, econometricians in the 1950s and 1960s adopted classical methods of spectral analysis, which had been developed for very long time series, and applied these to the short time series of macroeconomics. They focused mainly on financial series, for which frequent observations were available, but which were not those in which cycles had previously been observed. These decisions virtually guaranteed that no cycles would be found.

When methods appropriate for analysing short time series were developed in the natural sciences in the 1970s, they were not adopted by econometricians. As is demonstrated in Chapter 3, these methods clearly lead to the inference of quasi-cycles.

The following examples of the views of prominent economists regarding the stylized facts will make the discussion more concrete. The first three examples will be taken from a more theoretical, the final three from a more empirical context.

Example 1

The initial statements of the NCM, such as Lucas (1972) and Sargent (1973), were completely static: the effects of shocks were limited to the period in which they occurred. These models do not account for the serial correlation of economic time series, which is one of their most obvious properties (even after trend removal). To correct this aspect, Lucas (1975) introduced lags into a NCM model. The fact that this was done as an afterthought shows that the explanation of dynamic phenomena was not a major concern of the NCM.

Very illuminating in this connection is the discussion of the stylized facts given by R. E. Lucas, which deserves to be quoted:

Technically, movements about trend in gross national product in any country can be well described by a stochastically disturbed difference equation of very low order.

These movements do not exhibit uniformity of either period or amplitude, which is to say, they do not resemble the deterministic wave motions which sometimes arise in the natural sciences. Those regularities which are observed are in the *comovements* among different aggregative time series. (Lucas 1977 : 217)

The statement is followed by a list of seven stylized facts, all referring to comovements, none to a temporal regularity.

With the statement that the data are not deterministic wave motions, a proposition never asserted by anyone, Lucas attacks a straw man. From this, he concludes that only comovement characterizes the data. In addition to being a *non sequitur*, this conclusion is in direct conflict with the earlier part of his statement and also his model, both of which assume that the data are generated by stochastic difference equations. These have perforce a temporal structure, and the spectra implied by the model (when estimated) should match the spectra of the data. Also, there is no a priori reason for excluding complex roots, in which case quasi-cycles would be implied.

Example 2

Sargent (1979) gives a theoretical discussion of quasi-cycles in terms of the complex roots of stochastic difference equations, or the corresponding peaks in the spectrum. This analysis is quite along the lines implied by the work of SEMECON. He computes spectra to see if they show evidence of a quasi-cycle. In doing so, he shows himself to be unaware of the descriptions traditionally given by the ICT. He does not consider investment data at all. He indicates that he is looking only for a cycle of about three years. Any longer cycle would not be observable, in any case, given the scaling of his spectra. Since the typical equipment cycle is eight years or longer, and even inventory cycles may be as long as five years, this procedure makes no sense. Finally, he gives no information about how he computed the spectra and how (if at all) he detrended his data. But these procedures are essential to judging the results.

Not surprisingly, positive serial and contemporaneous correlation is Sargent's only conclusion from his data analysis. Unintentionally, he has given a demonstration of how not to find cycles.

Example 3

Blanchard and Fischer (1989) examine the components of GNP including fixed and inventory investment. Their basic procedure is to fit ARIMA processes to these variables in order to *remove* the endogenous dynamics, and then to analyse the innovations. They make no effort to determine stylized facts in the sense of SEMECON, for which an examination of the spectra and cross-spectra of the variables would be relevant. I conclude that the empirical claims examined, made by contemporary theoreticians, are naïve, a fact somewhat disguised by the formal and technical apparatus employed.

Next, I turn to the perception of the stylized facts on the part of more empirically oriented authors. It turns out that their findings amount to a partial rediscovery of the stylized facts long associated with the ICT.

Example 4

One of the most striking stylized facts of economic fluctuations is that inventory investment, which on average amounts to only 1–2 per cent of GNP, accounts for 50–100 per cent of short-run fluctuations.

The contemporary discussion begins with papers by Blinder (1981) and a major examination of the US evidence by Blinder and Holtz-Eakin (1986). These papers confirmed the role of inventories in fluctuations. Various authors took up the question of whether the stylized facts are compatible with the production-smoothing model. This specific literature is referred to in Chapters 3 and 7.

As Abramovitz (1986) points out in his comment on Blinder and Holtz-Eakin, their findings basically reconfirm work done at the NBER going back to Kuznetz (1926). Abramovitz (1950), Hansen (1941), and many other authors have pointed to the role of inventories in the short, 3.5–5-year 'business' or inventory cycle. This strong stylized fact of the ICT, confirmed in Chapter 3 and explained in Chapter 4, is still being ignored in the current literature on inventory behaviour.

Example 5

A major stylized fact associated with the ICT is that longer cyclical movements are predominantly associated with equipment and more generally with fixed investment. There has not been a resurgence of interest in the behaviour of fixed investment, similar to that in inventory investment. A significant study, however, is that of Gordon and Veitch (1986). These authors do not distinguish between short and long cycles, but they show that for all cyclical downturns the role of fixed investment (including structures and consumer durables) is substantial, amounting to 51 per cent of prewar and 41 per cent of postwar declines (my averages of their figures).

The endogenous dynamics of the investment process is virtually ignored by the authors, but they do write that investment in producer-durable equipment appears to be substantially determined by its own lagged values. This points in the direction of a mainly endogenous explanation of the dynamics of this variable, as postulated by the ICT and made specific in Chapter 4.

The conclusion here, as for inventory behaviour, is that contemporary investigators who deal seriously with the empirical evidence are forced in the direction of the ICT, though they are not yet willing to go all the way.

Example 6

Finally, I turn to a recent discussion of the stylized facts which is in quite a different vein from those just discussed. Zarnowitz (1992) begins his analysis with the observation that there is no convergence in the perception of the stylized facts of economic fluctuation in the economics profession. He states:

In this chapter, an attempt is made to comprehend the problems behind this apparent impasse by reviewing the literature and historical evidence. This approach lacks the terse elegance, but also the frequently spurious precision, of a single quantitative model or formula: the informed judgment it yields may well be more dependable. (Zarnowitz 1992 : 232)

The most central conclusion he draws from his comprehensive examination of the evidence, and states at the outset, is:

On the whole, this line of work suggests the existence of a recursive system that plays a central role in the generation and propagation of business cycles. It stresses the endogenous and deterministic rather than the exogenous and random elements of the process . . . (Zarnowitz 1992 : 233)

    Juglar [1862] was the first to observe that fluctuations in prices, interest rates, and other financial variables often lasted about 7–11 years. Kitchin [1923] stressed the primacy of 3–4 year cycles; the major cycles were to him 'merely aggregates' of two or three minor ones (p. 10). In time it came to be widely believed that business investment in machinery and equipment plays a central part in the major, or Juglar, cycles, and inventory investment in the minor, or Kitchin, cycles. The former involve longer decision and implementation lags than the latter. Fixed capital lasts for years and cannot be adjusted to desired levels nearly as quickly as inventories that are normally disposed of in days, weeks, or at most months. (Zarnowitz 1992 : 239)

Similarly:

Studies of the historical record indicate that the relative importance of changes in business inventories is very large in short and weak fluctuations, much smaller in the long and strong ones, whereas the opposite is typically the case for investment in plant and equipment. Stocks of goods held for current production and sale are generally subject to prompter and less costly adjustments than stocks of structures and equipment on hand. (Zarnowitz 1992 : 245)

In a nutshell, this is the description of the stylized facts associated with the ICT and elaborated in Chapter 3. In addition, the explanation of the different typical durations of cycles in terms of different adjustment speeds is the essence of the *second-order accelerator* (SOA) explanation given in Chapter 4.

    To be fair, my quotations are selective. Writing in the tradition of the NBER, Zarnowitz generally emphasizes diversity and variability of the historical record. In particular, stressing the variation in duration and amplitude of specific cyclical episodes, he refuses to characterize them as 'periodic', using instead the well-known NBER terminology 'recurred but not periodic'. The problem with this phrase is that, as far as I know, its meaning has never been precisely defined. Moreover, the description given by Zarnowitz is in complete accordance with the hypothesis of quasi-cycles, associated with the roots of a disturbed dynamic system, of the type he himself suggests. The irregularity of the observation is easily accounted for by the presence, in addition to shocks, of observation errors, and the superposition of different cycles and trend.

The investigations of the more empirically oriented authors are much more successful than the empirical work of the theoreticians discussed earlier. These results tend to recover stylized facts long maintained in the ICT, but do not go all the way in this direction. In Chapter 3 it will be argued that contemporary data support the traditional stylized facts of the ICT not only partially, but fully, including properties of cyclicity.

8.3. The Empirical Content of the RBCT

This section examines in somewhat greater detail the empirical claims of the RBCT, since it is the major school claiming to explain macroeconomic fluctuations.

In so far as stylized facts are recognized by the RBCT, they are the typical very weak ones generally recognized in contemporary macroeconomics: Long and Plosser (1983) merely postulate strong serial and cross-correlations of the key variables. Kydland and Prescott (1982) emphasize that the normalized variance of fixed investment is large relative of consumption. Plosser (1989) presents a defence of the RBCT. He does not compare model predictions with stylized facts. The essential step in empirical validation is the comparison of predicted growth rates for the *GNP* and some components, as well as other variables, with the observed values. The predictions require a measure of postulated technology shocks as a model input and Plosser uses the Solow residual for this purpose. As Mankiw (1989) points out, the pattern of fluctuations of the Solow residual is virtually identical with that of output. This pattern, which dominates the movements of the other variables as well, is thus imported into the model and not explained by it.

Another telling criticism made by Mankiw is that, if technology shocks play an important role in the economy, we would expect that they would be identified and discussed, much as the oil shocks were. No technology shocks corresponding to short-run output movements have in fact been identified.

A criticism which, in comparison to the above, is perhaps minor is that Plosser includes among his dependent variables consumption of nondurables, which fluctuate little, and excludes inventory investment, which fluctuates more than any other component.

It is seen that even the most recent claim that the RBCT can explain the stylized facts cannot stand scrutiny.

8.4. Basic Assumptions

Whereas the preceding section examined the perception of stylized facts in contemporary macroeconomics, this section will look at theoretical motivations and basic assumptions. The two topics are not entirely separate, since the validity of assumptions can be and is discussed in terms of their correspondence to directly observable stylized facts.

The motivation of Keynes had been empirical: namely, to explain the Great Depression. To this end, he constructed a theory in which, in analogy to general equilibrium theory, the variables that characterize the economic system mutually determine each other. The principal modification, apart from aggregation, made by Keynes was that he allowed market imperfections and based these either on irrational behaviour (money illusion) or on assumptions for which he did not specify a rational basis (e.g. rigid nominal wages).

Both the NCM and the NKE are in large measure reactions to this construction. The basic aim of the NKE is to reconcile the assumptions of disequilibrium and rational behaviour. The NCM attempts to show that it is possible to explain economic fluctuations while retaining both of the basic assumptions of general equilibrium theory: rational behaviour and market-clearing. The NKE is generally perceived as having a stronger empirical, the NCM a stronger theoretical, orientation.

The following subsections will focus first on the assumption of rationality, then on market-clearing, and finally on the assumption of income labour substitution made by the NCM.

Rational expectations

The principal difference in the use of the rationality postulate, between on the one hand the NCM and on the other more traditional econometricians of either the Keynesian or the ICT variety, is that the former use rational expectations (RE) whereas the latter typically employ some variant of *adaptive expectations*. Are RE, as the term would seem to imply, somehow *more rational* than, and therefore superior to, adaptive expectations?

Simple adaptive expectation models, such as Friedman's permanent income hypothesis for consumption and Koyck's flexible accelerator for investment, were first motivated empirically, since they tend to give a good fit to data. Muth (1960) showed that these simple adjustment processes are optimal under certain assumptions. An alternative, deterministic derivation of both the flexible and second-order accelerators is given in Chapter 8.

In the case of RE, agents are supposed to solve a much more difficult problem. They focus not on the variables affecting them directly, but rather on the disturbances impinging on the economic system as a whole. Then they compute the effects these disturbances will have as they work their way through the structure of the economic system. This structure is assumed known to them and identical with the model being proposed by the NCM theoretician.

In addition to its severe implausibility in terms of our direct knowledge of economic agents, the assumption can also be criticized on theoretical and empirical grounds. A theoretical objection is that agents, with apparently infinite observational and computational powers, should consider strategic behaviour. The outcomes would then have to be computed in the context of game theory, something that NCM theorists have not done. At the empirical level, there are a number of studies indicating that the forecasts made by professional forecasters do not satisfy minimal requirements of rationality (Lovell, 1986). This finding is hard to reconcile with a general assumption of RE.

The conclusion is that RE are hardly a general requirement to be imposed on all researchers. Adherents of RE are of course free to demonstrate that the assumption helps them to construct empirically superior models. They have not succeeded in doing this.[8]

Equilibrium

That markets are cleared by prices in the short run is a position held only by the NCM. The assumption is refuted prima facie by the official data on unemployment and capacity utilization. The NKE has produced a large literature explaining why this is so. Arguments tending in the same direction were independently produced by such distinguished economists as Kaldor (1985), and with the major, but not exclusive, focus on the socialist economy by Kornai (1980). The 'fixprice method' advocated by Hicks (1965), which inspired a substantial literature, represents another attempt to deal with this phenomenon (cf. Silvestre 1987).

In conclusion, it seems safe to say that the assumption of market-clearing is not an asset to a theory of economic fluctuations. The NCM or RBCT have not produced any empirical successes which might tempt one to reconsider this view.

Income–leisure substitution

That observed unemployment results from a voluntary substitution of leisure for income is a basic tenet of the NCM and RBCT. I feel that the assumption can be rejected out of hand as being merely silly, since it implies:

1. that official unemployment statistics and payments are fraudulent *in toto*;
2. that the Great Depression was the first manifestation of societies being able to enjoy leisure on a mass scale.

---

[8] Detailed criticisms of the RE approach are found in Frydman and Phelps (1983) and Pesaran (1987).

Not surprisingly, econometricians willing to test the assumption empirically have also come up with negative results (cf. Mankiw 1989).

8.5. Conclusion

A student of contemporary macroeconomics might well conclude that what is needed is a theory of macroeconomic fluctuation that meets:

1. the requirement of the RBCT that it be a small dynamic model, derived from intertemporal maximization and capable of quantitatively explaining economic fluctuation;
2. the requirement of the NKE that it be based on disequilibrium quantity adjustments.

Such a theory is fortunately vigorously alive. It is the *disequilibrium econometrics of cyclical growth*, described in the next section.

For the NCM and RBCT the key concepts are: *equilibrium*, primarily *real*, but shocks may be *monetary*, *fluctuation*, both *micro* and *macro*, *exogenous*, both *investment* and *consumption*, *speculative*, *formal*, for a time *central*, but now *peripheral*.

The NKE is characterized by: *disequilibrium*, *real*, *micro*, both *empirical* and *formal*, *central*.

9. Disequilibrium Econometrics of Cyclical Growth

9.1. Introduction

In Section 5, I argued that the ICT was incorporated in the early econometric cycle models (EECM), but that the entire approach was ultimately abandoned under the impact of static Keynesianism. Hicks, who with his *IS–LM* model had been the most successful promoter of static Keynesian theory, later attempted a fusion of the EECM with Keynesian ideas, but in this he failed. The mainstream work on economic fluctuation of the past twenty years has been completely separate from the earlier tradition.

Outside of the mainstream, a small number of economists did continue a tradition which may be regarded as a fusion of Keynesian ideas and the EECM. The main references are Phillips (1961), Bergstrom (1962, 1967, 1976, 1988), Bergstrom and Wymer (1976), Gandolfo (1981), Gandolfo and Padoan (1984, 1987, 1990), Hillinger (1966, 1986, 1987), and Hillinger and Schueler (1978). I refer to this tradition as the *disequilibrium econometrics of cyclical growth (DECG)*. While there are considerable differences between these authors in detail and in problems chosen for emphasis, there is also a surprising amount of agreement on purpose, methodology, and substantive assumptions. These common features will be discussed in the following subsections.

9.2. Purpose and Methodology of the DECG

The principal aim of the DECG, as the name implies, is to explain the cyclical growth of output of the macroeconomy. The explanations take the form of a small or medium-sized econometric model, derived from economic theory and estimated and tested against macroeconomic data. The DECG emphasizes the need to take into account the actual process by which data are generated. Virtually all economists who have considered the subject have argued that the generation of data is more nearly continuous than discrete. In the DECG, this aspect is reflected in the methods used for empirical estimation. This is discussed in Chapter 4, where references are given.

9.3. Substantive Aspects of the DECG

Economic fluctuations are explained in all of these models in terms of the dynamics of disequilibrium adjustment processes. All the models emphasize the importance of fixed and inventory investment in the fluctuations of GNP (GDP). Furthermore, all of the models use the *second-order accelerator (SOA)* to model the output–inventory decisions. This means that the *rate of change* (not the level) is influenced by the difference between actual and desired levels of stocks. In the models of Gandolfo and SEMECON, the SOA is used also to model fixed investment. This means that the *rate of change* (not the level) of investment depends on the difference between actual and desired fixed capital.

The importance of the SOA as a distinct explanation of investment cycles is stressed in the SEMECON literature.

9.4. Conclusion

After several decades of essentially static macroeconomic theorizing and atheoretical time-series analysis, the need for a theory-based dynamic modelling approach to macroeconomics is increasingly being recognized. In his recent Nobel Price lecture, Solow (1988) has pointed to the need to construct small dynamic econometric models of macroeconomic disequilibrium. The DECG has been carrying out this enterprise with considerable sophistication and success for about three decades.

The key concepts are: *disequilibrium*, primarily *real*, but also *monetary*, *fluctuation* or *cycle*, *macro*, primarily *endogenous* but with *exogenous* influences, *investment* and *consumption*, *speculative* and *empirical*, *formal*, as yet *peripheral*.

10. Economic Fluctuations under Socialism

This section provides a background for the papers of the Hungarian contributors to this volume. Neither space nor competence allows me to go into much detail. Fortunately, recent surveys by Nove (1987), Nuti (1987), and van Brabant (1989) discuss many of the relevant issues and cite the associated literature.

The principal theory of capitalism is the model of general equilibrium under perfect competition, for which the main ideas are already found in Adam Smith. Socialism has lacked a similar theory. More recently, Taylor, Lange, and Lerner proposed a general equilibrium model for socialism in which appropriate prices are set by the planning agency.[9] The theory of socialist planning developed in the Soviet Union may also be regarded as a theory of a full-employment, though not necessarily efficient, socialist economy.

Both sets of theories have been allied with their respective ideologies, and it has been difficult under either system to develop theories dealing with deviations from the presumed optimum, including theories of unemployment and of economic fluctuations. In the capitalist economies such theories formed, in the phrase of Keynes, the 'underground of economics', a situation altered only by the impact of Keynes himself. Criticisms of socialism from within were initially prohibited by the ruling communist parties. Such criticism began in two of the less repressive socialist countries, Hungary and Poland, in the 1960s and 1970s. In the following paragraphs I discuss a few selected contributions to the theory of economic fluctuations under socialism.

A remarkable early contribution was made by Aftalion, who was a leading member of the Accelerationist school of economists dealing with economic fluctuations, and specifically with investment cycles under capitalism. In Aftalion (1909) he argued that the accelerator mechanism would be equally operative under socialism and would lead to similar fluctuations. The prescience of this thought is illustrated by the fact that accelerator-based investment cycles are the central mechanism of both the Hungarian and the SEMECON contributions in this volume.

Aftalion's reflections about investment cycles under socialism were soon forgotten. Apart from the contributions of Bródy and Tarjan in Chapters 5 and 6, writers on economic disequilibrium and fluctuations under socialism focused on institutional features, particularly on the planning process and the constraints facing planners, as explanatory factors.

Two streams of literature of this type have been prominent recently. The first stream, the so-called 'shortage' approach, is associated with the name of Kornai, the most important statement being Kornai (1980). Kornai points to the pervasive presence of shortages in planned economies, which directly contradict the claim of a rationally planned, consistent outcome. His discus-

---

[9] For a discussion and reference see Kowalik (1987).

sion is microeconomic and essentially static. The constraints and motivations of economic agents are analysed in great detail, and it is shown why the system has no tendency to a market-clearing solution. The discussion is remarkably similar to that offered by the NKE for market economies. Of course, the institutional detail differs greatly.

The other school is the so called 'disequilibrium' approach associated with the name of Portes, the seminal contribution being Portes (1981), who uses non-Walrasian equilibrium analysis in which the algebraic sum of excess demands is zero. The disequilibrium school builds small macroeconometric models. The results are interpreted as denying the general shortage phenomenon, which the shortage economists regard as evident.

The evaluation of the two schools by van Brabant (1989) is quite similar to my evaluation of the NCM and NKE in Section 8 above: the disequilibrium approach is implausible as it denies the obvious; the shortage approach is more realistic, but lacks a dynamic dimension. The dominant macroeconomic schools for both types of economies have run out of steam without producing convincing explanations of economic fluctuations. They have all tended to focus on institutional aspects of the respective systems. Both sets of writers have missed the remarkable stability of the phenomenon of economic fluctuations over time and over different economic systems. Basically, they have remained investment cycles, the longer movements being in fixed, the shorter ones in inventory, investment. This makes it plausible that the simpler, more fundamental, technology-oriented, explanation connected with the ICT deserves consideration as an explanation of the fluctuations in both types of systems.

11. Economic Fluctuations and Paradigm Changes: A Conclusion

Primarily abstract and primarily empirical schools of thought have alternated or coincided in macroeconomics, particularly in the study of economic fluctuations, for centuries. The abstract theories have had a large ideological component, expressed either in a support of general equilibrium theory or in opposition to it, as in the case of Keynes and the Keynesians. Given the greater prestige of theoretical as compared with empirical work in economics, and given also that most economists see themselves as suppliers of policy advice, it is not surprising that the abstract, ideological, policy-oriented schools have attracted the most attention. Their evident failure has also been the prime ingredient in a general disillusionment with macroeconomics.

The ICT is the one macroeconomic tradition which, by staying clear of the ideological battles, attracted less attention, but made steady and impressive progress. It can now meet the highest standards and criteria that can be proposed, in relation to both economic and econometric theory.

TABLE 1.1 Economic paradigms and the associated key concepts

	Equilibrium	Disequilibrium	Real	Monetary	Fluctuation	Cycle	Micro	Macro	Exogenous	Endogenous	Investment	Consumption	Speculative	Empirical	Formal	Informal	Central	Peripheral
Before 1600	*						*						*	*		*	*	
Mercantilism, 1600–1760		*		*	*			*					*	*		*	*	
Dominant tradition, 1760–1930			*	*			*								*		*	*
Subsidiary traditions, 1790–1870		*	*	*	*	*		*		*	*		*	*		*		*
Marxism, 1870–		*	*	*	*	*		*		*	*	*	*	*				*
Investment cycle theories, 1870–1930		*	*	*	*	*		*	*		*	*		*				*
Keynesianism, 1930–1960		*	*	*	*	*	*	*			*		*	*	*		*	
Macroeconomic dynamics, 1930–1960		*	*		*	*	*	*		*	*	*	*	*	*			*
Empirical macroeconomics, 1930–1960		*	*				*	*						*		*		*
Monetarism		*		*	*		*	*	*		*	*	*	*	*	*	*	
New Classical macroeconomics and real business cycle theory	*		*				*	*	*				*	*	*		*	*
New Keynesian economics		*	*				*							*	*		*	
Disequilibrium econometrics of cyclical growth		*	*	*	*	*		*	*	*	*	*	*	*	*			*

References

Abramovitz, M. (1950), *Inventories and Business Cycles*, National Bureau for Economic Research, New York.

—— (1986), 'Comment', in Gordon (1986 : 214–23).

Aftalion, A. (1909), 'La realité des superproductions générales', *Revue d'économie politique*, 23(3) : 201–29.

Allen, W. R. (1987), 'Mercantilism', in Eatwell *et al.* (1987), pp. 445–9.

Bauer, T. (1978), 'Investment cycles in planned economies', *Acta Oeconomica*, 21(3) : 243–60.

Bergstrom, A. R. (1962), 'A model of cycles, technical progress, the production function and cyclical growth', *Econometrica*, 29 : 357–70.

—— (1967), *'The Construction and Use of Economic Models'*, English Universities Press, London. Also published as *Selected Economic Models and their Analysis*, American Elsevier, New York, 1967.

—— (1976), *Statistical Inference in Continuous Time Economic Models*, North Holland, Amsterdam.

—— (1988), 'The ET interview : Professor Albert Rex Bergstrom' (interviewed by P. C. B. Phillips), *Econometric Theory*, 4 : 301–27.

—— and Wymer, C. R. (1976), 'A model of disequilibrium neoclassical growth and its application to the United Kingdom', in Bergstrom (1976).

Blanchard, O. J., and Fischer, S. (1989), *Lectures on Macroeconomics*, MIT Press, Cambridge, Mass.

Blaug, M. (1980), *The Methodology of Economics*, Cambridge University Press.

Blinder, A. S. (1981), 'Inventories and the structure of macro models', *American Economic Review*, 71 : 11–16.

—— and Holtz-Eakin, D. (1986), 'Inventory fluctuations in the United States since 1929', in Gordon (1986).

Box, G. E. P., and Jenkins, G. M. (1970), *Time Series Analysis, Forecasting and Control*, Holden-Day, San Francisco.

Davis, C., and Charameza, W. (eds.), (1989), *Models of disequilibrium and Shortage in Centrally Planned Economies*, Chapman & Hall, London/New York.

Domar, E. (1946), 'Capital expansion, rate of growth and employment', *Econometrica*, 14 : 137–47.

Eatwell, J., Milgate, M., and Newman, P. (eds.), (1987), *The New Palgrave : A Dictionary of Economics*, Macmillan, London/Stockton, New York/Maruzen, Tokyo.

Friedman, M. (1953), 'The methodology of positive economics', in *Essays in Positive Economics*, University of Chicago Press.

—— (ed.) (1956), *Studies in the Quantity Theory of Money*, University of Chicago Press.

—— (1968), 'The role of monetary policy', *American Economic Review*, 58(1) : 1–17.

—— and Schwarz, A. J. (1963), *A Monetary History of the United States 1867–1960*, Princeton University Press.

Frisch, R. (1933), 'Propagation problems and impulse problems in dynamic economics', in *Economic Essays in Honour of Gustav Cassel*, George Allen & Unwin, London. Reprinted in R. A. Gordon and L. R. Klein (1965).

Frydman, R., and Phelps, E. S. (1983), *Individual Forecasting and Aggregate Outcomes*, Cambridge University Press.

Fusfeld, D. R. (1966), *The Age of the Economist*, Scott, Foresman, Glenview, Ill.

Gandolfo, G. (1981), *Qualitative Analysis and Econometric Estimation of Continuous Time Dynamic Models*, North-Holland, Amsterdam.

—— and Padoan, C. P. (1984), *A Disequilibrium Model of Real and Financial Accumulation in an Open Economy*, Springer, Berlin.

—— —— (1987), 'The mark V version of the Italian continuous time model', *Quaderni dell' Instituto di Economia dell' Universita di Siena*, 70.

—— —— (1990), 'The Italian continuous time model, theory and empirical results', *Economic Modelling*, 7 : 91–132.

Gordon, R. A., and Klein, L. R. (1965), *Readings in Business Cycles*, Richard D. Irwin, Homewood, Ill.

Gordon, R. J. (ed.) (1986), *The American Business Cycle : Continuity and Change*, University of Chicago Press.

—— and Veitch, J. M. (1986), 'Fixed investment in the American business cycle', in Gordon (1986).

Haberler, G. (1958), *Prosperity and Depression*, Harvard University Press, Cambridge, Mass. Originally published 1937 by the League of Nations.

Hahn, F. (1990), 'John Hicks the theorist', *Economic Journal*, 100 : 401, 539–49.

Hansen, A. H. (1941), *Fiscal Policy and Business Cycles*, W. W. Norton, New York.

Harrod, R. F. (1939), 'An essay in dynamic theory', *Economic Journal*, 49 : 14–33.

Hicks, J. R. (1937), 'Mr Keynes and the "Classics" ', *Econometrica*, 5 : 147–59.

—— (1950), 'A contribution to the theory of the trade cycle', Clarendon Press, Oxford.

—— (1965), *Capital and Growth*, Oxford University Press.

Hillinger, C. (1966), 'An econometric model of business cycles', *Manchester School of Economics and Social Studies*, 34 : 269–84.

—— (1986), 'Inventory cycle and equipment cycle interaction', in A. Chikan (ed.), *Inventories in Theory and Practice*, Elsevier, Amsterdam.

—— (1987), 'Business cycle stylized facts and explanatory models', *Journal of Economic Dynamics and Control*, 11 : 257–63.

—— and Schueler, K. W. (1978), 'Cyclical fluctuations of the German economy : a continuous time econometric model', *Social Science Review*, 2 : 75–88.

Juglar, C. (1862), *Crises commerciales et leur retour périodique en France, en Angleterre et aux Etats-Unis*, Guilaumin, Paris, 1889.

Kahn, J. A. (1987), 'Inventories and the volatility of production', *American Economic Review*, 77(4) : 667–79.

Kaldor, N. (1985), *Economics without Equilibrium*, M. E. Sharpe, Armonk, NY.

Kalecki, M. (1933), 'Outline of a theory of the business cycle', trans. from Polish in 1966; in Kalecki (1971).

—— (1935), 'A macrodynamic theory of business cycles', *Econometrica*, 3 : 327–44.

—— (1954), *Theory of Economic Dynamics*, George Allen & Unwin, London.

—— (1971), *Selected Essays on the Dynamics of the Capitalist Economy, 1933–1970*, Cambridge University Press.

Keynes, J. M. (1936), *The General Theory of Employment, Interest and Money*, Macmillan, London.

Kitchin, J. (1923), 'Cycles and trends in economic factors', *Review of Economics and Statistics*, 5(1) : 10–17.

Kornai, J. (1980), *Economics of Shortage*, 2 vols., North-Holland, Amsterdam.

Kowalik, T. (1987), 'Lange–Lerner mechanism', in Eatwell *et al.* (1987), pp. 129–31.

Kuznets, S. (1926), *Cyclical Fluctuations : Retail and Wholesale Trade, United States 1919–1925*, Adelphi, New York.

Kydland, F., and Prescott, E. C. (1982), 'Time to build and aggregate fluctuations', *Econometrica*, 50(6) : 1345–70.

Lee, M. W. (1971), *Macroeconomics : Fluctuations, Growth and Stability*, Richard D. Irwin, Homewood, Ill.

Long, J. B., and Plosser, C. I. (1983), 'Real business cycles', *Journal of Political Economy*, 19(1) : 39–69.

Lovell, M. C. (1986), 'Tests of the rational expectations hypothesis', *American Economic Review*, 76(1) : 110–24.

Lucas, R. E. Jr. (1972), 'Expectations and the neutrality of money', *Journal of Economic Theory*, 4(2) : 103–23. Reprinted in Lucas (1981).

—— (1975), 'An equilibrium model of the business cycle', *Journal of Political Economy*, 83(1) : 113–44. Reprinted in Lucas (1981).

—— (1977), 'Understanding business cycles', in K. Brunner and A. H. Meltzer (eds.), *Stabilization of the Domestic and International Economy*, Carnegie-Rochester Series on Public Policy, v, 5 North-Holland, Amsterdam. Reprinted in Lucas (1981).

—— (1981), *Studies in Business Cycle Theory*, Basil Blackwell, Oxford.

Lundberg, E. (1937), *Studies in the Theory of Economic Expansion*, P. S. King & Sons, London; Basil Blackwell, Oxford, 1955.

Malinvaud, E. (1980), *Profitability and Unemployment*, Cambridge University Press.

Mankiw, N. G. (1989), 'Real business cycles : a new Keynesian perspective', *Journal of Economic Perspectives*, 3(3) : 79–90.

Matthews, R. C. O. (1959), *The Business Cycle*, University of Chicago Press.

Metzler, L. A. (1941), 'The nature and stability of inventory cycles', *Review of Economic Statistics*, 23 : 113–29. Reprinted in R. A. Gordon and L. R. Klein (1965).

Miron, J. A., and Zeldes, S. P. (1988), 'Seasonality, cost shocks and the production smoothing of inventories', *Econometrica*, 56(4) : 877–908.

Muth, J. F. (1960), 'Optimal properties of exponentially weighted forecasts', *Journal of the American Statistical Association*, 55 : 299–306.

Nove, A. (1987), 'Socialism', in Eatwell *et al.* (1987), pp. 398–407.

Nuti, D. M. (1987), 'Cycles in socialist economies', in Eatwell *et al.* (1987), pp. 744–6.

Okun, A. M. (1981), *Prices and Quantities : A Macroeconomic Analysis*, Brookings Institution, Washington, DC.

Pesaran, M. H. (1987), *The limits to rational expectations*, Basil Blackwell, Oxford.

Phelps, E. S. (1968), 'Money wage dynamics and labour market equilibrium', *Journal of Political Economy*, 76(4) : 687–711.

Phillips, A. W. (1961), 'A simple model of employment and prices in a growing economy', *Economica*, 28 : 360–70.

Plosser, C. I. (1989), 'Understanding real business cycles', *Journal of Economic Perspectives*, 3(3) : 51–77.

Portes, R. (1981), 'Macroeconomic equilibrium and disequilibrium in centrally planned economies', *Economic Inquiry*, 19(4) : 559–78.

Ravetz, J. R. (1971), *Scientific Knowledge and its Social Problems*, Oxford University Press.

Robertson, D. H. (1936), 'Some notes on Mr. Keynes's general theory of employment', *Quarterly Journal of Economics*, 51 : 168–91.

Samuelson, P. A. (1939), 'Interaction between the multiplier analysis and the principle of acceleration', *Review of Economic Statistics*, 4 : 75–8.

—— (1948), *Economics*, McGraw-Hill, New York (11th edn. 1980).

Sargent, T. J. (1973), 'Rational expectations, the real rate of interest, and the natural rate of unemployment', *Brooking Papers on Economic Activity*, 2 : 429–72.

—— (1979), *Macroeconomic Theory*, Academic Press, New York.

Schumpeter, J. A. (1939), *Business Cycles*, McGraw-Hill, New York.

—— (1954), *The History of Economic Analysis*, Oxford University Press; paperback edition, George Allen & Unwin, London, 1986.

Silvestre, J. (1987), 'Fixprice models', in Eatwell *et al.* (1987), pp. 388–92.

Solow, R. M. (1956), 'A contribution to the theory of economic growth', *Quarterly Journal of Economics*, 70 : 65–94.

—— (1988), 'Growth theory and after', *American Economic Review*, 78(3) : 307–17.

Spiegel, H. W. (1971), *The Growth of Economic Thought*, Prentice-Hall, Englewood Cliffs, NJ.

Stigler, G. J. (1988), 'Palgrave's Dictionary of Economics', *Journal of Economic Literature*, 26(4) : 1729–36.

Swan, T. W. (1956), 'Economic growth and capital accumulation', *Economic Record*, 32 : 334–61.

Tibergen, J. (1930), 'Ein Schiffsbauzyklus?', *Weltwirtschaftliches Archiv*. Reprinted in L. H. Klaasen et al. (1959), *Selected Papers*, North-Holland, Amsterdam.

—— (1939), *Statistical Testing of Business Cycle Theories*, 2 vols., League of Nations, Geneva.

van Brabant, J. M. (1989), 'Socialist economics : the disequilibrium school and the shortage economy', *Journal of Economic Literature*, 4(2) : 157–75.

Walters, A. (1987), 'Friedman, Milton', in Eatwell *et al.* (1987), pp. 422–7.

Waugh, F. V. (1964), 'Cobweb models', *Journal of Farm Economics*, 46 : 732–50.

Zarnowitz, V. (1985), 'Recent work on business cycles in historical perspective', *Journal of Economic Literature*, 23(2) : 523–80.

—— (1990), 'A guide to what is known about business cycles', *Business Economics*, 25(3) : 5–13.

—— (1992), *Business Cycles : Theory, History, Indicators and Forecasting*, University of Chicago Press for NBER.

Zellner, A. (1985), 'Bayesian econometrics', *Econometrica*, 53(2) : 253–69.

2

The Methodology of Empirical Science

Claude Hillinger

1. Introduction

A principal aim of Chapter 1 was to show that the investment cycle tradition which is continued in the present volume, was by no means empirically refuted. Its basic findings were unjustifiably forgotten and are now in a process of being rediscovered. I have argued that the reason for the lack of steady progress in macroeconomics is the failure to apply the standard precepts of the scientific method. This theme will be elaborated further in the present chapter.

Methodological debates typically flare up in immature sciences when the lack of progress becomes painfully evident. Economics, particularly macroeconomics, is in just such a situation. This is reflected in a sharp rise in the number of articles suggesting fundamental changes in economic methodology. Three broad streams may be distinguished in this literature. First, there are the econometricians: some advocate changes in technical econometric methodology.[1] Others stress new approaches to model validation.[2] Second, there are the authors who are oriented towards the philosophy of science. They tend to criticize the insufficient emphasis on hypothesis-testing in economics.[3] And third, there are the advocates of 'rhetoric' who are allied with the counterculture in the philosophy of science, whose best-known representative is Paul Fayerabend. The members of this group deny the existence of a scientific method with prescriptive value.[4]

It is impossible to deal with the literature on economic methodology in detail here.[5] Generally, it takes on part of the problematic characteristics of economics itself. It is highly abstract, programmatic, and devoid of examples showing that the methodology advocated leads to the reliable accumulation of knowledge.

The notion that empirical science can be learned abstractly must, at any rate, be treated with caution. The philosophy of science developed after physics

---

[1] The completely atheoretical Vector autoregression (VAR) methodology advocated by Sims (1980) may be mentioned in this connection.

[2] An example is the exchange between McAllen *et al.* (1985) and Leamer (1985).

[3] A highly readable contribution in this vein is Blaug (1980).

[4] A forceful statement of this position is given by McCloskey (1983).

[5] Selections from the diverse streams and positions in the literature on economic methodology are found in Caldwell (1984).

had achieved astounding successes and focused on those aspects of physics that seemed interesting from a philosophical point of view. This left out most of the social aspects of science as well as its craft aspect. I believe that the successful conduct of empirical science involves much more pedestrian issues than those discussed by philosophers of science or by econometricians. The discussion of these elementary issues is a major concern of this chapter.

The idea that there is a single method of science applicable to the natural and the social sciences generally and to economics in particular is controversial. In recent decades, many economists have accepted the position of Popper on falsification as being of universal validity. However, Popper's views, or economists' understanding of them, appear to be too non-specific to be a sufficient guide for actual research practice. Also, Popper's analysis may be challenged as being partial. This is discussed in Section 4. First I turn to the question of whether there is a universal scientific method and, if so, what its outstanding characteristics are.

2. The Unity of Science

That the scientific method, as practised in the natural sciences, is universally applicable in the empirical sciences is a proposition that cannot be proven, but can be made extremely plausible.

In order to be as concrete as possible, I will start with a discussion of the role of scientific method in my own research on economic fluctuations which was inspired by the above viewpoint.

As a graduate student at the University of Chicago, I studied intensively the philosophy of science as well as the writings on methodology of prominent physicists.[6] I was motivated by the belief that the most advanced sciences should naturally serve as models for the less advanced ones, such as economics. The outcome of these studies was that they confirmed and deepened the elementary notion that hypothesis-testing, at the empirical and theoretical levels, is the essence of the scientific process.

When I came to look for a dissertation topic, I noticed that at the time it was generally accepted that economic fluctuations in the postwar US economy roughly followed a 40-month cycle and were dominated by inventory investment and disinvestment. Metzler's model of inventory cycles was well known, but there was no effort either systematically to establish the *stylized facts* characterizing these cycles, or to test Metzler's model as a hypothesis to explain them. From the point of view of the scientific method, this appeared to be a gross negligence. For my dissertation, therefore, I decided to test the

[6] From my studies of that period, I would like to recommend four books of outstanding depth and scope. Two are by philosophers: Hempel (1966), which I still consider to be the best short introduction to the scientific method, and Nagel (1961); the remaining two are by a physicist (Frank 1957) and a historian (Mason 1962).

stylized facts of inventory cycles and Metzler's explanation. Regarding the former, I was quite successful; regarding the latter, the results were mixed.

The step from the philosophy of science to an appropriate econometric methodology was greatly smoothed for me by R. L. Basmann, who at that time taught econometrics at Chicago. He had also studied the philosophy of science and had come to similar conclusions regarding hypothesis-testing, and the general failure to conduct such tests in the context of the large-scale macroeconomic model methodology that was then prevalent. He became the chairman of my dissertation committee.

The econometric methodology that was developed in connection with my dissertation became the basis for the subsequent work at SEMECON, in the course of which it was greatly refined. My conviction that the SEMECON methodology is simply the methodology of the natural sciences has been confirmed in conversations on methodological problems that I have had over the years with natural scientists. More recently, Thilo Weser obtained his Ph.D. at SEMECON after previously receiving a Ph.D. in experimental physics. He participated intensively in our discussions of the applied econometric work, and it can be said that we found no basic distinctions between his approach, based on his training in physics, and the empirical research at SEMECON.

One reason for believing in the universality of the scientific method is the success with which it has spread to new areas. Beginning with physics, it later entered and transformed other physical sciences, such as chemistry and geology. The full-fledged entry of the scientific method into biology is quite recent; Watson (1968) describes the immense resistance that the scientific method, and the associated revolution in molecular biology, encountered from traditional biologists.

Economists and econometricians have shown little interest in the natural sciences and their methodology. Two outstanding exceptions are R. L. Basmann, who, as mentioned, was my mentor at Chicago, and A. Zellner. A strong defence of the unity of science is given in Chapter 1 of Zellner's (1984) *Philosophy and Objectives of Econometrics*.

3. The Non-intellectual Aspects of Science

3.1. Background

There is a tendency in the social sciences and particularly in economics to view scientific and methodological problems as being primarily intellectual. This view of the problems cannot explain why the social sciences tenaciously cling to ineffective methodologies even though the effective methodology of the natural sciences has by now been practised for centuries. To understand this phenomenon, it is necessary to look at some non-intellectual and social aspects of science.

There are two very fundamental aspects of science that are non-intellectual and are not much discussed in the standard philosophy of science. They are science as a social activity, and science as a craft activity. Fortunately, there are a few first-rate books that focus on these aspects. At a general philosophical level, the writings of Michael Polanyi, particularly Polanyi (1958, 1966), are of pivotal importance. His basic message is that the most human knowledge is *tacit*, i.e. non-formalizable. This is true of almost all of the activities of daily life, such as recognizing a face, or riding a bicycle. Knowledge that can be expressed verbally corresponds to the one-tenth of an iceberg that is above water, tacit knowledge to the nine-tenths that is below. Knowledge that can be expressed in mathematical and even more restrictively, axiomatic terms represents not much more than the tip of the iceberg.

A detailed description of the social and craft aspects of science is given by the historian and philosopher of science Ravetz (1971). This book is particularly valuable because of his discussion of immature sciences or fields of inquiry. An 'immature' science is defined as one that lacks generally agreed upon criteria for establishing factual truth. This definition is certainly applicable to economics and other social sciences.

Similar themes have been explored in several books by the physicist Ziman, particularly in Ziman (1978). He stresses the central role played in science by the recognition and communication of patterns, both essentially non-formalizable activities, which join the craft and social aspects of science at the most elementary level. I will return to both of these aspects below.

It is a telling fact that the *critical* attention of social scientists has been deflected almost entirely away from their own analysis of their own activities and participation in a social system. An important exception is Tullock (1966): in addition to dealing with many aspects of the social structure of science, he deals also with 'the backwardness of the social sciences'.

3.2. The Social Aspect of Science

The incentives facing scientists and the efficiency of the social system of science

There is a widespread *ideology* of science, according to which the social structure of science is such that competition between scientists automatically leads to the most efficient production of new knowledge, analogously to the efficient production of commodities in a competitive economy. This idealized picture of science is valid only if the leaders of the discipline, i.e. those deciding on promotion and access to journals, possess appropriate criteria for evaluating scientific research: by this I mean criteria, the application of which leads to the separation of truth and falsehood. If the criteria possessed by the leaders are ineffectual, the process of accumulating knowledge will not occur. Moreover, the leaders are likely to oppose the introduction of methods and criteria that are effective, since these would tend to undermine their authority and devalue the human capital that they have acquired.

After analysing and rejecting various explanations for the relative backwardness of the social sciences, G. Tullock comes to the following conclusion:

The real difference between the social sciences and the natural sciences, then, is a difference in motivation. Investigators in the natural sciences are motivated by a desire to make practical applications of new knowledge, by curiosity, or by a desire to make money out of research in a field where only research leading to increases in knowledge is profitable. In the social sciences the possibility of practical applications is very limited, and curiosity is likely to be directed at non-scientific ends. As a result, the induced researchers are not subject to the strict controls that cover the activities of those in the natural sciences. Further, there are no significant motives for attempting to obscure or conceal the truth in the natural sciences, while social fields abound with such motives. The 'organization of inquiry' in the natural sciences is a system of voluntary co-operation in which the work of each investigator not only meets his own desires but also helps other investigators. The system works largely because of the similarity of the ends and presuppositions of the scientists. In the social studies, there is less similarity of ends and presuppositions and, consequently, less voluntary co-operation. (Tullock 1966 : 193–4)

This discussion points at still another non-intellectual aspect of science, namely, the moral dimension. The improvement of an immature discipline may require the efforts of individuals whose commitment to truth is stronger than the material incentives provided by the discipline.

Replication and the social character of knowledge

No aspect of science is more important than replication, because it is what establishes the *social* character of science and distinguishes it from more subjective areas of human experience such as religion or art. Recently there has been concern in economics regarding the replicability of published results, in the sense that another investigator, starting with the same body of data, should be able to compute the same statistical measures (cf. Dewald *et al.* 1986). This notion of replication is only trivially related to replication as understood in natural science.

The archetypical form of replication involves the independent replication of an experiment by another investigator and the demonstration that the results are essentially similar. This is not possible in many sciences such as astronomy, geology, or evolution. In spite of this, all of these fields succeed in unambiguously establishing facts. The same can even be said of history, though it is not a science in the sense of establishing theoretically relevant facts and then being able to agree on their explanation.

The essential process leading to an expanding factual consensus in the non-experimental disciplines is the careful scrutiny of all the available evidence by independent investigators.[7] The failure to accumulate factual knowledge in economics is a failure of effort and of competence which cannot be corrected by merely checking the arithmetic of published results. The inability of macroeconomists to establish convergence regarding the stylized facts of macroeconomic fluctuations is a major theme of this volume.

Another dramatic example is the history of the quantity theory of money. The fame of Copernicus, as everyone knows, is due to his advocacy of the heliocentric hypothesis in the sixteenth century. What is less known is that he was also one of the first advocates of the quantity theory (cf. Spiegel 1971: Chapter 4). The subsequent history of the two propositions could not differ more starkly. The heliocentric hypothesis was strongly opposed by the Church and consequently also by the secular authorities. In this area, the dogmatic opposition to scientific evidence ultimately collapsed, and today the heliocentric hypothesis is doubted only by a handful of cranks. The quantity theory never came into conflict with formidable institutions intending to enforce their own version of the truth. Over the centuries, economists simply did not make the effort carefully to marshal the enormous amount of relevant evidence. The major exception is the work of Friedman and his associates at Chicago, which did succeed in establishing the quantity theory for a while (cf. Ch. 1, Sect. 7 above). Owing to the failure continuously to train new economists in the replication. of basic empirical knowledge, the belief in the validity of the quantity theory is again fading. I return to this topic in the following section on the craft aspect of science.

3.3. The Craft Aspect of Science

The craft tradition in natural science

A crucial factor in the rise of modern science was the merging in the sixteenth century of two previously separate social traditions: a scholarly speculative tradition, which had found its home in the monasteries, the Church, and the early universities, and the tradition of the artisans and craftsmen. When the two streams joined, the craftsmen became the instrument-makers and experimenters; the scholars became the theoreticians who furnished the explanatory hypotheses for the regularities discovered by the experimenters. While the craftsmen had been of inferior social status, in the context of science, both their scientific and social prestige became at least equal to that of the theoreticians.[8]

---

[7] The social validation of scientific knowledge is discussed by Ravetz (1971), particularly in Chs. 6 and 10, and by Ziman (1978), particularly in Chs. 1 and 2.
[8] This period is described in Mason (1962: Ch. 13).

The social sciences never absorbed a similar craft tradition. In economics, the scholarly empirical schools of historical or institutional economics never entered a symbiosis with the dominant theoretical school. Instead, they fought against theory and lost. In the following subsections I deal with various aspects of craft knowledge in relation to the generation and interpretation of data that are particularly important for understanding and evaluating the SEMECON approach.

Data generation and data properties

The determination of 'facts' in the natural sciences has usually been the result of extraordinary efforts involving great skill and determination and in many cases huge costs. In contrast to this, the attitude towards facts in economics unfortunately often borders on indifference. Ravetz, who analyses at great length the social and craft aspects of determining scientific facts, writes:

The difficulty of achieving genuine facts will vary enormously over different fields of study. In fields which are well matured in their methods of work and controlling judgements, and which are descriptive rather than theoretical in character, facts are easy to come by; indeed, the transition from refined data to facts may be hardly noticeable. At the other extreme are fields which are both immature and strongly theoretical, so that the objects of investigation are replaced with dizzying speed. In such cases, one can find libraries full of research reports, all of it the product of hard work and some of it of inspiration as well; but no facts. (Ravetz 1971 : 19)

Very illuminating is the following statement by Ziman:

Through our natural facility for *pattern recognition* we may become aware of significant features of our experience, and transfer consensible messages, in the form of diagrams and pictures, whose 'meaning' cannot be deduced by formal mathematical or logical manipulation. For this reason, scientific knowledge is not so much 'objective' as 'intersubjective', and can only be validated and translated into action by the intervention of human minds.

These messages are not merely poured into the archives nor passively received by other scientists. Consensuality implies strong interactions between the human actors in the drama. Thus, for example, elementary errors and misunderstandings are eliminated by the independent repetition of experiments, or by theoretical criticism. . . . trivial errors are endemic in scientific research and must be continually corrected if the system is to generate anything approaching 'the truth'. (Ziman 1978 : 6, 7)

In economics, concern with the careful establishment of facts is most highly evolved in experimental economics. In contrast to this, macroeconomists take a formalistic approach to data. Empirical research for them is pretty much limited to finding data with an appropriate sounding caption in an official source book. Scarcely any interest is shown in the likely properties of the data.

Econometric practice revolves very largely about the use of complicated procedures for estimation and inference, based on assumptions whose applicability to the data remains largely unexamined and often highly implausible. Regarding this attitude, Medawar writes:

another distinguishing mark of unnatural scientists is their faith in the efficacy of statistical formulae, particularly when processed by a computer—the use of which is in itself interpreted as a mark of scientific manhood. There is no need to cause offence by specifying the unnatural sciences, for their practioners will recognize themselves easily: the shoe belongs where it fits. (Medawar 1982 : 167)

The most widely used statistic in the natural sciences is the signal–noise ratio, which describes the quality of the data and hence the inferences that may reasonably be made from it. It is revealing that this statistic is virtually never used in economics. The reporting of such ratios should be a prime responsibility of the statistical agencies, but this is wholly alien to the spirit in which they operate.

The following are some examples of craft knowledge regarding properties of data which are particularly important in evaluating the empirical work of SEMECON discussed in this volume.

1. The key variable in short-run economic fluctuations is inventory investment and disinvestment. Basically, it is estimated as the difference between the 'sources' and 'uses' sides of the national accounts and thus contains a compounding of the errors made on both sides. Many countries do not show a statistical discrepancy separately, but simply include it in the figure for inventory investment. Indicative of the quality of the data is the fact that the revisions are sometimes of the same order of magnitude as the data themselves.

2. Regarding fixed investment, or capital formation as a whole, the situation is different, but not necessarily better. Many problems are discussed in Usher (1976). I will here mention two: (1) Economic theory suggests that real capital should be defined in terms of the output it can produce in co-operation with other given factors. The practice, however, is to define real capital in terms of the cost of producing it. (2) A considerable amount of capital is invested in unfinished projects and cannot produce any output at all. Curiously, this elementary fact is recognized in the accounting practice of the former communist countries, but not in the West.

The improvement and analysis of these two types of data would plausibly have contributed more to an understanding of macroeconomic fluctuation than all the ideologically motivated macroeconomic controversies of the last decades.

3. Economists appear to believe that as, far as data are concerned, more is always better. Specifically, since the availability of quarterly national accounts data, the annual data have been neglected. There is no basis for this assumption. The quarterly data are blowups of smaller samples and, for this and other reasons, significantly noisier. Even after seasonal adjustment, which is never unproblematic, they are likely to contain short-run systematic movements not corresponding to the theory being tested. At SEMECON we have

often found that the use of annual data, as in the present volume, yields more stable and significant results than the use of quarterly data.

The analysis of data

It has already been mentioned that formal statistical inference, the main content of econometrics, has been little used in natural science. There, the main form of inference has been the visual detection of patterns in data, objectivity being guaranteed by *consensuability*, i.e. the ability of different skilled investigators to detect the same pattern. Ziman (1978) discusses this process in great detail and gives many examples.

The use of sophisticated statistical methods in natural science is relatively recent and is concentrated in areas where observations are few and there is little theory to guide the investigator. The evaluation of medical treatments is a prime example.

The work of SEMECON combines the visual approach, particularly in the preliminary analysis of data, with sophisticated methods of inference, specifically the maximum entropy spectrum (Chapter 3) and maximum likelihood estimation in continuous-time econometric models (Chapter 4).

4. The Logic of Scientific Inference

4.1. Alternative Views

The preceding sections have stressed the social and craft aspects of science. In addition to these, it is certainly highly desirable to have an understanding of the basic logic involved in scientific inference. Unfortunately, philosophers of science have advanced views in this area which appear mutually irreconcilable, and the views of economists on this subject have changed completely. Here I shall briefly describe the different positions, in the next subsection I shall present what I believe to be the incisive, though little known, solution of the puzzle due to the philosopher Wesley Salmon.

The views of economists

Roughly coincident with the rise of the econometric movement, there has been a 180-degree turnabout in the basic assumptions economists make regarding the source of validity of economic hypotheses. I will refer to these contradictory positions as the traditional view of methodology and the econometric view of methodology.

According to the traditional view, economists proceed by deductive reasoning from assumptions that are self-evident, on the basis of either introspection, or common knowledge about the economic system. The truth of the premises is assumed to guarantee the truth of the conclusions. Under these circumstances there is no need for hypothesis-testing. The econometric view of methodology derives from the statistical theory of hypothesis-testing and is also closely allied with Popper's *falsificationism* in the philosophy of science. In this view, no factual proposition is ever certain: at best it can be corroborated by surviving repeated testing.

The econometric view has been given a particular twist as a consequence of Friedman's influential position, which regards the 'realism' of the assumptions of a theory as irrelevant, as long as the theory as a whole cannot be rejected by testing it. I believe that this extreme view is wrong and that it has had a damaging effect on how economics is currently approached.[9]

Regarding Friedman's methodology, I would like to make the following points. First, it has been highly influential. In particular, I believe that the NCM could not have gathered adherents otherwise: it would have been rejected out of hand as being based on completely unrealistic assumptions. Secondly, Friedman himself did not follow his methodology most of the time. He is in fact a master in the analysis of economic issues, based on realistic and standard microeconomic assumptions. Thirdly, the methodology appears to have been invented to serve as an ideological weapon. Friedman's position of extreme *laissez-faire* is well known; in fact, it is often labelled 'Friedmanian'. This policy is theoretically justifiable only under the assumption of perfect competition.

Friedman argued that the competitive model yields correct prediction at the market level and therefore has not been refuted. This argument involves a mistake, which in fact demolishes Friedman's position quite generally. The assumption of perfect competition, or most other assumptions in economics, is directly testable in a variety of ways. There exists in fact a substantial empirical literature on the degree of monopoly in American industry, which is quite independent of predictions concerning price and quantity movements.

Both the traditional and the econometric views of methodology are extreme and one-sided. The apparent need to reconcile them acquires an additional urgency from the failure of econometrics progressively to establish well corroborated empirical regularities and scientific laws.

The views of philosophers[10]

In the writings on the philosophy of science and on the foundations of statistical inference, three broad strands of reasoning can be found. Each can be identified with a central concept.

---

[9] Friedman's methodology, sometimes referred to as 'instrumentalism', and the literature that has accumulated in relation to it, are discussed by Blaug (1980; Ch. 4). A recent book devoted to this theme is Arni (1989). That instrumentalism has had a deleterious influence on economic theorizing has been the view of several authors quoted or cited by Blaug (1980: Ch. 15).

[10] This section is based on Salmon (1966: Ch. VII).

1. *Confirmation*. This is the view that the probability in some sense, which may be left vague or defined precisely, increases with the number of instances in which a theory predicts correctly. The Bayesian concept of posterior likelihood fits into this framework.
2. *Falsification*. This is the approach of Popper. In his view, a hypothesis that resists attempts of falsification becomes corroborated. Popper vehemently denies that corroboration can be expressed as a probability. A puzzling aspect of Popper's theory is that he regards as highly corroborated a theory that makes improbable predictions which turn out to be true.
3. *Plausibility*. According to this criterion, scientists consider only those hypotheses that do not contradict the established knowledge of their field. The philosopher of science Hanson points out that hypotheses failing this criterion are typically rejected outright as the work of a crank.

4.2. A Bayesian Synthesis

The positions discussed in the preceding two subsections appear to be highly disparate and even contradictory. It is the great merit of Salmon to have shown that the issues can be clarified and the positions reconciled in a Bayesian framework.

The following notation will be used:

$P(H)$ prior probability that a hypothesis H is true.
$P(E)$ probability that some particular evidence E will obtain.
$P(E/H)$ probability of the evidence E given that the hypothesis H is true.
$P(H/E)$ posterior probability that the hypothesis H is true given that the evidence is E.

Other probabilities are defined analogously in an obvious manner. Using the law of conditional probability, the probability that both H is true and E will occur can be expressed in two ways:

$$P(H \cap E) = P(H/E)P(E) = P(E/H)P(H)$$

From the second equality,

$$P(H/E) = \frac{P(E/H)P(H)}{P(E)},$$

which is Bayes's formula. A more useful formulation for our purposes is

$$P(H/E) = \frac{P(E/H)P(H)}{P(E/H)P(H) + P(E/\bar{H})P(\bar{H})}$$

where

$$P(\bar{H}) = 1 - P(H)$$

is the probability that H is false.

The three criteria can now be identified with terms in Bayes's formula. This identification is straightforward for the likelihood $P(E/H)$ and for the prior probability $P(H)$ which can be identified with Hanson's plausibility criterion. More novel and highly illuminating is Salmon's interpretation of Popper's falsifiability criterion as referring to $P(E/\bar{H})$ as the probability of the evidence if the hypothesis is false, i.e., if some alternative hypothesis is true. The role of $P(E/\bar{H})$ in the formula is understood most easily by looking at some extreme cases. $P(E/\bar{H}) = 0$ implies $P(E/H) = 1$. If the observed evidence contradicts all rival hypotheses, then H must be true. $P(E/\bar{H}) = P(E/H)$ implies $P(H/E) = P(H)$. If the evidence is equally likely on all hypotheses, it cannot distinguish between them. A strong and highly falsifiable hypothesis must thus be interpreted as one for which $P(E/\bar{H})$ is very small.

The extension to more than two hypotheses is straightforward. If $H_1, \ldots, H_n$ are all of the mutually exclusive hypotheses being considered as relevant to the evidence E, then

$$P(H_i/E) = \frac{P(E/H_i)\,P(H_i)}{P(E/H_i)P(H_i) + P(E/\bar{H}_i)P(\bar{H}_i)}. \qquad i = 1, \ldots, n$$

where $P(\bar{H}_i)$ is the probability that a hypothesis alternative to H_i is true. Relevant for the acceptance of $P(H_i/E)$ is not the absolute value of H_i but rather its value relative to the posterior probabilities of alternative hypotheses.

To summarize the discussion in relation to explanatory economic theories, (1) they should be based on plausible assumptions (high prior likelihood); (2) they should make strong predictions regarding stylized facts, which are difficult to explain in terms of alternative theories; (3) they should have a good fit to the data (high value of likelihood function).

5. The Work of SEMECON

The connection between the preceding discussion of the scientific method and the work on economic fluctuations carried out at SEMECON may be summarized as follows.

1. The stylized facts are established independently (Chapter 3) of the explanatory model (Chapter 4).
2. The basic stylized facts (a three- to four-year quasi-cycle in inventory investment, an eight- to ten-year cycle in equipment investment) are explained by the proposed theory, but are highly unlikely given the alternative theories of economic fluctuations that have been proposed.
3. The assumptions entering the theory (essentially the second-order accelerator mechanism of production and investment) are plausible. They are closely related to assumptions that have a long history in macroeconomics and also figure prominently in applied discussions of fluctuations and in

forecasting. (High inventory–sales ratios and low capacity utilization are prime indicators for expecting downturns in production and fixed investment.) The assumptions and models are also plausible in the sense of being derivable from basic economic theories of intertemporal maximization (Chapter 8) and aggregation (Chapter 9).

4. In spite of their extreme simplicity, the models provide satisfactory fits to the data and post-sample predictions for several countries.
5. The process of validation, in the sense that results are replicated by independent investigators working with new sets of data, has also been successful to a considerable extent. Generations of students and collaborators at SEMECON have found essentially the same stylized facts using different methodologies and data-sets. Moreover, the findings are broadly consistent with those of many investigators writing at different times in different countries.

I hope that the present volume will motivate other economists to participate in the replication process. This process is the only way to acquire the requisite craft knowledge for further progress. We at SEMECON will be happy to assist with our expertise any investigator undertaking this task.

References

Arni, J.-L. (1989), *Die Kontroverse um die Realitätsnähe der Annahmen in der Ökonomie*, Verlag Rüegger, Chur.

Blaug, M. (1980), *The Methodology of Economics*, Cambridge University Press.

Caldwell, B. (ed.) (1984), *Appraisal and Criticism in Economics*, George Allen & Unwin, Boston.

Colander, D. (1989), 'Research on the economics profession', *Journal of Economic Perspectives* 3(4) : 137–48.

—— and Klamer, A. (1987), 'The making of an economist', *Journal of Economic Perspectives* 1(2) : 95–111.

DeMarchi, N. (1988), *The Popperian Legacy in Economics: Papers Presented at a Symposium in Amsterdam*, Cambridge University Press.

Dwyer, G. P., and Hafer, R. W. (1988), 'Is money irrelevant?', *Federal Reserve Bank of St Louis Review*, 70(3) : 3–17.

Dewald, W. G., Thursby, J. G., and Anderson, R. G. (1986), 'Replication in empirical economics: the Journal of Money, Credit and Banking Project', *American Economic Review*, 76(4) : 587–603. See also 'Comment' by J. J. Merrick, Jr. and 'Reply', *American Economic Review*, 78 (1988) : 1160–1 and 1162–3.

Frank, P. (1957), *The Philosophy of Science*, Prentice-Hall, Englewood Cliffs, NJ.

Hempel, C. G. (1966), *The Philosophy of Natural Science*, Prentice-Hall, Englewood Cliffs, NJ.

Leamer, E. E. (1985), 'Sensitivity analyses would help', *American Economic Review*, 75(3) : 308–13.

Mason, S. F. (1962), *A History of the Sciences*, Collier Books, New York.

McAllen, M., Pagan, A. R., and Volker, P. A. (1985), 'What will take the con out of econometrics?', *American Economic Review*, 75(3) : 293–307.

McCloskey, D. (1983), 'The rhetoric of economics', *Journal of Economic Literature*, 21(2) : 481–517.

—— (1986), *The Rhetoric of Economics*, University of Wisconsin Press, Madison.

Medawar, P. (1982), *Pluto's Republic*, Oxford University Press.

Morgan, T. (1988), 'Theory versus empiricism in academic economics: update and comparisons', *Journal of Economic Perspectives*, 2(4) : 159–64.

Nagel, E. (1961), *The Structure of Science*, Harcourt, Brace & World, New York.

Platt, J. R. (1964), 'Strong inference', *Science*, no. 146 : 347–53. Reprinted in J.R. Platt, *The Step to Man*, John Wiley, New York, 1966.

Polanyi, M. (1958), *Personal Knowledge*, University of Chicago Press.

—— (1966), *The Tacit Dimension*, Doubleday, Garden City, NJ.

Ravetz, J. R. (1971), *Scientific Knowledge and its Social Problems*, Clarendon Press, Oxford.

Salmon, W. C. (1966), *The Foundations of Scientific Inference*, University of Pittsburgh Press.

Sims, C. A. (1980), 'Macroeconomics and reality', *Econometrica*, 48 : 1–4.

Spiegel, H. W. (1971), *The Growth of Economic Thought*, Prentice-Hall, Englewood Cliffs, NJ.

Tullock, G. (1966), *The Organization of Inquiry*, Duke University Press, Durham, NC.

Usher, D. (1980), *The Measurement of Capital*. University of Chicago Press.

Watson, J. D. (1968), *The Double Helix*, Atheneum, New York.

Zellner, A. (1984), *Basic Issues in Econometrics*, University of Chicago Press.

—— (1985), 'Bayesian econometrics', *Econometrica*, 53(2) : 253–69.

Ziman, J. (1978), *Reliable Knowledge: An Exploration of the Grounds for Belief in Sciences*, Cambridge University Press.

PART II

Economic Fluctuations in Market Economies

3

The Stylized Facts of Macroeconomic Fluctuations

Claude Hillinger and Monika Sebold-Bender

1. Introduction

A central tenet of the SEMECON methodology, as elaborated in Chapter 2, is the determination of *stylized facts* independently of the models constructed to explain them. Accordingly, this chapter elaborates the stylized facts of macroeconomic fluctuations. These empirical regularities are explained in the following chapter. The methods used in obtaining the stylized facts are also described, though it is not possible to go into every detail. Particular emphasis is placed on the visual examination of the data for making preliminary inferences (cf. Chapter 2, Section 3.3).

The major stylized facts regarding economic fluctuations have been described many times and some were noted more than a century ago (cf. Chapter 1, Sections 3.6 and 6). Moreover, the stylized facts are not marginal: they dominate the movements of macroeconomic time series. To obtain a rough picture of the stylized facts it is enough to look at the relevant data, using some simple transformations in order to bring out relevant features. More refined methods are used at later stages of the investigation in order to obtain more quantitative precision and to test hypotheses.

What are the major stylized facts? First and foremost, that economic fluctuations occur in the investment components of the GDP. Secondly, that these fluctuations have characteristic average durations, so that it makes sense to refer to them as *cycles*. The characteristic durations or *periods* of the cycles are specific to particular categories of investment. Inventory investment is characterized by a three- to four-year cycle, fixed investment, particularly the equipment component, by a seven- to ten-year cycle; the building component of fixed investment often exhibits a sixteen- to twenty-year cycle. These cycles are often referred to by the names of their discoverers or by the component of investment in which they are most prominent—the inventory or Khitchin cycle, the equipment or Juglar cycle, and the building or Kuznetz cycle.

Not all cycles are visible in the data of all countries at all times and the irregularity varies substantially. Nevertheless, together they typically account for roughly 50 per cent of the fluctuations of GDP.

Given the distinctiveness of the stylized facts and the obvious need to understand economic fluctuations, which are associated with enormous social costs, it is natural to ask why they are not better known. The basic explanation concerns the general ineffectiveness of economics as an empirical science, which was the topic of the previous chapter. We repeat here the following characteristics of the natural science methodology for establishing stylized facts:

1. familiarity with the procedures generating the data and with properties of the data such as the signal–noise ratio;
2. the visual examination of data in conjunction with transformations designed to bring out characteristic features;
3. the fact that the establishment of scientific truth is a *social* process: a basic precondition for this process to take place is that the training of scientists must concentrate on the replication of known facts, thereby developing the skill and judgement required in order ultimately to establish new facts.

Unfortunately, the training of economists is often more in the nature of an assault on the ability to form common sense and intuitive judgement rather than a strengthening of these abilities. In reading the empirical sections of this chapter, therefore, readers are strongly urged to suspend their acquired beliefs regarding both facts and methods. Since the features of the data that we infer are quite strongly present, readers approaching the evidence with open minds should have no difficulty in accepting it.

We have endeavoured to describe our procedures completely so that our result can be replicated by interested readers. Even more importantly, such readers should be able to apply these methods to *any* body of data.

Before we summarize the empirical results for fifteen countries, our procedures are explained in relation to German data. Starting with visual examination and simple transformations of the data, we proceed to more sophisticated methods. The theoretical background is explained when necessary, but the practical procedures and the possible interpretations are emphasized.

The starting point (Section 2) is the visual examination. This gives first impressions concerning the structure of the data. The results won by visual examination also serve as a control for the more sophisticated methods. Results that contradict the obvious structure should be regarded with scepticism.

The next step (Section 3) is the separation of growth and fluctuations. The data are often dominated by the trend to such an extent that many details regarding the fluctuations cannot be recognized by looking at the original data. For this reason we either transform the data to growth rates or use the deviations from a smooth function fitted to the data.

More detailed insights into the nature of fluctuations are provided by the correlogram and the periodogram of the detrended data, which can be defined as rather simple data transformations (Section 4). These transformations help in the identification of periodic components of the fluctuations and in the assessment of their importance.

The statistical theory of time-series analysis attempts to move beyond descriptive transformations of the data to obtain test statistics and estimates with known and desirable properties. For this purpose it is stipulated that the data are generated by a stochastic process. Classical time-series analysis employs various procedures for smoothing the periodogram to obtain an estimate of the spectrum characterizing the generating process of the time series. These nonparametric methods require large samples and in our judgement have failed in economics where samples are short, particularly relative to the length of the cycles identified.

In the last two decades parametric methods that are much more efficient have been developed in the natural sciences and have become the methodology of choice in many applications. In the most widely used method, known as *maximum-entropy spectral analysis*, the data are parametrized by fitting an AR *process* and the spectrum is derived from the estimated parameters. In Section 5 we explain this methodology and then apply it to the data.

In Section 6 the results for 15 OECD countries are summarized. The results establish and deepen the stylized facts described above, and enlarge them by two further results concerning the role of the noise. Section 7 summarizes the chapter.

2. Visual Examination of Data

We begin with a look at the original data. The gross domestic product (GDP) is divided into gross fixed capital formation (GFCF), inventory investment (II), and residual demand (RD), defined as the remainder after subtracting the two investment series. These components of GDP are plotted against time, analysed visually, and compared with the aggregate. The examination has two aims: to get an idea about the relative importance of growth and fluctuations, and to analyse the fluctuations in more detail; if there is a cyclical component present, the length of the cycle(s) is roughly determined by counting the years between major troughs or peaks.

2.1. Analysis of the German Data

The procedure will be demonstrated using the GDP of Germany and its components. They are plotted in Figs. 3.1–3.4. The original data are marked by solid squares and connected with a dashed line. It is easily seen that the GDP and RD (Figs. 3.1 and 3.2) are dominated by trend, while the two investment series (Figs. 3.3 and 3.4) have strongly fluctuating components. If the GDP is examined in greater detail, one can recognize quite regular fluctuations around the trend. The troughs of these fluctuations are placed at the years 1968, 1976, and 1984. So the GDP seems to exhibit a cycle of about eight years.

FIG. 3.1.   GDP, Germany, 1960–1986 (1982 DM billions)

Where does this come from? The RD deviates only slightly and irregularly from the dominating upward movement. Here we can find no regular behaviour that could be called a cycle. So we expect to find the cycle in the two strongly fluctuating investment series. In the GFCF the presence of a cyclical component is striking, while the trend plays a lesser role than in the GDP.

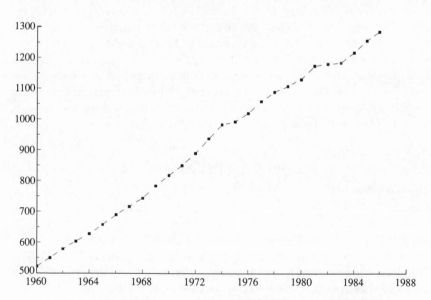

FIG. 3.2.   Residual demand, Germany, 1960–1986 (1980 DM billions)

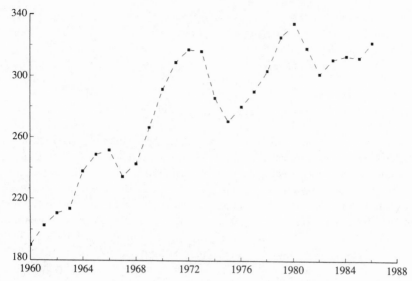

FIG. 3.3. Gross fixed capital formation (GFCF), Germany, 1960–1986 (1980 DM billions)

After the 1970s the trend flattens, while the amplitudes of the cycles strongly increase. The major troughs are located at the years 1967, 1975, and 1981. Thus, the fluctuations repeat themselves after about seven or eight years.

The inventories fluctuate strongly and have no recognizable trend. At 1967, 1975, and 1981 very deep troughs are present. Between these, at 1963, 1971,

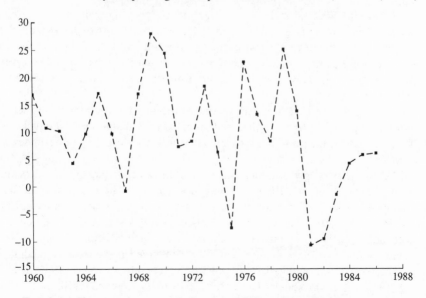

FIG. 3.4. Inventory investment, Germany, 1960–1986 (1980 DM billions)

and 1978, more moderate troughs can be found. This suggests the superposition of a long cycle of about six to eight years over a short one of about three or four years. The troughs of the shorter cycle amplify the troughs of the longer cycle and reduce its peaks.

2.2. Conclusions

Comparing the three components, one can conclude that the fluctuations of the GDP come from the investment series. Residual demand contributes to the growth, but not to the cycles, that can be found in the GDP. While the cycles of GFCF are superposed by a trend, which has been flattened since the seventies, the inventories fluctuate around a constant level. In addition to the long six- to eight-year cycle that is present in the GFCF, the inventories exhibit a shorter one of about four years. The long cycle has about twice the amplitude of the short one. This shorter cycle cannot be found by visual examination in the aggregate: it is dominated by the other components. It must be remembered in this context that II is only about 1 per cent of GDP on average.

In order to obtain better pictures of the cyclical movements, particularly of the GDP, it is necessary to remove the trend from the data. This is done in the next section.

3. Separation of Growth and Economic Fluctuations

As shown in Section 2, it is necessary to separate growth and economic fluctuations in order to get detailed information about the two phenomena. We use two methods for this purpose: the transformation of the data into growth rates, and the fit of a smooth function as an estimate for the trend. We apply both methods and show that for our questions the second alternative is more appropriate.

For the discussion of both cases, we assume that the economic time series can be separated into a smooth trend component and stationary fluctuations. That means that the noise has no permanent influence on the long-term development.

The alternative view of stochastic trends allows a permanent effect of the noise. Usually it is modelled by a unit root which can be removed by differencing the data. This hypothesis has become more and more popular during the 1980s. Different tests (see e.g. Nelson and Plosser 1982) favoured the unit-root hypothesis against the deterministic smooth trend. Perron (1989) demonstrated that these results cannot be confirmed if the trend is modelled as a linear function with structural breaks corresponding to the 1929 crash and the 1973 oil price shock. Extensive experimentation at SEMECON with diverse trend functions, including some with a structural break, have led us to conclude that a smooth flexible trend leads to a better representation of the deviations than the linear trend with structural breaks.

3.1. The Growth Rates

First, the growth rates of the series containing trend—GDP, RD, GFCF—are investigated.

Definition and basic properties

Denoting the original data by x_t, $t = 1, \ldots, N$, the growth rates g_t are defined by

$$g_t = \frac{x_t - x_{t-1}}{x_{t-1}}, \qquad t = 2, \ldots, N \tag{3.1}$$

There are two advantages of growth rates:

1. Because they are dimensionless, they allow the comparison of series with different dimensions or orders of magnitude. For example, one can compare the RD and GFCF, although the RD is larger, or one can compare different countries.
2. Most models of economic growth imply constant growth rates. Empirical and theoretical work can be connected via the analysis of growth rates.

The main purpose of this chapter is to analyse the data to get information about cyclical components of the economic fluctuations. This raises the question, Does the transformation to growth rates have an effect on the cyclical structure? In order to answer this question, we suppose that the cyclical structure can be represented by a sum of two cosines with short-period p_a and long-period p_b. With $T(t)$ denoting the trend, the time series is represented by

$$x(t) = T(t) + a \cos\left(\frac{2\pi}{p_a} t\right) + b \cos\left(\frac{2\pi}{p_b} t\right).$$

The continuous expression for the growth rates is

$$\frac{Dx(t)}{x(t)} = \frac{DT(t)}{x(t)} + A \sin\left(\frac{2\pi}{p_a} t\right) + B \sin\left(\frac{2\pi}{p_b} t\right),$$

where D is the differential operator and

$$A = \frac{a}{x(t)} \frac{2\pi}{p_a}, \qquad B = \frac{a}{x(t)} \frac{2\pi}{p_b}$$

It follows that

$$\frac{A}{B} = \frac{a}{b} = \frac{p_b}{p_a}.$$

It is seen that the transformation to growth rates reduces the relative amplitude of the longer cycle proportional to the relative length of the period.

An additional problem with the transformation to growth rates is that the random or irregular component of the data is amplified. The irregular appearance of differenced data is well known.

Application to German data

In Figs. 3.5–3.7 the growth rates of GDP, RD, and GFCF are plotted. Since II exhibits no growth, as shown in Section 2, and is sometimes negative, growth rates cannot be calculated and will not be considered in the following analysis.

The growth rates for all three series are decreasing. For GDP they fluctuate around a descending line, while the growth rates of RD vary around a constant level, which is shifted downwards at about 1974. In the case of GFCF, the growth rates tend to a constant level at zero.

The transformation to growth rates has eliminated most of trend and the fluctuations have become prominent. The amplification of the short cycles and the noise is obvious. The growth rates of GDP (Fig. 3.5) are characterized by an M-shape produced by the superposition of a short and a long cycle. The troughs of the long cycle are located at 1967, 1975, and 1982. That yields the seven- to eight-year cycle already detected in Section 2. The moderate troughs are placed at 1963, 1971, and 1979. This, together with the major troughs, indicates a short cycle of between three and four years. So, in contrast to the visual examination of the original data, one can now observe a quite similar shape as present in the original data of the inventories (Fig. 3.4). The removal

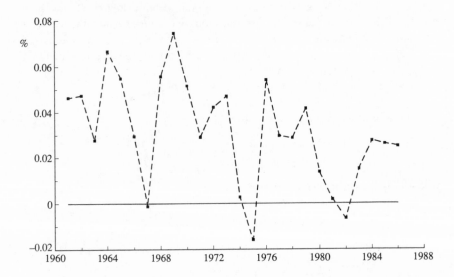

FIG. 3.5. Growth rates in GDP, Germany, 1960–1986, constant prices

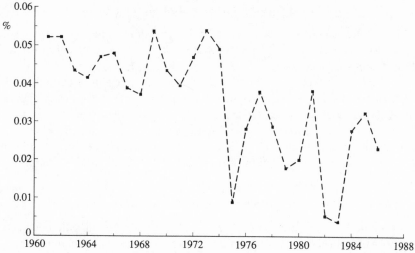

FIG. 3.6. Growth rates in residual demand, Germany, 1960–1986, constant prices

of the main part of the growth and the amplification of short cycles enables us to see the short inventory cycle in the GDP.

The growth rates of RD (Fig. 3.6) do not exhibit any clear pattern. The shape looks quite irregular and no cyclical structure can be identified.

The growth rates of GFCF do not produce new results concerning its cyclical structure. The troughs at 1967, 1974, and 1982 again evidence a long cycle of about seven or eight years. No further cycle can be found.

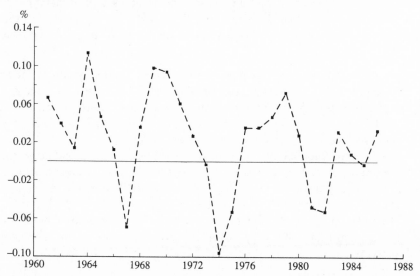

FIG. 3.7. Growth rates in gross fixed capital formation (GFCF), Germany, 1960–1986, constant prices

3.2. Fit of a Trend Function and Deviations from Trend

The amplification of the short cycles in the growth rates motivates the desire
to remove the trend in another way, which does not distort the cyclical structure. Supposing that economic cycles and growth are independently additive
phenomena, one can fit a smooth function representing the trend. Then the
deviations from the estimated trend are the economic fluctuations. A bias can
arise if the fitted trend is not appropriate. This problem will be discussed
together with two different possibilities used for trend functions in the first
subsection. In the second subsection the German data are detrended and analysed according to the questions already asked for visual examination.

The trend functions, their properties, and the estimation

An optimal trend function should describe the secular growth path and separate growth from economic fluctuations. Separation means that there is no trend
component left in the fluctuations, nor is a part of the fluctuation included in
the trend. We try to fulfil this task with two different trend types.

The polynomial trend. First we consider a polynomial trend, which is defined as

$$T_1(t) = a_0 + a_1 + \ldots + a_n t^n, \qquad t = 1, \ldots, N \qquad (3.1)$$

where N stands for number of observations. Polynomials are smooth and very
flexible functions. The theorem of Weierstraß (cf. Rudin 1964 : 147) recommends polynomials as optimal approximations to any smooth function. The
parameters can be estimated easily using OLS (ordinary least squares). Unfortunately, there are also some problems associated with the use of polynomial
trends:

1. Their ability to separate growth and fluctuations is strongly dependent on
   the correct determination of the trend order n, which demands a lot of
   experience, because no objective rule exists. Simulations carried out at
   SEMECON have demonstrated that the periods—especially the long
   ones—can be shortened by too high a trend order.
2. The fit of polynomials by least squares can be strongly dependent on the
   beginning and ending of the series. If the fluctuations have just reached a
   peak (trough), at such a point the trend would be lifted up (down).
3. The polynomial trend lacks an economic interpretation.
4. The polynomial trend cannot be extrapolated for forecasting purposes,
   because the shape of the polynomial is not stable outside the sampling
   interval.

The logistic trend. The traditional model for time series with decreasing
growth rates is the *logistic* curve, which was first used in demography. It also

proved to be useful for the study of the reaction of the market to a special product. The logistic trend is defined by

$$T_2(t) = \frac{a}{1 + be^{-ct}}, \qquad t = 1, \ldots, N \qquad (3.3)$$

for all parameters taking positive values. The parameters determine the typical symmetric S-shape of the curve. The logistic trend takes values between two asymptotes. The lower bound is 0 and the upper bound, the so-called 'saturation level', is fixed by the parameter a.

The growth rates are characterized by the Verhuelst differential equation:

$$g(t) = \frac{DT_2(t)}{T_2(t)} = c \left(1 - \frac{T_2(t)}{a} \right) \qquad (3.4)$$

They are dependent on the ratio of the actual value $T_2(t)$ and the saturation level a and decrease with increasing $T_2(t)$. If $T_2(t)$ is small relative to the saturation level a, the second factor tends to 1. The growth rate is nearly constant in this range and the logistic curve behaves like an exponential. As $T_2(t)$ tends to the saturation level, the growth rate tends to 0.

The logistic curve is fitted to the data by minimizing the sum of squared residuals:

$$\sum_{t=1}^{N} \left(x_t - \frac{a}{1 + be^{-ct}} \right)^2.$$

The nonlinear character of the logistic curve demands a numerical solution. The resulting NLS (nonlinear least squares) estimates have asymptotically the same properties as the OLS estimates (Judge *et al.* 1988: Ch. 12).

The logistic curve has two major advantages relative to a polynomial trend: the number of parameters is fixed and does not have to be determined for each application; and the function is stable outside the sampling interval and is therefore suitable for extrapolation, which a polynomial trend is not. The missing flexibility of the logistic trend causes it to be quite stable relative to the phases of the added fluctuations. The ending of the series has only a slight influence on the fit, as a study by Sigrid Viergutz at SEMECON has shown.

Application to German data

For the German data the logistic trend proves to be appropriate. The results for the logistic trend and the polynomial differ only slightly. For example, the optimal polynomial and the logistic trend of the GDP (Figs. 3.8 and 3.9) are very similar. The adjusted R^2 confirms this impression. For both trend types it is 0.994. Figure 3.10 exhibits the deviations from the polynomial trend as a

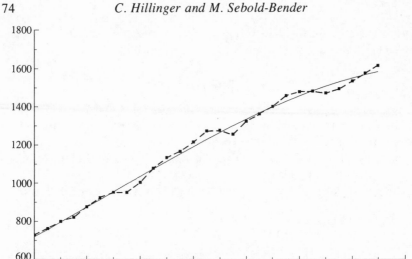

Fɪɢ. 3.8. Polynomial trend of order 3 for GDP, Germany, 1960–1986 (1980 DM billions)

dashed line and logistic trend as a solid line. They differ only slightly. Therefore the further analysis employs only the logistic trend.

The trend analysis supports earlier results. Figures 3.9, 3.11, and 3.12 exhibit the plots of data and of the fitted logistic trend. The R^2, listed in Table 3.1, of the fitted trends quantifies the impression of the visual examination. RD is almost totally explained by a smooth trend, while GDP and especially GFCF exhibit additional structure.

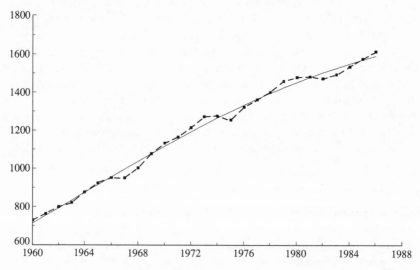

Fɪɢ. 3.9. Logistic trend for GDP, Germany, 1960–1986 (1980 DM billions)

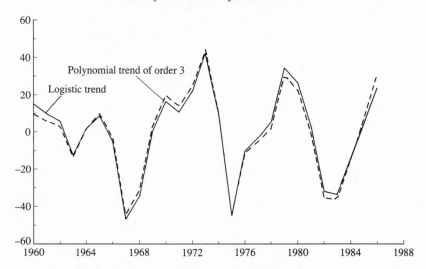

FIG. 3.10. Detrended data for GDP, Germany, 1960–1986 (1980 DM billions)

TABLE 3.1 R^2 of trends

	$R^2(\%)$
GDP	97.8
RD	99.9
GFCF	87.1

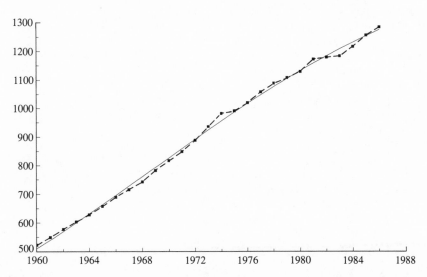

FIG. 3.11. Logistic trend for residual demand, Germany, 1960–1986 (1980 DM billions)

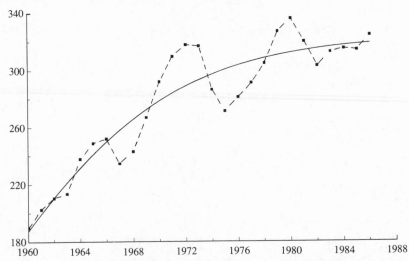

FIG. 3.12. Logistic trend for gross fixed capital formation (GFCF), Germany, 1960–1986 (1980 DM billions)

The investigation of the detrended data establishes the previous results concerning the cyclical structure. A comparison of the troughs and maxima of the detrended series of GDP and GFCF (Figs. 3.10 and 3.14) and the data of II (Fig. 3.4) shows that the cycles in all series are in phase. That means that the locations of maxima and minima of the long cycle as well as the short cycle coincide for all series.

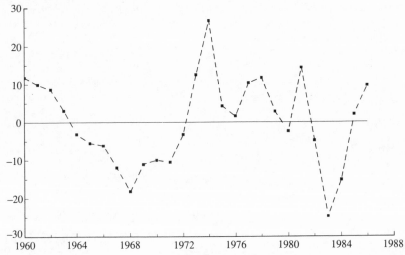

FIG. 3.13. Detrended data for residual demand, Germany, 1960–1986 (1980 DM billions)

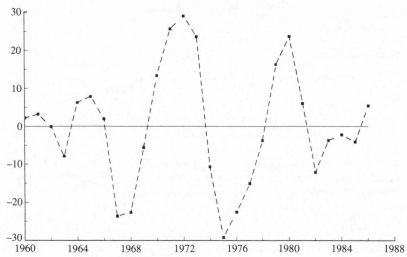

FIG. 3.14. Detrended data for gross fixed capital formation (GFCF), Germany, 1960–1986 (1980 DM billions)

3.3. Conclusions

The investigation of growth rates together with the trend analysis enlarges the results. Both methods isolate the economic fluctuations. For a detailed analysis of the cyclical character of the resulting fluctuations the trend analysis is suitable, because the growth rates lead to biases concerning the amplitudes.

All series considered are characterized by decreasing growth rates. They can be described adequately by a logistic trend model. The investigation of the original data and trend functions as well as of the growth rates and the detrended data can be summarized as follows. The RD exhibits no cycles; the variation of the data is explained by the trend, as reflected by an R^2 of nearly 100 per cent. The cyclical character of the mild fluctuations around the trend of GDP is caused by the investment series. The long cycle detected in the GDP corresponds to the eight-year cycle of the GFCF. Additionally, the amplification of short cycles by growth rates enables us to identify a short cycle, which corresponds to the four-year cycle already identified in the original data of the inventories. The long cycles of GFCF, II, and GDP as well as the short cycles are in phase.

4. Characterization of the deviations from trend or mean

In this and the following section the deviations are investigated more carefully. For this purpose, two transformations of the data are employed in this section: the correlogram and the periodogram. Both provide insight into the dynamic structure which may not be evident when looking at the original data.

4.1. The Correlogram

Definition and properties

The autocovariance coefficient of the detrended time series $x_t, t = 1, \ldots, N$

$$r_\tau = \frac{1}{N} \sum_{t=\tau+1}^{N} x_t x_{t-\tau}, \tag{3.5}$$

measures the average dependence between x_t and $x_{t-\tau}$ The plot of r_τ normalized by the variance against the lag τ is called *correlogram* of the data.

Given a cycle of period p in the data, the correlogram will exhibit a maximum at $\tau = p$ and a minimum at $\tau = p/2$.

Application to German data

Looking at the correlograms of the GDP and its investment components, some obvious structure is found. The GDP (Fig. 3.15) is dominated by a cycle of about eight years, which can also be found in the GFCF (Fig. 3.16). This pattern is clearer in the GFCF, suggesting the presence of some other factor in the GDP. However, the four-year cycle, which owing to the amplification was visible in the growth rates of GDP, cannot be identified here. The correlogram of II (Fig. 3.17) looks rather different. The values of the correlogram are low and the shape is quite irregular. If there is any structure in the data,

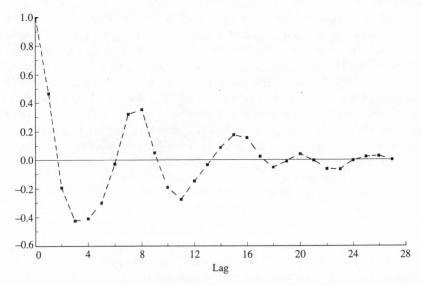

FIG. 3.15. Autocorrelation function for GDP, Germany, 1960–1986, constant prices

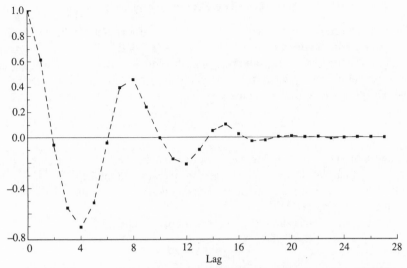

FIG. 3.16. Autocorrelation function for gross fixed capital formation (GFCF),
Germany, 1960–1986, constant prices

its weight is relatively low compared with that of the added noise. While a
four-year cycle is suggested, particularly at the beginning of the correlogram,
the entire impression is so irregular as to suggest an essentially random phenomenon.

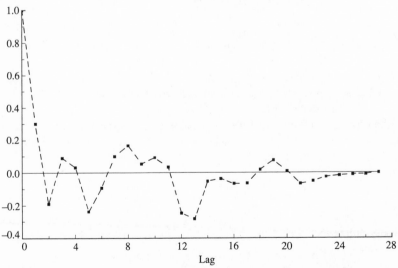

FIG. 3.17. Autocorrelation function for inventory investment, Germany, 1960–
1986, constant prices

4.2. The Periodogram

The correlogram and the visual examination of the data indicate cyclical components in the deviations of the GDP, GFCF, and II. To get more precise information regarding the number, length, and relative importance of the cyclical components, we employ the *periodogram*. After a short description, the periodogram is applied to the German data.

Idea and interpretation of periodogram

We will motivate and define the periodogram in terms of least squares, an approach that should be much more intuitive to economists than the usual definition using Fourier transforms. Subsequently, we will show how various definitions are related.

The simplest description of a cycle is a cosine function,

$$\alpha \cos(\omega t + e),$$

with frequency ω corresponding to period

$$p = \frac{2\pi}{\omega},$$

amplitude α, and phase e. It is equivalent to

$$b_1 \cos(\omega t) + b_2 \sin(\omega t),$$

with

$$\alpha = \sqrt{b_1^2 + b_2^2},$$

$$\tan(e) = -\frac{b_2}{b_1},$$

for any fixed frequency of the range $[0, \pi]$ and can be fitted to data by OLS. The fit of several cosines can be compared by their respective R^2. The plot of R^2 against the frequency is the *periodogram* $I(\omega)$.[1]

The cosine functions for different values of ω are generally correlated, but they are uncorrelated at a set of orthogonal frequencies ω_i. Given a data set x_t, $t = 1, \ldots, N$, they are defined by

$$\omega_i = \frac{i}{N}, \qquad i = 1, \ldots, N/2 \tag{3.6}$$

For these frequencies the above definition of the periodogram is equivalent to the normalized square of the expansion of the series into a Fourier series:

[1] Although most people are more familiar with thinking in terms of periods, we chose the plot against frequencies. This decision was induced primarily by two advantages: (1) the finite frequency range corresponds to an infinite period range; (2) the orthogonal frequencies (see (3.6)) are equi-spaced in the frequency domain.

$$I(\omega) = a(\omega)^2 + b(\omega)^2,\tag{3.7a}$$

where $a(\omega)$ and $b(\omega)$ are defined by the following relations:

$$a(\omega) = \sqrt{\left(\frac{2}{N}\right)} \sum_{t=1}^{N} x_t \sin(\omega t)$$

$$\tag{3.7b}$$

$$b(\omega) = \sqrt{\left(\frac{2}{N}\right)} \sum_{t=1}^{N} x_t \cos(\omega t).$$

This again is, except for a constant factor, the same as the Fourier transform of the empirical autocovariance function r_τ, $\tau = 1, \ldots, N-1$

$$I(\omega) = \frac{1}{2\pi} \sum_{\tau=-N}^{N} r_\tau e^{-i\omega\tau}.\tag{3.8}$$

Expressions (3.7a), (3.7b), and (3.8) are the usual definitions of the periodogram (Priestley 1981). At the orthogonal frequencies the periodogram computed according to (3.7a), (3.7b), or (3.8) and normalized is exactly equal to the R^2 obtained when a cosine is fitted to the observations by OLS. For the

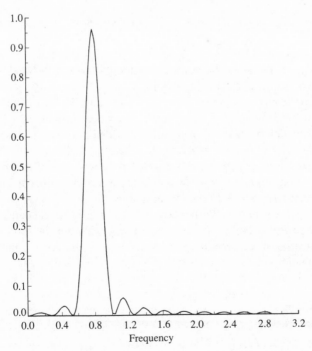

FIG. 3.18. Periodogram of artificial data: cosine of frequency 0.78

Peak periods: 8.00, 5.56, 14.29

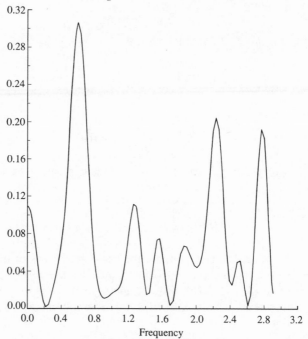

FIG. 3.19.   Periodogram of artificial data: standard Gaussian noise

Peak periods: 10.53, 2.82, 2.27

non-orthogonal frequencies, a study by Jochen Meiners at SEMECON showed that the two measures differ only slightly.

The properties of the periodogram are illustrated in Figs. 3.18 and 3.19.[2] Since the appearance of the periodogram is strongly influenced by the length of the observation horizon, we have used artificial data with the same number of observations (27) as are available for the empirical part, considering the two extreme cases of a time series generated by white noise and by a simple cosine function. Figure 3.18 is the periodogram of a cosine function with a period of eight years corresponding to a frequency of 0.78. A cosine of this frequency explains nearly 100 per cent of the variation of the data. In contrast to that, the periodogram of white noise (Fig. 3.19) exhibits no prominent peak. The explanation of any one frequency does not exceed 25 per cent.

The problems arising in connection with the use of the periodogram are illustrated by the periodograms of the two artificial series. In Fig. 3.18 not only is there a peak at the frequency of the real cycle, but the periodogram also exhibits lower peaks called *side lobes* to the left and right of the dominating peak. Since a cosine of period p is just uncorrelated with its harmonics, defined by multiples of the basic period p $(\ldots 3p, 2p, p/2, p/3, p/4, \ldots)$, cosines of periods in between explain a certain fraction of its variance.

[2] For a detailed discussion and formal explanation, see e.g. Priestley (1981).

This effect causes difficulties of interpretation. One may be unable to distinguish between side lobes of a dominating cycle and peaks of additional cycles with lower power. The noise (Fig. 3.19) presents additional problems. If the noise causes a high percentage of the variation of the data, it may be impossible to discriminate between real and pseudo peaks due to the random variation. These two effects—side lobes and peaks caused by noise—can interact and strengthen artificial peaks. So one must be cautious and take into account visual examination and the results of the analysis of the correlogram to judge the periodogram.

The difficulties just described suggest the need for a test for significance of the structure. For this purpose we use the test of Durbin (1969), which uses the fact that the periodogram of a random time series has no concentration at any frequency. Because the periodogram of white noise looks very irregular (cf. Fig. 3.19), one uses the cumulated periodogram normalized with the variance, which is much smoother. The theoretical cumulated periodogram of white noise is a diagonal straight line. Using a Kolmogoroff–Smirnoff-like statistic, one can test whether the empirical cumulated periodogram differs significantly from this diagonal. The significance level and the degrees of freedom fix two parallels to the diagonal. If the cumulated spectrum lies outside the fixed range, the hypotheses of white noise can be rejected.

If the tested data are residuals of a least-squares regression—like the deviations from trend—the test must be modified. The parallels to the diagonal are replaced by two lines. If the cumulated periodogram lies in the intermediate region, no decision can be drawn; if the cumulated periodogram exceeds the outer line, significant structure is present in the residuals.

Application to German data

The periodograms analysed in this section were first tested for significance by the procedure just described. As was to be expected after the previous analysis, the detrended data of GDP and GFCF exhibited significant structure using a significance level of 0.05. The suspicion that the II is generated by noise could be rejected. In Fig. 3.23 the cumulated periodogram of II and the limits for a significance level of 0.05 are plotted. The cumulated periodogram slightly exceeds the bounds.

The periodogram of the deviations from trend of the GDP (Fig. 3.20) is clearly dominated by a peak at eight years, which accounts for 45 per cent of the variation of the data. The lower peak at about four years accounts for just 13 per cent. The fact that this cycle is clearly present in the growth rates and in II suggests that in spite of its low R^2 it is real rather than artificial. The lower peaks at 5 and 16 years are of doubtful significance. They reach just about 10 per cent. A superposition of a four- and eight-year cycle produces a quite similar shape, with side lobes located at five and 16 years. So one can assume that the GDP contains just a four- and an eight-year cycle.

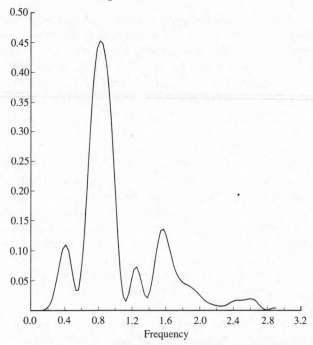

FIG. 3.20.   Periodogram of GDP, Germany, 1960–1986, constant prices

Peak periods: 7.69, 4.00, 15.38

The periodogram of the GFCF (Fig. 3.21) is clear. It indicates an eight-year cycle and nothing more.

More difficult to interpret is the periodogram of the II (Fig. 3.22). An R^2 of about 20 per cent for a period of 3.8 years and about 26 per cent for a period of 8.9 years suggests that these two cycles are real ones. The peak at 4.8 years is probably a side lobe strengthened by the noise.

4.3. Conclusions

Analysis of correlogram and periodogram confirms the results of Sections 2.1 and 2.2. The lengths of the cycles are determined more precisely by the periodogram. The R^2 reflects the dominance of the long cycle. The correlogram as well as the periodogram show that the II exhibits a strong noise component, while the GFCF is dominated by the cycle.

5. Spectral Analysis of Fluctuations

In previous sections the data were analysed without any assumptions about how they were generated. Simple descriptive transformations were employed. All this was done under the heading of *exploratory data analysis*.

The next step—to obtain stronger and testable results—involves the move from *descriptive* to *inferential* statistics. For this purpose, a generating probability distribution for the data must be assumed. In classical statistics it is assumed that the data are identically and independently distributed (*IID*). This assumption does not allow us to search for structure in a time series. For this purpose we must assume a joint distribution over time. The resulting theory is that of *stochastic processes*, and the branch of statistics dealing with inference from such processes is *time-series analysis*.

Both classical statistics and time-series analysis may be done by parametric and non-parametric methods. Classical statistics has from the beginning been mainly parametric, with non-parametric methods acquiring some importance more recently. Time-series analysis was in the beginning entirely non-parametric, and parametric methods have come to the fore only in the last twenty years. As we explain below, this fact had a rather fateful consequence for the application of time-series analysis in economics.

Parametric representations generally involve the assumption of a *specific* (e.g. normal) distribution and allow stronger inferences than are possible in

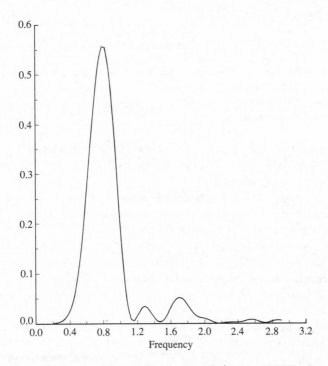

FIG. 3.21. Periodogram of gross fixed capital formation (GFCF), Germany, 1960–1986, constant prices

Peak periods: 8.00, 3.70, 4.88

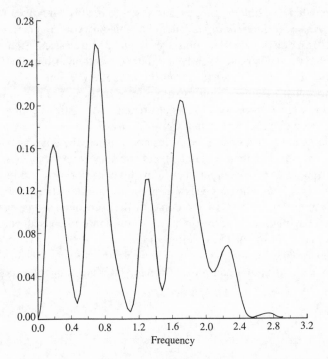

FIG. 3.22. Periodogram of inventory investment, Germany, 1960–1986, constant
· prices

Peak periods: 9.09, 3.70, 33.33

the non-parametric case. This is particularly important if there are few observations. The problem, of course, is that the assumed distribution may be a serious misspecification.

In the 1950s and 1960s a considerable amount of non-parametric spectral analysis was done with economic time series in order to determine if 'business cycles' could be found. They were not. Granger (1966) summarized these results and claimed a 'typical spectral shape' of economic time series which is monotone, thus rejecting the hypothesis of cycles in the data. Later, when the Box–Jenkins methodology (which is parametric) became popular in econometrics, it was not used to search for cycles, in the apparent belief that their non-existence had been demonstrated.

The work of SEMECON conclusively shows this view to be mistaken. The negative results were due to the inappropriateness of the non-parametric method for the available short-time series. (Other considerations, such as use of inappropriate time series and inadequate detrending, also played a role.) The parametric method described in this section confirms and strengthens our earlier findings regarding cycles.

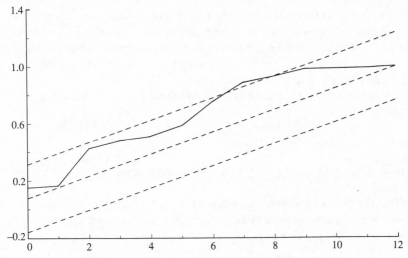

FIG. 3.23.   Test of Durbin for significance level 0.05: inventory investment, Germany, 1960–1986, constant prices

The next section defines some concepts and discusses briefly some of the difficulties connected with non-parametric estimation. We assume the data to be generated by a *weakly stationary process*, i.e. one that is characterized by constant mean, constant variance, and shift-invariant autocovariance. Formally, it is required that for all t

$$E(X_t) = \mu$$

$$\text{var}(X_t) = \sigma^2 \qquad (3.9)$$

$$\text{cov}(X_t, X_{t-\tau}) = \rho_\tau, \qquad \text{for all } \tau > 0 \text{ and } \tau \neq t.$$

Because we are interested primarily in the cyclical characteristics of the process, we use the spectrum of a stationary stochastic process. The spectrum reflects the behaviour of a process in respect to its cyclical pattern. After a short description of the theoretical spectrum, the *maximum-entropy spectrum* (ME spectrum) is introduced as the optimal estimate for the theoretical spectrum for time-series data. The interpretation of the ME spectrum is the next step. The application to German data follows after a short discussion of the estimation procedure.

5.1. The concept of a spectrum

The spectrum is the theoretical equivalent to the periodogram. While the periodogram reflects the cyclical pattern of a time series, the spectrum is related to a stationary stochastic process. Periodogram analysis decomposes a time series into cosine functions and investigates their contributions to the total variance. This concept can be transferred to stationary processes, because any stationary process can be represented as the limit of the sum of cosine functions with uncorrelated, random coefficients—the so-called *Cramér representation* (for details see Priestley 1981: Sect. 4.11). The distribution of variance over these random cosines yields the spectrum.

The meaning of the spectrum is best understood looking at a cyclical *process* of frequency ω^*:

$$X_t(\omega) = A \cos(\omega^* t + \theta),$$

where $\omega^* \in [0, \pi]$ and $A > 0$ are constants and θ is rectangularly distributed on $[-\pi, \pi]$.

The variance of the process is totally explained by just one 'random cosine'—the cyclical process of frequency ω^*. The spectrum $S_d(\omega)$ is discrete and consists of only one line at ω^*:

$$S_d(\omega) = \frac{1}{2} A^2 \quad \text{if } \omega = \omega^*,$$

$$S_d(\omega) = 0 \quad \text{otherwise.}$$

The variance of a sum of k such cyclical processes of frequencies ω_i can be decomposed into k components. The again discrete spectrum exhibits k lines, the heights being determined by the respective amplitude:

$$S_d(\omega) = \frac{1}{2} A^2 \quad \text{if } \omega = \omega_i,$$

$$S_d(\omega) = 0 \quad \text{otherwise.}$$

General stationary stochastic processes cannot be explained by a finite number of such 'random cosines'. One needs an uncountably infinite number of components for decomposing the process into 'random cosines'. This is done by the Cramér-representation of a stationary process. In this case the variance of the process is distributed over the whole frequency range. The spectrum becomes *continuous*. It is clear that no single component explains a certain amount of the variance. As in the case of continuous probability distributions, mass corresponds only to an interval. The integral below the spectrum normalized by total variance measures the R^2 belonging to an interval.

According to the theorem of Wold, the continuous spectrum is the Fourier transform of autocovariance function of the process (X_t).

$$S(\omega) = \frac{1}{2\pi} \sum_{\tau = -\infty}^{\infty} \rho_\tau \, e^{-i\omega\tau}. \tag{3.10}$$

For most applications the case of a discrete spectrum can be neglected. In time-series analysis, for example, a generating process is commonly assumed from the family of linear processes which have a continuous spectrum and are defined by

$$X_t = u_t + a_1 u_{t-1} + a_2 u_{t-2} + \ldots, \qquad (3.11)$$

where u_t denotes a white-noise process. The class of the linear processes includes the autoregressive (AR), the moving average (MA), and their combination, the ARMA process.

5.2. The Maximum-Entropy Spectrum as the Optimal Estimate

The most intuitive way to estimate a theoretical spectrum is to substitute the theoretical autocovariance function in (3.10) with the empirical autocovariance function (3.5). Normalizing with the variance, this leads to (3.8), one of the three equivalent formulations for the periodogram. Therefore the periodogram can be considered as an estimate for the spectrum. The examples with artificial data in Section 4.2 proved that this leads to many problems concerning artificial peaks. The traditional techniques of windowing the data, the correlogram, or the periodogram itself (for details see Priestley 1981) cannot offer a satisfying solution to this problem. The removal of artificial peaks is accompanied by a loss of resolution. The peaks become broad and often merge. Short-time series in particular cannot be analysed by the traditional methods. So the traditional spectral analysis fails for economic time series, which are typical short series.

A totally different approach, proposed by Burg (1967), solves these problems. Assuming that the first n autocovariances of a time series generated by a Gaussian, linear process are known, all spectra are considered that do not contradict the given autocovariance function. Since a continuous spectrum is given by the Fourier transform of the whole autocovariance function, many different spectra could belong to the given part of an autocovariance function. Therefore the problem is to choose an optimal one from all spectra that are compatible with the given part of the autocovariance function. Common sense demands that we choose the spectrum that is (1) is compatible with the given autocovariance function and (2) non-informative regarding the non-given values. Using the entropy as an information measure, the problem can be formalized (Burg 1967), and calculus of variation (Parzen 1983) yields the *maximum-entropy spectrum*:

$$S(\omega) = \frac{1}{2\pi} \frac{\sigma_u^2}{\left| 1 - \sum_{k=1}^{n} a_k e^{-i\omega} \right|^2}, \qquad (3.12a)$$

where the parameters a_i and σ^2 are determined by the Yule–Walker equations:

$$\sigma_u^2 = a_1\rho_1 + a_2\rho_2 + \ldots + a_n\rho_n$$

$$\rho_1 = a_1\rho_0 + a_2\rho_1 + \ldots + a_n\rho_{n-1}$$

$$\ldots$$

(3.12b)

$$\rho_n = a_1\rho_{n-1} + a_2\rho_{n-2} + \ldots + a_n\rho_0$$

where ρ_τ, $\tau = 1, \ldots, n$ denotes the given autocovariance function.

The theoretical spectrum determined by the above equations is equivalent to the spectrum of an nth-order autoregressive process with parameters $a_1 \ldots a_n$ (Koopmans 1974). That means that, given an autocovariance function to lag n, a finite autoregressive process determined by the Yule–Walker equations is the 'best' representation of the generating process considering all linear normal processes (Choi 1986).

After this discussion it is also clear that the ME spectrum cannot exhibit artificial peaks. It is a theoretical spectrum; its shape is uniquely determined by its functional form (3.12a). So it is an ideal instrument for identifying cyclical components in short-time series (Hillinger and Sebold 1989). In contrast to the periodogram, no further considerations are necessary to determine if a peak is artificial.

5.3. The Interpretation of the ME Spectrum

As mentioned above, the ME Spectrum is equivalent to the spectrum of an autoregressive process. The interpretation of the ME spectrum is easier if one takes this equivalence into account. So we will first discuss the basic assumptions and properties of an autoregressive process[3] and then elucidate the interpretation of the ME spectrum. This interpretation is divided into two parts. First, the shape of the ME spectrum and its relation to the properties of an AR process are discussed. Secondly, the information that can be drawn from an ME spectrum is summarized.

Basic assumptions and properties of the AR process

An AR process of order n is defined by a stochastic nth-order difference equation:

$$x_t = a_1 x_{t-1} + a_2 x_{t-2} + \ldots + a_n x_{t-n} + u_t,$$

(3.13)

where u_t is identically and independently distributed with mean 0 and variance σ_u^2.

---

[3] A detailed discussion of autoregressive processes can be found in the fundamental books of Box and Jenkins (1970) or Anderson (1971).

The AR process is stationary if the n roots λ_k, $k = 1, \ldots, n$ of the associated polynomial equation,

$$\lambda^n - a_1 \lambda^{n-1} - \ldots - a_{n-1} \lambda^1 - a_n = 0, \qquad (3.14)$$

are less than one in absolute magnitude.

We can see how an autoregressive process models cyclical behaviour by setting $u_t \equiv 0$ for all t. The resulting homogeneous difference equation can easily be solved using the roots of (3.14). The solution is a superposition of declining exponentials due to the real roots and damped cosines due to pairs of conjugate complex roots. These terms are referred to as the *components* of the solution. In particular, we speak of components associated with positive or negative real roots, or of *cyclical components* associated with the pairs of complex roots.

The noise u_t prevents the process from dying out and disturbs the functional relationship.

The stochastic impulse influences the cyclical pattern caused by the conjugate complex roots, and the cyclical components do not repeat themselves at strict periods. The added noise causes random phase shifts. The actual duration of a cycle varies around the period determined by the complex root (Priestley 1981 : 131–2). These periods, respectively frequencies, are often called *natural periods/frequencies* of the AR process.

It is obvious that the more strongly damped the homogeneous solution is, the more the noise influences the behaviour of the process. Therefore the actual duration of a cycle varies in a wider range, the more strongly damped a cycle is. Near the stationarity bound the cycle is just slightly damped and the process is less noisy; as one approaches the stationarity bound, the frequency band corresponding to a complex root becomes narrower.

These heuristical arguments are supported by the complete solution of the stochastic difference equation (3.13), which is given by

$$x_t = \sum_{\tau = 0}^{\infty} \delta_\tau u_{t-\tau} \qquad (3.15)$$

with

$$\delta_\tau = \sum_{i=1}^{n} k_i \lambda_i^\tau,$$

where k_i are arbitrary constants and λ_i, $i = 1, \ldots, n$, the roots of (3.14) (Anderson 1971 : 171–3). In the case of an AR process of order 2 with complex roots $\lambda_1 = re^{i\omega}$, $\lambda_2 = re^{-i\omega}$, (3.15) simplifies to

$$x_t = \sum_{\tau = 0}^{\infty} \frac{\sin [\omega(\tau + 1)]}{\sin (\omega)} r^\tau u_{t-\tau}. \qquad (3.16)$$

The periodic pattern of the coefficients induces a periodic influence of previous u_s on x_t, $t = s + 1$, $s + 2, \ldots$, and an oscillating behaviour of x_t. The more strongly damped the coefficients are, the lower is the influence of previous realizations of u_s and the stronger is the influence of the new impulse. Therefore x_t is governed by the noise.

The ME spectrum and the AR process

The cyclical behaviour represented by the conjugate complex roots of the characteristic equation is expressed by the ME Spectrum (3.12a):

$$S(\omega) = \frac{1}{2\pi} \frac{\sigma_u^2}{\left| 1 - \sum_{k=1}^{n} a_k e^{-i\omega} \right|^2}.$$

At once one can see that the spectrum is always positive.

The shape of the spectrum is governed by the denominator. Its minima determine the peaks. The denominator of the AR-spectrum can be expressed in terms of the roots λ_i of (3.14) and the spectrum (3.12a) can be represented (Anderson 1971 : 407–9)

$$S(\omega) = \frac{1}{2\pi} \frac{\sigma_u^2}{\prod_{i=1}^{n} \left| e^{i\omega} - r_i e^{i\omega_i} \right|^2}. \tag{3.17}$$

The roots determine the range, where the minima of the denominator and so the peaks of the spectral density are located. Real roots, characterized by $\omega_i = 0$ if positive and $\omega_i = \pi$ if negative, attribute most of the mass to the limits 0 to π. The pairs of conjugate complex roots λ_i, λ_i^* can be combined to give (Anderson 1971 : 408):

$$(1 - r_i^2)^2 + 4r_i^2(\cos \omega_i - \cos \omega)^2 - 4r_i(1 - r_i)^2 \cos \omega_i \cos \omega. \tag{3.18}$$

Therefore the pairs of conjugate complex roots produce peaks inside the frequency range $[0, \pi]$ in the neighbourhood of the natural frequencies of the AR process (see also Box and Jenkins 1972 : 62–3).

The shape of the maxima is dependent on the magnitude r of the roots. Approaching 1, the peak becomes sharper. That means that the corresponding cyclical component is concentrated in a narrow frequency band. In the limit the spectrum has a pole, and the corresponding frequency band degenerates to a singular point; the spectrum tends to infinity at this frequency.[4]

The numerator displays the influence of the stochastic component. It increases with its share of total variance. A numerical measure for the share of

---

[4] This case is excluded because of the stationarity condition.

the noise is the *signal–noise ratio* (SNR), which is defined as the ratio of the variance of the signal $a_1 x_{t-1} + a_2 x_{t-2} + \ldots + a_n x_{t-n}$ to the variance of the noise u_t (see Koopmans 1974 : 148).

Information from the ME spectrum

Three main aspects of cyclical components can be analysed by ME spectral analysis. First, one can extract the dominating cyclical components. Their lengths are marked by the peak frequencies. Since the ME spectrum is a continuous spectrum the cyclical components are not strictly periodic, but roughly repeat themselves at periods concentrated around these peak periods.

Second, the width of the interval in which the periods are concentrated can be determined. This depends on the damping parameter of the corresponding root of the AR process as well as on the signal–noise ratio. The sharper a peak is, the smaller the interval. To get a quantitative measure, the *half-bandwidth* is calculated. This is defined as the range in which a peak halves. With the half-bandwidth the spread of different waves can be compared.

The third aspect is the question, How important is a specific wave? The usual measure is the variance and its decomposition. Since the ME spectrum is continuous, only intervals can be classified by variance (Section 5.1). To simplify and visualize the analysis, the integrated spectrum normalized by total variance is calculated:

$$I(\omega) = \frac{\displaystyle\int_0^\omega S(\varepsilon)\,d\varepsilon}{\displaystyle\int_0^\pi S(\varepsilon)\,d\varepsilon}, \qquad \omega \in [0, \pi]. \tag{3.19}$$

The normalized integrated spectrum ranges from 0 to 1. Sharp peaks are displayed by steep ascents over the range marked by the peak. The difference between two frequencies reflects the variance explained by the defined range. To classify the peak frequencies ω_k we use the frequency range of $(1 \pm 0.1)\omega_k$.

5.4. Estimation Procedure

The derivation of the ME spectrum is based on the assumption that a part of the autocovariance function of the process is given. In fact, in most applications the autocovariance function must be estimated by the empirical autocovariance function (3.5). The quality of the estimate decreases with increasing lag. Therefore the theoretical relationship cannot simply be transferred. In fact, the empirical determination of the ME spectrum of a time series involves two steps: the determination of the order of the AR process, and parameter estimation. These are discussed in the following two sections.

Order determination

The determination of the order of the AR process is an instance of the more general problem of model selection. One approach to this problem involves the use of a criterion derived from information theory in order to estimate the distance between the real model and the fitted one for each alternative; the one for which the criterion reaches its minimum is chosen. In the last two decades several criteria were developed for estimating the distance in different ways.

We decided to use the CAT criterion, because the CAT (criterion for autoregressive transfer functions) is constructed to search for the best finite AR representation of a general linear process. Other commonly used criteria like the AIC (Akaike information criterion) or the FPE (final prediction error) restrict the class of generating processes to finite AR processes. The derivation from the ME principle recommends the ME spectrum as the best spectrum not only for finite AR process, but also for general linear processes. So the CAT criterion is the optimal instrument for determining the order of the fitted process.

The CAT criterion is based on the integrated relative mean square error of the spectral density of the fitted model. This idea results in calculating the quantity (for a detailed derivation see Priestley 1981)

$$\text{CAT}(k) = \left(\frac{1}{N} \sum_{j=1}^{k} \frac{1}{\hat{\sigma}_j^2} \right) - \frac{1}{\hat{\sigma}_k^2} , \qquad (3.20a)$$

where

$$\hat{\sigma}_j^2 = \frac{1}{N-J} \sum_{t=1+j}^{N} [x_t - (a_1 x_{t-1} + a_2 x_{t-2} + \ldots + a_j x_{t-j})] \qquad (3.20b)$$

denotes the unbiased residual variance of a j-order model. The k, where CAT attains its minimum, is chosen as the optimal order if it is lower than the CAT of a model of order 0, which is computed by

$$\text{CAT}(0) = -\left(1 + \frac{1}{N}\right). \qquad (3.21)$$

Otherwise it is not useful to fit an autoregressive model. The comparison of CAT(k), $k = 1, \ldots, N-1$, with CAT(0) supplements the Durbin test for white noise (Section 4.2) and indicates structure in the data.

Parameter estimation

The Yule–Walker equations relate the parameters of the AR process to its autocovariance function. Substituting the autocovariance function with the empirical autocovariance function (3.5) would yield simple estimates. But the empirical autocovariance function is a poor estimate for the theoretical auto-covariance function, so it seems better to estimate the parameters directly from the data.

Usually the least-squares principle is employed. But a modification of Burg, which takes into account the stationarity assumption, proved to be superior (Swingler 1979). Since a stationary process must not have any direction, the parameters of a stationary AR process must be valid both for a forward and a backward regression. This leads to the following modification (Burg 1975). Minimize the so-called *Burg-norm* in respect to the parameters a_k:

$$\frac{1}{2(n-m)} \sum_{t=1}^{n-m} \left[\left(x_{t+m} - \sum_{k=1}^{m} a_k x_{t+m-k} \right)^2 + \left(x_t - \sum_{k=1}^{m} a_k x_{t+k} \right)^2 \right]. \quad (3.22)$$

Unfortunately, the resulting parameter estimates do not always fulfil the stationarity condition. To force stationary parameters the *Levinson recursion* is used, which relates the parameters of AR models of order $1, 2, 3, \ldots$ Denoting by $a_{i,j}$ the jth parameter of the i-order AR model, the Levinson recursion reads as follows:

$$a_{i,j} = a_{i-1,j} + a_{i,i} a_{i-1,i-j}. \quad (3.23)$$

So the parameters of an AR model of order p are determined by the so-called *reflection coefficients* $a_{i,j}$ of the AR model of order p and the preceding AR models of order $1, \ldots, p-1$. To guarantee stationary parameters, it is sufficient that the reflection coefficients lie between -1 and 1 (Burg 1975).

Therefore using the Levinson recursion, stationary estimates are obtained minimizing the Burg-norm (3.22) under the constraint that the reflection coefficients $a_{i,j}$ are in magnitude lower than 1. Technically this is done by substituting $a_{i,j}$ with

$$a_{i,i} = \varepsilon \cos(\theta_i) \quad (3.24)$$

where ε is a constant slightly less than 1, and minimizing the Burg-norm in respect to θ_i. For a detailed discussion we refer readers to Fougere (1985).

5.5. Application to German Data

The determination of the order of the generating AR process for the deviations from trend/mean of the GDP, GFCF, and II is unambiguous. The example GDP is representative. The CAT criterion leaves no doubt and indicates that the time series is best approximated by an AR process with five parameters (Fig. 3.24). A comparison with $CAT(0) = -1.04$ confirms that it is reasonable to fit an AR process. Similar plots lead to an order of 5 also for the GFCF and II.

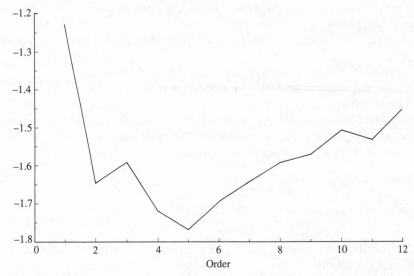

FIG. 3.24.   CAT-criterion: GDP, Germany, 1960–1986, constant prices

In harmony with the previous results, the GDP (Fig. 3.25) exhibits two maxima: a rather sharp one at a period of 8.0 years and a flatter and much lower peak at 3.6 years. The GFCF (Fig. 3.26) is dominated by a spike at 8.2 years. No additional cycle is indicated. The sharp peaks of the long cycle in GDP and GFCF are contrasted by the spectrum of II (Fig. 3.27). The two peaks displayed are very broad, and the peak at the long 10.1-year period is even flatter than the maximum at 3.4 years.

The half-bandwidths are listed in Table 3.2 together with the peak frequencies, and the periods, and the R^2 of peak frequency ± 10 per cent (see Section 5.3).

TABLE 3.2 Peak period, frequency, bandwidth, R^2

	GDP		GFCF	II	
	(i)	(ii)	(i)	(i)	(ii)
Period	8.00	3.76	8.20	10.10	3.43
Frequency	0.79	1.68	0.77	0.62	1.84
Half bandwidth	0.11	—	0.09	—	0.58
R^2	0.55	0.07	0.64	0.07	0.22

As can be seen, the peak of the GFCF is the sharpest. The frequency band belonging to the long cycle of the GDP is two-thirds wider. The peaks of the inventories are spread over ranges that are at least three times as wide. The short cycle in the GDP and the long cycle in the II are so flat that no half-bandwidth can be calculated.

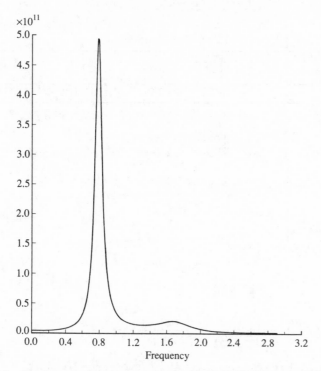

FIG. 3.25. Maximum-entropy spectrum of order 5: GDP, Germany, 1960–1986, constant prices

Peak periods: 8.00, 3.76

The integrated spectra confirm these results. The GDP (Fig. 3.28) is characterized by a steep ascent at the frequency of the long cycle. The symmetric 10 per cent interval explains 55 per cent of the variation of data. The ascent at the short cycle is very flat. No beginning or end can be defined. The R^2 is low and reaches just 7 per cent.

The long cycle is dominating in the GFCF (Fig. 3.29). The ascent at the peak frequency defines a step of the integrated spectrum which explains about 90 per cent of the data variation; the ± 10 per cent interval explains more than 60 per cent. Apart from the long cycle, no additional details can be seen.

The integrated spectrum of the inventories (Fig. 3.30) is a strong contrast to the previous one. While for the short cycle a beginning and end can be defined, this is impossible for the longer one. The shorter is more important than the longer. Its R^2 is about three times higher than the R^2 of the long cycle. Nevertheless, it is essentially lower than the R^2 of the long cycle in the GFCF.

In addition to the half-bandwidths and the R^2, an analysis of the parameter r and the SNR is useful. They are listed in Table 3.3. As stated above (Section 5.2), these measures reflect the influence of noise.

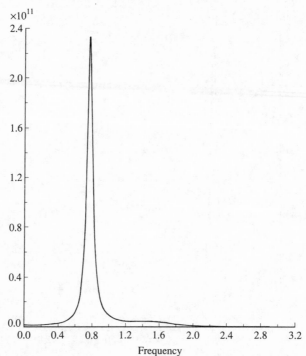

FIG. 3.26.   Maximum-entropy spectrum of order 5: gross fixed capital formation
(GFCF), Germany, 1960–1986, constant prices

Peak period: 8.23

TABLE 3.3   SNR, peak periods, and their damping parameter

	GDP		GFCF	II	
	(i)	(ii)		(i)	(ii)
Peak period	8.00	3.76	8.23	10.10	3.43
Parameter r	0.95	0.78	0.96	0.66	0.79
SNR		9.15	19.1		6.04

The table confirms that the II is dominated by the noise. The signal–noise ratio
is very low. Also, the two cycles are strongly damped.

The most deterministic series is the GFCF. An SNR of 19.1 indicates a
signal that dominates the process. The damping parameter is near the stationarity bound. The corresponding cycle is only slightly damped. Without noise
it lasts about five times longer than the long cycle of the inventories until it
reaches its half time after about 17 years.

In addition to the strong deterministic component of the GFCF, the GDP
also exhibits the strongly stochastic short cycle of the II. So the SNR is
significantly lower than the SNR of the GFCF. Nevertheless, a value of 9.15

indicates again a strong deterministic part. This is confirmed by the damping parameter of the longer cycle. It is also near the stationarity bound. The undisturbed cycle halves after about 14 years. In contrast, the short cycle is strongly damped. Like the cycles of the inventories, it needs just about three years to halve the amplitudes if no noise is present.

5.6. Conclusions

We conclude that the fluctuations of the GDP contain two cyclical components in the range of about four and eight years. The longer one can be found in the GFCF as well as in the II, while the short one comes just from the II. The GFCF is strongly dominated by the deterministic part. The period of the wave is concentrated in a narrow range. The inventories are strongly affected by noise. Both cycles are present in the II range over a broad frequency band.

The empirical application of the ME spectrum demonstrates the usefulness of this tool. The CAT criterion clearly determines the order of the AR process in each case. The spectra determine the peak periods without introducing

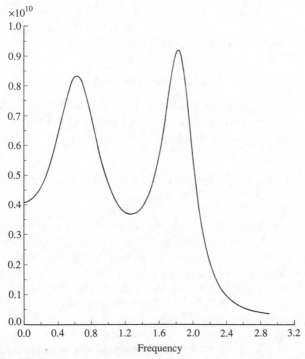

F IG. 3.27. Maximum-entropy spectrum of order 5: inventory investment, Germany, 1960–1986, constant prices

Peak periods: 10.00, 3.44

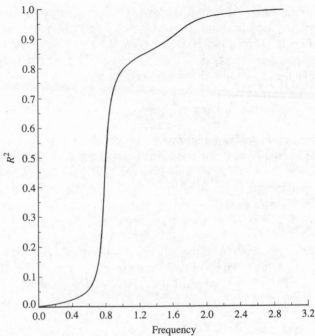

FIG. 3.28.   Integrated maximum-entropy spectrum: GDP, Germany, 1960–1986, constant prices

Peak periods: 8.00, 3.76

artificial peaks. Even minor cycles such as the short one in the GDP of Germany could be uncovered. The further analysis of the peaks and roots of the characteristic polynomial help to judge the periods indicated by the maxima.

6. Summary of 15 OECD Countries and Resulting Stylized Facts

The evidence is broadened in this section to 15 countries. In addition to Germany, we chose 14 further OECD countries (OECD 1988), which were not involved in breaks in continuity such as major wars or change of political system: Australia, Austria, Belgium, Canada, Denmark, France, Italy, Japan, Netherlands, Norway, Sweden, Switzerland, the UK, and the USA. The data are annual, from 1960 until 1986, and in constant prices.

The step-by-step method of analysis described in the preceding sections was employed and produced similar results. Visual examination and trend analysis again locate the economic fluctuation in the investment series. As in the case of Germany, II exhibits no trend. GDP, GFCF, and RD are characterized by decreasing growth rates. So it is not astonishing that the logistic trend is appropriate in all cases.

The R^2 of the trend, listed in Table 3.4, are a measure of the share of the trend in total movements. The table confirms the results for Germany. The residual demand is almost totally explained by the trend function, the median R^2 being 99.6 per cent. The share of trend decreases for GDP and GFCF: while in the GDP the median is placed at 99.2 per cent, for the GFCF it is noticeably smaller at 88.6 per cent.

The preceding section demonstrated that the ME spectrum is an ideal instrument for the analysis of the deviations. We shall therefore report only the results obtained in this manner. Before fitting an autoregressive process to the detrended data, the data are investigated to see whether it is reasonable to assume structure. The test for white noise (Section 4.2) together with the check of the CAT criterion against CAT (0) (Section 5.4) indicate that it is not reasonable to analyse the II of Belgium, Denmark, and the Netherlands. For these series the hypothesis of white noise cannot be rejected.

The analysis again starts with the plot of the spectra and integrated spectra. The typical findings from the spectra and integrated spectra of Germany (Figs. 3.25–3.30) can be confirmed. Most of the variance of GFCF is explained by the long periods, while II exhibits strong components in the long and the short range. The shape of the spectra of GDP is similar to the GFCF, but exhibits

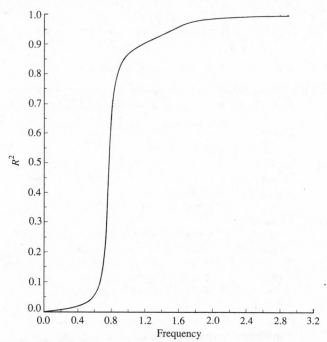

FIG. 3.29. Integrated maximum-entropy spectrum: gross fixed capital formation (GFCF), Germany, 1960–1986, constant prices

Peak period: 8.23

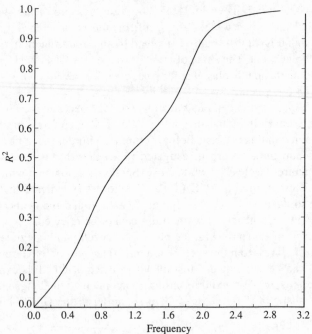

FIG. 3.30.   Integrated maximum-entropy spectrum: inventory investment, Germany, 1960–1986, constant prices

Peak periods: 10.00, 3.44

an additional weak component concentrated at short periods. In contrast to Germany, for some countries two long peaks can be identified.

TABLE 3.4 R^2 of the trend

	GDP	GFCF	RD	II
Australia	0.992	0.969	0.990	—
Austria	0.994	0.948	0.994	—
Belgium	0.994	0.841	0.996	—
Canada	0.995	0.975	0.997	—
Denmark	0.986	0.674	0.991	—
France	0.998	0.978	0.997	—
Germany	0.993	0.869	0.998	—
Italy	0.995	0.857	0.999	—
Japan	0.994	0.974	0.999	—
Netherlands	0.992	0.881	0.993	—
Norway	0.996	0.889	0.985	—
Sweden	0.992	0.945	0.998	—
Switzerland	0.953	0.707	0.990	—
UK	0.984	0.910	0.993	—
USA	0.987	0.886	0.997	—
Median	0.992	0.886	0.996	—

In Table 3.5 the peak periods of the spectra are summarized. The R^2 (in brackets) as defined in Section 5.3 help to judge the importance of the peaks. The SNR displays the influence of the noise.

Countries that have similar cycles can be classified into four groups. Similarity of cyclical structure is seen to be determined almost entirely by geographical proximity. The only exceptions are Australia and Italy in group 1, who are not close to each other or the North European countries. The second group has central and western Europe, the third North America. Japan, which is geographically isolated, is by itself in group 4.

TABLE 3.5 Peak periods, R^2, and SNR

	Period R^2	Period R^2	Period R^2	SNR
Group 1				
Norway				
GDP	11.7	6.60	3.9	11.26
	(0.36)	(0.10)	(0.06)	
GFCF	13.9	5.5	—	6.23
	(0.21)	(0.10)		
II	—	5.0	3.0	4.56
		(0.37)	(0.23)	
Sweden				
GDP	14.5	5.0	3.0	15.2
	(0.71)	(0.13)	(0.03)	
GFCF	14.3	4.5	—	9.29
	(0.62)	(0.10)		
II	—	5.0	2.5	10.2
		(0.37)	(0.05)	
UK				
GDP	12.5	5.8	2.6	8.18
	(0.16)	(0.26)	(0.11)	
GFCF	12.4	5.8	—	9.70
	(0.44)	(0.17)		
II	—	5.1	2.9	6.11
		(0.25)	(0.13)	
Australia				
GDP	13.9	5.1	2.5	9.82
	(0.60)	(0.10)	(0.02)	
GFCF	12.4	4.5	—	7.87
	(0.17)	(0.18)		
II	—	5.1	2.6	6.13
		(0.24)	(0.29)	
Italy				
GDP	—	6.1	3.5	5.57
		(0.80)	(0.05)	

TABLE 3.5 cont.

	Period R^2	Period R^2	Period R^2	SNR
GFCF	11.8 (0.13)	5.8 (0.36)	—	12.3
II	—	5.4 (0.39)	3.2 (0.24)	6.18
Group 2				
Austria				
GDP	13.2 (0.18)	—	3.0 (0.06)	9.16
GFCF	16.1 (0.09)	7.1 (0.56)	—	12.6
II	—	6.38 (0.52)	3.3 (0.14)	5.76
Belgium				
GDP	13.0 (0.26)	—	3.6 (0.06)	8.29
GFCF	13.8 (0.55)	—	—	12.33
II	—	—	—	—
Denmark				
GDP	—	9.7 (0.37)	3.2 (0.05)	6.45
GFCF	14.5 (0.79)	6.7 (0.03)	—	8.83
II	—	—	—	—
France				
GDP	15.4 (0.14)	6.8 (0.14)	3.5 (0.07)	7.85
GFCF	—	7.4 (0.61)	—	11.53
II	—	—	4.0 (0.10)	4.64
Germany				
GDP	—	8.0 (0.55)	3.6 (0.07)	9.15
GFCF	—	8.2 (0.64)	—	19.1
II	—	10.1 (0.07)	3.4 (0.22)	6.04
Netherlands				
GDP	—	9.8 (0.22)	—	7.19

TABLE 3.5 cont.

	Period R^2	Period R^2	Period R^2	SNR
GFCF	—	8.8 (0.25)	—	7.50
II	—	—	—	—
Switzerland				
GDP	—	10.9 (0.38)	3.8 (0.02)	15.55
GFCF	—	10.6 (0.32)	—	12.5
II	—	8.3 (0.20)	3.2 (0.19)	5.82
Group 3				
Canada				
GDP	13.8 (0.30)	6.3 (0.24)	4.0 (0.09)	7.99
GFCF	—	6.8 (0.30)	—	7.12
II	—	5.0 (0.16)	2.4 (0.22)	5.45
USA				
GDP	—	6.3 (0.34)	2.5 (0.05)	11.7
GFCF	—	6.3 (0.58)	—	15.1
II	—	—	2.6 (0.84)	5.96
Group 4				
Japan				
GDP	13.5 (0.25)	—	3.3 (0.05)	14.7
GFCF	—	10.8 (0.41)	—	8.23
II	—	—	—	—

Geographical proximity is, of course, only an indirect factor. It tends to promote cultural and economic homogeneity. In addition, these countries tend to transact much of their trade with each other. This may lead to a synchronization of cycles along lines similar to those discussed by Weser in Chapter 9 below. This is a topic that should be investigated further.

The most homogeneous group is group 1. Sweden, Norway, and the United Kingdom are characterized by three cycles. As in all other countries, the shortest one of about three years cannot be identified in the GFCF. The GFCF is dominated by two longer cycles, one of more than 12 years and one between five and six years. The mass concentrates on the longer one. In the GFCF for all three countries the R^2 of the longer is essentially higher than that of the shorter one. But this five- to six-year cycle plays an important role in the II. An R^2 of between 25 and 37 per cent reflects the dominating character of this cycle for the inventories. In the case of Sweden and the United Kingdom, this even raises the R^2 of the five- to six-year cycle in the GDP relative to the GFCF. Such a cycle is also observed for Italy and Australia. Again, its dominance occurs in the II.

Although many countries of western or central Europe (group 2) exhibit a cycle longer than 12 years, it does not have the same weight as in the case of group 1. Except for Belgium and Denmark, the GFCF of all countries is dominated by a second long cycle. This second cycle is significantly longer than in the case of group 1 and ranges from seven to ten years. The increase of the SNR and the R^2 of the long cycles from GDP to GFCF emphasize the impression that the long cycles of GDP come mainly from the GFCF. In II the short cycle of about three to four years, which cannot be found in the GFCF, reaches the highest R^2. The longer components have a relatively low R^2. In contrast to the GFCF, which is characterized by a strong signal, the II are dominated by noise: the low SNRs, and the fact that the II of three countries (Denmark, Belgium, and Netherlands) do not exhibit significant structure, prove that.

The third group contains Canada and the USA. Both countries are characterized by a longer cycle of about 6.5 years and a very short one of about 2.5 years. The short cycle dominates the II. In the case of the USA it even reaches an R^2 of 84 per cent.

Japan, which comprises the fourth group, has a totally different behaviour. In contrast to all other countries, the long cycles of the three series are not placed in the same range. Only the typical short inventory cycle can be fixed, at three years.

Although the length and relative importance of the cyclical components depend on the respective country, a common structure of all countries can be extracted. No short cycles can be found in the GFCF of any country. The additional short cycle that can be detected in the GDP is obviously caused by the II. Its R^2 rises for almost all cases substantially comparing II with GDP. For most countries the R^2 of the short cycle is essentially larger than the R^2 of the longer components, which can also be found in the II. This behaviour of the R^2 confirms the importance of the short cycle in the II. The long cycles seem to come from the GFCF, where they reach the highest R^2. An exception to this rule seems to be the five- to six-year cycle of group 1. It plays an important role in the II as well as in the GFCF.

Comparing the SNR of GDP with the SNR of GFCF and II confirms that GFCF is dominated by a deterministic pattern while II exhibits a strong noise component. For almost all countries, the SNR of GFCF is higher than the SNR of GDP, while the SNR of II is less.

Additional information can be drawn from the damping parameter r. Since its pattern does not differ from country to country, just the medians are listed. In Table 3.6 cycle 1 denotes the longest cycle, which exceeds 12 years, cycle 2 the second long cycle, of between five and ten years, and cycle 3 the short cycle.

TABLE 3.6 Medians of damping parameter (r)

	Cycle 1	Cycle 2	Cycle 3
GDP	0.93	0.93	0.83
GFCF	0.96	0.94	—
II	0.88	0.87	0.90

The GDP is characterized by two slightly damped long cycles and one essentially stronger damped short cycle. Without stochastic impulse the longer cycles halve after about ten years, while the short one reaches its half after only four years. That means that the duration of the long cycles is quite constant, but the short cycle varies strongly.

In GFCF the damping parameters r of the two long cycles are close to the stationarity bound, but very low in the II. In contrast to the clear cyclical pattern of the long cycles in the GFCF, they are strongly influenced by the noise in the II. The short cycle of II has a higher parameter r, indicating that in the II the short cycle is less influenced by noise than the long cycles. Compared with the GDP, the short cycle is much more precise in the II. Arguing that the series that caused the cyclical components should exhibit them in a clear pattern, the damping parameter suggests, as in the previous discussion, that the long cycles are due to the GFCF and the short to the II.

Summing up the investigation of the 15 OECD countries, one can recognize typical patterns, which one can call stylized facts (SF) of economic fluctuations. Visual examination and trend analysis locate the fluctuations in the investment series and lead to:

SF1. The fluctuations are concentrated in the investment series—inventory investment and gross fixed capital formation. The II does not exhibit any trend: it fluctuates around a constant level. Residual demand, defined as the remainder of GDP after removal of the II and the GFCF, is dominated by trend, which explains almost 100 per cent of the movement.

ME spectral analysis extracts the cyclical components of GDP and its investment components. The length and R^2 of the cycles characterizes the series as well as the country:

SF2. GFCF exhibits cycles in the range of six to ten years often superposed by a cycle longer than 12 years. II contains a typical two- to four-year cycle additional to the longer cycles.

SF3. The periods of the cycles, as well as their relative importance, depend on the respective country. Neighbouring countries tend to have similar patterns.

The SNR calculated from the ME spectrum reflects the role of the cyclical components in the fluctuations.

SF4. The II are more affected by noise than the GFCF.

The extracted cyclical components are not strictly periodic, but have a stochastic phase. The duration of a cycle fluctuates about the value indicated by the peaks of the spectrum. Where the duration varies, the damping of the homogeneous solution of the AR process gives us an idea of how wide the range is. The two longer cycles are characterized by a different range than the shorter one.

SF5. The longer cycles are just slightly damped. They concentrate in a narrow frequency band.
SF6. The short cycle is strongly damped. The corresponding frequency band is essentially wider than for the longer cycles.

Finally, we discuss a hypothesis that is implied by Weser's work on aggregation in Chapter 9. According to this hypothesis, we may expect a 2 : 1 relationship between the periods of the equipment and inventory cycles.

To examine this hypothesis, we select from Table 3.5 all the available pairs of long cycles in fixed investment and short cycles in inventory investment. These are listed in Table 3.7. Sometimes there are two long cycles present in the fixed investment (see e.g. Norway). We assume that in this case the longer one is caused by the building component of fixed investment, so we concentrate on the shorter cycle.

TABLE 3.7 The relation of the inventory and equipment cycle

	II	GFCF
Australia	2.6	4.5
Austria	3.3	7.1
Canada	2.4	6.8
France	4.0	7.4
Germany	3.4	8.2
Italy	3.2	5.8
Norway	3.0	5.5
Sweden	2.5	4.5
Switzerland	2.3	10.6
UK	2.9	5.8
USA	2.6	6.3
Median	3.0	6.3

Looking at Table 3.7, although the median indicates a 2 : 1 relationship between the inventory and equipment cycle, there is no striking evidence for this relation. The relationship varies considerably. A correlation coefficient of 0.62 and a Spearman rank correlation coefficient of 0.58 between the inventory and equipment cycle indicate a mild positive correlation. That means a longer equipment cycle is generally accompanied by a longer inventory cycle.

Also relevant to the 2 : 1 hypothesis is that the 'M-shape' discussed by Weser has recently entered German policy discussions in relation to growth cycles of the GDP. We were able to confirm this phenomenon in Section 3.1.

We conclude that, while the 2 : 1 hypotheses cannot be strongly tested, owing to data limitations, it is certainly not rejected by the international data set. In addition, isolated data-sets, such as the German growth rates discussed at the beginning of this chapter, show an impressive conformity not only for the 2 : 1 relationship, but also for the precise phase relationship given by Weser.

7. Summary and Conclusions

The basic stylized facts developed in the course of about a century, in the context of investment theories of economic cycles, could be convincingly confirmed with contemporary data from 15 industrialized economies. The same basic results are obtained from the simple visual examination of economic time series as well as by using classical and modern methods of time-series analysis.

The use of modern methods developed in the physical sciences over the past twenty years, in order to analyse short-time series efficiently led to particularly impressive results. By using these methods, we were able to quantify the traditional SF as well as to obtain new ones and to assess their statistical significance.

This chapter *described* the stylized facts and the methodology used to obtain them. In Chapter 4 they will be *explained*, using structural econometric modelling. Together, the two chapters describe the substantive findings as well as the methodology developed at SEMECON.

References

Anderson, T. W. (1971), *The Statistical Analysis of Time Series*, John Wiley, New York.

Box, G. E. P., and Jenkins, G. M. (1970), *Time Series Analysis, Forecasting and Control*, Holden Day, San Francisco.

Burg, J. P. (1967), 'Maximum entropy spectral analysis', reprinted in D. G. Childers (ed.), *Modern Spectrum Analysis*, IEEE Press, New York.

—— (1975), *Maximum Entropy Spectral Analysis*, Ph.D. dissertation, Stanford University.

Choi, B. S. (1986), 'On the relation between the maximum entropy probability density function and the autoregressive model, IEEE', *Transactions on Acoustics, Speech and Signal Processing*, 34 : 1659–61.

Durbin, J. (1969), 'Test for serial correlation in regression analysis based on the periodogram of least-squares residuals', *Biometrika*, 56(1) : 1–15.

Fougere, P. F. (1977), 'A solution to the problem of spontaneous line splitting in maximum entropy power spectrum analysis', *Journal of Geophysical Research*, 82(7) : 1051–4.

—— (1985), 'A review of the problem of spontaneous line splitting in maximum entropy power spectral analysis', in C. R. Smith and W. T. Grandy (eds.), *Maximum-Entropy and Bayesian Methods in Inverse Problems*, D. Reidel, Dordrecht.

Granger, C. W. J. (1966), 'The typical spectral shape of an economic variable', *Econometrica*, 34 : 150–61.

—— and Newbold, P. (1986), *Forecasting Economic Time Series*, 2nd edn., Academic Press, New York.

Hillinger, C., and Sebold, M. (1989), 'Identifying discrete cycles in economic data: maximum entropy spectra and the direct fitting of sinusoidal functions', in J. Skilling (ed.), *Maximum Entropy and Bayesian Methods*, Kluwer, Amsterdam.

Judge, G. G. *et al.* (1988), *Introduction to the Theory and Practice of Econometrics*, 2nd edn., John Wiley, New York.

Koopmans, L. H. (1974), *The Spectral Analysis of Time Series*, Academic Press, New York.

Nelson, C. R., and Plosser, C. I. (1982), 'Trends and random walks in macroeconomic time series', *Journal of Monetary Economics*, 10 : 139–62.

OECD (1988), *National Accounts Main Aggregates*, i, OECD, Paris.

Parzen, E. (1983), 'Autoregressive spectral estimation', in D. R. Brillinger and P. R. Krishnaiah (eds.), *Handbook of Statistics*, iii, Elsevier, Amsterdam.

Perron, P. (1989), 'The great crash, the oil price shock, and the unit root hypothesis', *Econometrica*, 57(6) : 1361–1401.

Priestley, M. B. (1981), *Spectral Analysis and Time Series*, i: *Univariate series*, Academic Press, New York.

Rommelfanger, H. (1986), *Differenzengleichungen*, B.I.-Wissenschaftsverlag, Mannheim.

Rudin, W. (1964), *Principles of Mathematical Analysis*, McGraw-Hill, New York.

Schlittgen, R., and Streitberg, B. H. J. (1987), *Zeitreihenanalyse*, R. Oldenbourg Verlag, Munich.

Swingler, D. N. (1979), 'A comparison between Burg's maximum entropy method and a nonrecursive technique for the spectral analysis of deterministic signals', *Journal of Geophysical Research*, 84 : 679–85.

4

The Quantitative and Qualitative Explanation of Macroeconomic Investment and Production Cycles

Claude Hillinger and Michael Reiter

1. Introduction

This chapter describes an econometric test of the models developed at SEME-CON to explain economic cycles. The historical background of this work has been explained in Chapter 1, particularly Section 9, and the methodological background in Chapter 2.

A major postulate of the SEMECON methodology is that stylized facts must be determined independently. For present purposes, this has been done in Chapter 3. The principal findings there were that economic fluctuations occur primarily in fixed investment, where they take the form of a seven- to ten-year equipment cycle and sometimes a longer building cycle. In addition there is a shorter, three- to four-year, cycle in production and inventory investment.

The central conceptual tool in the SEMECON approach to the explanation of economic cycles is the *second-order accelerator* (SOA). The SOA and its usefulness in the explanation of the stylized facts of economic cycles is discussed in Chapter 8 below. There it is shown that, under certain assumptions regarding adjustment costs, the SOA can be derived from the intertemporal profit maximization of the firm.

The present chapter differs from the previous contributions[1] in the following ways:

1. The econometric methodology has been refined and now includes predictions beyond the sample period; a more comprehensive analysis of the estimation problem for continuous time systems is given.
2. The models thus far have been fitted only to German data: now they are also fitted to data for the USA and the United Kingdom.
3. Former versions of the models contained a modified Harrod–Domar growth path, the modification allowing for the decreasing growth rates to be observed in the Western economies after the Second World War. But previous

---

[1] The following remarks refer to the work of Hillinger and associates (cf. Hillinger 1987; Hillinger and Schueler 1977, 1978). Independently from this, Gandolfo (1981) and Gandolfo and Padoan (1984) used SOA equations in their model for the Italian economy.

estimates (Reiter 1988) showed that this growth path is inadequate for the German economy (and probably for other economies as well). To account for this, the models in this chapter are formulated as deviations from an equilibrium growth path and are applied to detrended data.

4. In addition to a simplified version, the general version of the SOA is tested.

The structure of the chapter is as follows. In Section 2 the reasons for separating fluctuations from trend are discussed and the method for this purpose is described. Sections 3–5 contain the derivation of the models and the empirical results. Section 3 discusses the equipment cycle model, which contains only the equipment sector, and applies the model to the German economy. Section 4 derives the inventory model, which explains production and inventory behaviour with final demand given exogenously. The model is estimated using UK data. In Section 5 these two models are combined to explain the interaction of equipment and inventory cycles. The larger model is tested with US data. Each of the three models is also re-estimated for a shorter time period, and out-of-sample-forecasts are made to demonstrate the stability of the results and the usefulness of the models for forecasting. Section 6 gives a general discussion of the merits and problems of the models. In Section 7 the econometric problems and methods are considered: subsections 7.1–7.3 explain the methodology for estimating a continuous-time dynamic model; subsection 7.4 gives the formulas for the estimator and some statistics used in previous sections. The Appendix contains the sources of the data.

2. Separating Fluctuations from Growth

Former versions of the SOA models (Hillinger and Schueler 1977, 1978; Hillinger 1987) were models of cyclical growth. The time path generated by them took the form of a superposition of a smooth equilibrium growth path, called *trend*, and a cyclical fluctuation about this trend. As in most equilibrium growth models, the trend in the SOA models followed an exponential function, or, in some generalized versions, an exponential function plus a constant. But as the data analysis of Chapter 3 above shows, the long-term growth of the industrialized countries often differs from this picture, and it is necessary to adopt flexible ways to separate the trend from the fluctuations. Underlying this separation is the idea that all movements in the data with a duration of more than, say, 12 years should be classed with the trend. An examination of whether long-run fluctuations may be due to long waves is impossible using the short-time series of this chapter.

It is clear, not only from the results of the data analysis but also from former estimates of the SOA models (Reiter 1988), that their trend component cannot explain the actual trend paths of the postwar economies. Furthermore, theoretical investigations in the microeconomic foundations (cf. Chapter 8) of the

SOA showed that the SOA can be most convincingly derived for variables that are defined as deviations from a long-term growth path.

For the above reasons, this chapter tests the models of Chapter 8, which are formulated in deviations from trend. It is assumed that the actual path of the economic variables is determined by an equilibrium growth path, which is not modelled in this chapter, and fluctuations around the trend, which will be explained by the SOA models.

The variables of all the following models refer to deviations from trend, and the models are therefore estimated with detrended data.[2] The data were detrended by the following method. For the flow variables (production, investment, residual demand) a third-order polynomial was fitted by least squares and then subtracted from the original data. This is a linear transformation of the data and has the advantage that the accounting identities are preserved. For finding the trend of capital stock, it must be taken into account that capital is the integral of investment. The trend of capital is therefore a fourth-order polynomial, and its parameters, except for an integration constant, are determined by the trend polynomial of investment. The integration constant was estimated by least squares.

3. The Equipment Cycle Model

3.1. Analysis of the Model

The fundamental dynamic equation for the equipment cycle model is the SOA investment equation:

$$DI_e = - b_e c_e K_e - c_e I_e \tag{4.1}$$

Here K_e denotes net equipment capital or net fixed capital[3] and I_e the corresponding investment series. Equation (4.1) is derived from optimality conditions in Chapter 8 as equation (8.29), after reparametrization according to (8.33). The variables Dk, k of Chapter 8, denoting deviations from long-term planning, can be identified with our detrended series I_e, K_e.

The model is remarkably simple. The paths of capital and investment are determined completely by their inherent dynamics, without being influenced by demand conditions. It should be noted that this concerns only the deviations from trend. Of course, the long-term growth rates of capital and demand are interrelated.

Equation (4.1), together with the identity $DK_e = I_e$, can be written as a vector differential equation

---

[2] The reasons for fitting flexible, deterministic trend functions is discussed in Ch. 3, Sect. 3.

[3] Fixed capital includes equipment and buildings. The model works equally well for both aggregates. In the following sections, net fixed capital is used.

$$Dx = Ax, \tag{4.2}$$

with

$$x = (I_e, K_e)^T$$

$$\tag{4.3}$$

$$A = \begin{pmatrix} -c_e & -b_e c_e \\ 1 & 0 \end{pmatrix},$$

where the superscript T indicates the transposition of a matrix or vector.

The solution of (4.2) is characterized by the eigenvalues $\lambda_{1,2}$ of A, which are

$$\lambda_{1,2} = \frac{1}{2}\left(-c_e \pm \sqrt{c_e^2 - 4b_e c_e}\right). \tag{4.4}$$

The solution is stable for all b_e, $c_e > 0$. For $b_e > c_e/4$, the eigenvalues are conjugate complex and the solution of (4.2) takes the form

$$I_e(t) = A_1 e^{\rho t} \cos(\omega t - \phi_1) \tag{4.5}$$

$$K_e(t) = A_2 e^{\rho t} \cos(\omega t - \phi_2).$$

The damping factor ρ, frequency ω, and period P are given by

$$\rho = \frac{-c_e}{2}$$

$$\omega = \frac{1}{2}\sqrt{4b_e c_e - c_e^2} \tag{4.6}$$

$$P = \frac{2\pi}{\omega}.$$

The factor ρ describes the rate at which the cycle would dampen out in the absence of shocks.

Because it is plausible that desired values can change much faster than real ones, an interesting special case is given when c_e, the adjustment coefficient of real investment (cf. Section 8.1), tends to 0 (with $b_e c_e$ held constant). Then the dampening factor vanishes and (4.1) converges to a model with cycles of constant amplitude:

$$DI_e = -a_e K_e \tag{4.7}$$

$$DK_e = I_e,$$

with

$$a_e = b_e c_e. \tag{4.8}$$

The roots of the corresponding system matrix are

$$\lambda_{1,2} = \pm i\sqrt{a_e}. \tag{4.9}$$

In this case the real part of the eigenvalues is 0, implying cycles of constant amplitude. This means that cycles originating from an initial disequilibrium never die out, even in the absence of shocks. Adding a shock term to (4.7) would lead to fluctuations of growing amplitude.

In former applications of SOA models by Hillinger and associates (e.g. Hillinger and Schueler 1978), only the simplified version (4.7) was tested.[4] In the following sections, both versions are examined and compared.

3.2. Empirical Results for Germany

The equipment cycle model was applied to annual German data over 1960–87. Section 7 presents detailed information about the estimation procedures.

TABLE 4.1 Parameter estimates for Germany: two-parameter model

Variable	Estimated value		Standard error
b_e	4.000		2.633
c_e	0.154		0.099
ρ_e	-0.077		0.050
P_e	8.055		0.422
Equation	R^2	MSE	Autocorr.
Equipm. investment	0.806	6.614	0.154
Equipment	0.968	3.522	0.161

Table 4.1 summarizes the estimates. For every parameter, its estimated value and the standard error are listed. The second part of the table gives some descriptive statistics: the R^2, mean squared error (MSE), and the empirical autocorrelation of the estimated errors, computed separately for every equation of (4.2), using the formulas of subsection 7.4. Note that the dynamic equation for capital, which is an identity in the continuous model, becomes stochastic in the discrete analogon that is actually estimated. (See Section 7 for details.)

The estimated values of the parameters all lie in the expected range. They imply a cycle of 8.055 years, which conforms to the stylized facts. The value of c_e gives a damping factor $\rho_e = -0.077$ (minus half the absolute value of c_e). This means that in an undisturbed model the amplitude of the cycle would halve within roughly nine years. This result may be surprising: the inertia of investment leads to very strong overshooting processes during the adjustment of capital, so that the convergence towards equilibrium takes a long time, even when no shocks disturb the adjustment.

A first impression of the performance of the model is provided by the statistics given in the second part of Table 4.1. An R^2 of 0.806 is very high

---

[4] Gandolfo (1981) and Gandolfo and Padoan (1984) applied an equation very similar to (4.1).

for a detrended time series, given the simplicity of the model. The autocorrelation of errors is positive, but not large.[5] A more careful evaluation of the fit can be obtained from Fig. 4.1, where the actual and the estimated values of equipment investment are plotted. To interpret the figure, it is useful to remember that the econometric model is a system of difference equations that make assertions about the *changes* of the level of the variables. To assess whether the assertions are true, one has therefore to compare the predicted change $\hat{I}_{e,t} - I_{e,t-1}$ (not $\hat{I}_{e,t} - \hat{I}_{e,t-1}$!) with the actual change $I_{e,t} - I_{e,t-1}$.

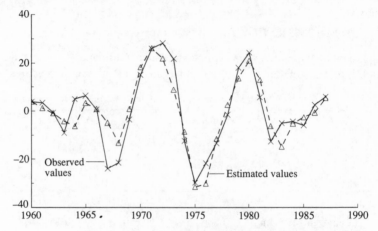

FIG. 4.1. Deviations from trend in net fixed capital formation, Germany: two-parameter model (1980 DM billions)

The picture shows that the fit is good, particularly for the big movements occurring after 1965. Also, for the first years of the sample, it can be seen that the sign of the change is predicted correctly for almost all years.

TABLE 4.2 Parameter estimates for Germany: one-parameter model

Variable	Estimated value	Standard error
a_e	0.612	0.062
P_e	8.032	0.406

Equation	R^2	MSE	Autocorr.
Equipm. investment	0.795	6.800	0.106
Equipment	0.967	3.604	0.105

The value of c_e is low; the model is therefore very similar to the single-parameter version (4.7). For comparison, the results using this simplified version are given in Table 4.2. It can be seen that the single-parameter version gives very similar results to the more comprehensive one. The value of the adjust-

---

[5] The value of the autocorrelation refers to a transformed model, see equation (4.51) below.

ment parameter implies a cycle of period 8.032 years, which is close to the previous result. The R^2 are only slightly lower than in Table 4.1.

It is worth while comparing the two models more carefully. For this purpose we construct out-of-sample forecasts for the last six years. That is, we re-estimate the models using only the data for 1960–81 and then predict the values for 1982–7, starting from the 1981 value. This procedure serves two purposes. First, it is a test of model reliability. One of the fundamental requirements of a model is its stability over time; therefore, the estimated parameters should not change too much when the model is re-estimated for a different sample period. Secondly, predictive power is a good criterion for the comparison of models with different numbers of free parameters. While it is obvious that a model with more parameters yields a higher R^2, it is by no means obvious that it will provide better forecasts. The predictions presented in Table 4.4 are dynamic; i.e., the prediction of year t is based on the predicted (not the actually observed) value of year $t - 1$.[6]

TABLE 4.3 Parameter estimates for Germany: comparison of sample periods

Variable	Estimated value for the period	
	1960–87	1960–81
Two-parameter model		
b_e	4.000	4.518
c_e	0.154	0.133
ρ_e	-0.077	-0.067
P_e	8.055	8.136
One-parameter model		
a_e	0.612	0.604
P_e	8.032	8.087

In Table 4.3 the parameter estimates for the different periods are compared. The cycle length is very stable for both models, the estimated damping $\rho_e = -0.067$ is even a bit lower for the shorter sample period.

TABLE 4.4 Predictive performance of models: Germany

Equation	MSE of the prediction, 1982–7	
	Two-parameter model	One-parameter model
Equipm. investment	5.591	7.222
Equipment	5.636	8.241

Table 4.4 compares the predictive accuracy of the two versions of the model. It can be seen that the two-parameter version performs slightly better. This indicates that the damping of the cycle is small but significant and plays an

---

[6] We made the forecasts by applying the exact discrete analogue (4.47), starting with the last observation of the shortened sample. The error is set to zero. This forecast is not optimal in the sense that it does not take account of the autocorrelation structure of the errors; cf. Sect. 7.3.

important role in forecasting. The MSE of the predictions are somewhat higher than those of the normal estimates (cf. Tables 4.1 and 4.2). This is natural because the forecasts are dynamic, the prediction for a period is based on the prediction for the former period, and therefore the errors of later periods are cumulating. Given that, the increase of the MSE is not much and the model shows a very reasonable behaviour.

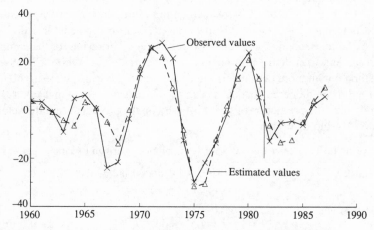

FIG. 4.2.   Deviations from trend in net fixed capital formation, Germany: two-parameter model, forecasts 1982–1987 (1980 DM billions)

Figure 4.2 shows the estimates for the two-parameter version. The values after the vertical bar are dynamic forecasts. The turning point of 1982 and the subsequent movement are modelled accurately, with the exception of an initial erratic movement in the data. This is a remarkable success for a forecasting period as long as six years.

In summary, this simple model, especially in the two-parameter version, performs excellently. It gives a high R^2, is very stable over time, and leads to reasonable predictions.

4. Inventory Model

4.1. Analysis of the Model

The behaviour of inventories can also be explained by an SOA-approach. The basic dynamic equation is derived in Chapter 8, equation (8.46). Reparameterized according to (8.33), it reads:

$$Dq = -c_i q - b_i c_i k_i. \tag{4.10}$$

The variables q and k_i denote production and inventories, respectively, measured as deviations from a medium-term optimal path. As explained in

Chapter 8, the time horizon involved in the determination of this path is shorter than the analogous time horizon for optimal equipment investment and shorter than the movements called trend. Therefore, the variables in (4.10) cannot be identified with our detrended values Q and K_i. To derive an equation that can be applied to the detrended values and is approximately equivalent to (4.10), we first rewrite it in a more extensive form:

$$D(\tilde{Q} - Q^{tr} - Q^m) = - c_i(\tilde{Q} - Q^{tr} - Q^m) - b_i[c_i(\tilde{K} - K^{tr} - K^m)]. \quad (4.11)$$

The variables q and k_i are expressed as the observations $\tilde{Q}$, $\tilde{K}_i$, minus the trend component (index tr) and the medium-term component (index m). Noting that our basic data Q, K_i are the detrended series, (4.11) simplifies to

$$D(Q - Q^m) = - c_i(Q - Q^m) - b_i[c_i(K_i - K_i^m)]. \quad (4.12)$$

The following further assumptions appear plausible:

$$K_i^m = vZ^*$$

$$Q^m = Z^* \quad (4.13)$$

$$DQ^m = DZ^*,$$

where Z^* denotes the medium-term expectation of sales. Because Z^* cannot be observed, it must be approximated in the empirical application. We approximate Z^* by Z, which contains in addition the short-run erratic movements, which average out to zero. A simple approximation of DZ^* is to set it equal to zero, since it is small relative to Z^*. To approximate DZ^* by DZ is not advisable, since DZ is dominated by the short-run movements. These considerations lead to the following assumptions:

$$K_i^m = vZ$$

$$Q^m = Z \quad (4.14)$$

$$DQ^m = 0.$$

Substituting (4.14) into (4.12) and adding the identity $DK_i = Q - Z$ yields the inventory model

$$DQ = b_i c_i(vZ - K_i) - c_i(Q - Z)$$

$$DK_i = Q - Z. \quad (4.15)$$

Within the context of the inventory model, Z must be taken as exogenous. The model describes the behaviour of production and of inventories in reaction to demand or, more precisely, to final sales.

Equations (4.15) can be written as a vector differential equation,

$$Dx = Ax + Bz, \tag{4.16}$$

where

$$x = (Q, K_i)^T$$

$$z = Z \tag{4.17}$$

$$A = \begin{pmatrix} -c_i - b_i c_i \\ 1 & 0 \end{pmatrix}$$

$$B = \begin{pmatrix} c_i(1 + b_i v) \\ -1 \end{pmatrix}.$$

The eigenvalues of A are given by

$$\lambda_{1,2} = \frac{1}{2}\left(-c_i \pm \sqrt{c_i^2 - 4b_i c_i}\right), \tag{4.18}$$

which is analogous to the equipment case. For $b_i > c_i/4$, the eigenvalues are conjugate complex. The general solution of (4.15) is a superposition of a particular solution of (4.15) and the general solution of the homogeneous part,

$$Dx = Ax, \tag{4.19}$$

which is formally equivalent to the equipment cycle case. The general solution of (4.19) can therefore be written as

$$Q(t) = A_1 e^{\rho t} \cos(\omega t - \phi_1) \tag{4.20}$$

$$K_i(t) = A_2 e^{\rho t} \cos(\omega t - \phi_2),$$

where the damping factor ρ and the frequency ω are given by

$$\rho = \frac{-c_i}{2} \tag{4.21}$$

$$\omega = \frac{1}{2}\sqrt{4b_i c_i - c_i^2}.$$

The particular solution of (4.16) depends on the path of the exogenous variable. As in the case of the equipment cycle, diminishing c_i leads in the limit to a version of the model with constant cycles:

$$DQ = a_i(vZ - K_i) \tag{4.22}$$

$$DK_i = Q - Z,$$

with

$$a_i = b_i c_i. \tag{4.23}$$

The roots of the corresponding system matrix are

$$\lambda_{1,2} = \pm \sqrt{a_i}. \tag{4.24}$$

4.2. Empirical Results for the UK

The inventory model is tested using annual data from the United Kingdom, 1960–86, because these show a regular inventory cycle so that the model can be expected to be fitted successfully. Table 4.5 gives the results for the two-parameter version. The values of b_i and c_i imply a cycle of period 3.615 years, reflecting the short-term movements typical for inventory investment and clearly seen in the data. In contrast to the equipment cycle, the inventory cycle is extremely damped: the damping factor $-c_i/2 = -1.534$ implies that in the absence of shocks the inventory cycle would reduce to one-fifth of its amplitude within one year! This does not agree with the findings of the data analysis: according to the results of Chapter 3, the dampening of the inventory cycle is much smaller. This is a problem for further investigation. We will make some remarks about it in Section 6.

TABLE 4.5 Parameter estimates for the UK: two-parameter model

Variable	Estimated value	Standard error
b_i	1.751	0.394
c_i	3.067	0.611
v	0.324	0.065
ρ_i	-1.533	0.032
P_i	3.615	0.704

Equation	R^2	MSE	Autocorr.
Production	0.925	1.163	0.234
Inventories	0.570	1.004	0.414
Invent. investment	0.493	1.163	0.234

The high R^2 of production is not surprising, because final demand, which amounts to the biggest part of production, is given exogenously and most of the variance of Q is explained simply as reaction to final demand. Interesting is the R^2 of inventories and inventory investment, which is the only component to be explained by the model. An R^2 of 0.493 for inventory investment can be regarded as a success, because this series is very volatile and erratic and also certainly contains a lot of measurement errors. A look at Figs. 4.3 and 4.4 confirms this positive view: the turning points of the short ups and downs are modelled adequately, even if the amplitude of the movement is underestimated in most cases. This is due to the extreme estimated dampening of the cycle.

The high value of c_i indicates that the single-parameter version is not a good approximation. The estimates contained in Table 4.6 verify this. The R^2 of inventory investment is negative: the model fails totally in explaining these movements. Therefore, the simplified version is not considered further.

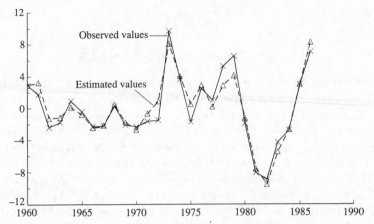

FIG. 4.3. Deviations from trend in GDP, United Kingdom: two-parameter model
(1980 £ billions)

TABLE 4.6 Parameter estimates for the UK: one-parameter model

Variable	Estimated value		Standard error
a_i	3.573		0.577
v	0.156		0.055
P_i	3.324		0.268
Equation	R^2	MSE	Autocorr.
Production	0.783	1.971	0.099
Inventories	0.301	1.228	0.298
Invent. Investment	− 0.465	1.971	0.099

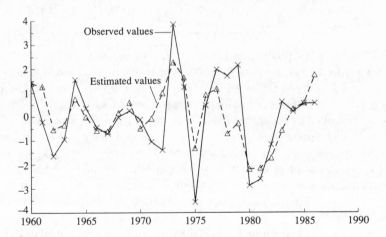

FIG. 4.4. Deviations from trend in inventory investment, United Kingdom: two-
parameter model (1980 £ billions)

TABLE 4.7 Parameter estimates for the UK: comparison of sample periods

Variable	Estimated value for the period	
	1960–86	1960–80
Two-parameter model		
b_i	1.752	1.913
c_i	3.067	2.654
v	0.324	0.507
ρ_i	− 1.533	− 1.327
P_i	3.615	3.450

In the rest of the section, the two-parameter version is re-estimated using the data for the period 1960–80 and its stability and forecasting performance is tested. Table 4.7 shows the parameter estimates for the different periods. The parameter values vary a bit, but the cycle length remains quite constant.

The forecasts were carried out as described in subsection 3.2, except that the observed values of the exogenous variable Z were used in making the forecasts, because the exogenous variable cannot be predicted. The MSE of the forecasts, listed in Table 4.8, is not much higher than for the normal estimates, but Fig. 4.5 shows that the predictions do not correspond satisfactorily with the qualitative features of the series. The last four data points actually exhibit very little movement, perhaps because these values are only preliminary and might be faulty. Also, with the normal estimation, the fit was not good for the last few years.

The results of this section show that the movement of inventories cannot be modelled as precisely as that of fixed investment. But the model explains the cyclical aspects of production and inventory behaviour and dates correctly the

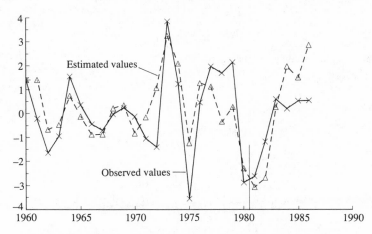

.FIG. 4.5. Deviations from trend in inventory investment, United Kingdom: two-parameter model, forecasts 1981–1986 (1980 £ billions)

turning points of the observed cycles. The high estimated damping rate indicates a deficiency of the model.

TABLE 4.8 Predictive performance of models: the UK

Equation	MSE of the prediction, 1981–6: two-parameter model
Production	1.411
Inventories	1.553

5. Equipment–Inventory Interaction

5.1. Analysis of the Model

The small models of the last two sections can be combined to show the interaction of the equipment and the inventory cycle.

In this more comprehensive model, a part of final sales Z is endogenous, namely the net fixed investment I_e. Therefore Z is split into I_e and Z_r. Z_r is called residual demand and must be treated as exogenous. It is a very heterogeneous variable, containing, among other things, such dissimilar series as consumption, export, import, and depreciation. An adequate explanation for its fluctuations could not yet be found within the framework of our model: export in particular resists a satisfactory cyclical analysis.

Combining (4.1) and (4.15), we have the complete model:

$$DI_e = -b_e c_e K_e - c_e I_e$$

$$DK_e = I_e$$

$$DQ = b_i c_i [v(Z_r + I_e) - K_i] - c_i(Q - Z_r - I_e)$$ \hfill (4.25)

$$DK_i = Q - Z_r - I_e.$$

In matrix notation it takes the form

$$Dx = Ax + Bz,$$ \hfill (4.26)

where

$$x = (I_e, K_e, Q, K_i)^T$$

$$z = Z_r$$ \hfill (4.27)

$$A = \begin{pmatrix} -c_e & -b_e c_e & 0 & 0 \\ 1 & 0 & 0 & 0 \\ c_i(1 + b_i v) & 0 & -c_i & -b_i c_i \\ -1 & 0 & 1 & 0 \end{pmatrix}$$

$$B = (0, 0, c_i(1 + b_i v), -1)^T.$$

The solution of (4.27) is very similar to the solution of the smaller models. The equipment cycle model is a self-contained subsystem of (4.27); therefore the system matrix A has a very simple structure. The eigenvalues are the same as in the single models:

$$\lambda_{1,2} = \frac{1}{2}\left(-c_e \pm \sqrt{c_e^2 - 4b_e c_e}\right)$$

$$\lambda_{3,4} = \frac{1}{2}\left(-c_i \pm \sqrt{c_i^2 - 4b_i c_i}\right)$$

(4.28)

If $b_e > c_e/4$ and $b_i > c_i/4$, the eigenvalues are complex conjugate and the solution of the homogeneous part of (4.26) is a superposition of two damped cycles. The frequencies and the damping factors are given by (4.6) and (4.21). As mentioned above, the dynamics of I_e and K_e is not influenced by Q and K_i; the solution for these variables therefore contains only one cycle. (This can be shown formally by an analysis of the eigenvectors of A.) Q and K_i contain an inventory cycle, generated by their own dynamics, and the equipment cycle because of the interrelationship with I_e.

If the single-parameter version of the SOA equations is used, the system matrix A takes the form

$$A = \begin{pmatrix} 0 & -a_e & 0 & 0 \\ 1 & 0 & 0 & 0 \\ a_i v & 0 & 0 & -a_i \\ -1 & 0 & 1 & 0 \end{pmatrix}$$

(4.29)

with eigenvalues

$$\lambda_{1,2} = \pm i\sqrt{a_e}$$

$$\lambda_{3,4} = \pm i\sqrt{a_i}.$$

(4.30)

Analogously to the previous case, the time paths of I_e and K_e are given by one cycle of constant amplitude, the paths for Q and K_i by a superposition of two cycles of constant amplitude.

5.2. Empirical Results for the USA

The complete model is applied to annual US data for 1960–86. Fixed private capital and its difference is used as K_e and I_e. (See Table 4.9). First, it must be noted that the results are very similar to those obtained in the last sections. The estimated values for b_e and c_e imply a weakly damped cycle of 6.637 years, those for b_i and c_i a strongly damped cycle of 2.713 years. These periods conform very well to the results of the data analysis in Chapter 3. The estimated damping of the short cycle is not so extreme as in the case of the UK: within one year the amplitude of the inventory cycle is reduced to one-third.

TABLE 4.9 Parameter estimates for the USA: Two-parameter model

Variable	Estimated value	Standard error
b_e	2.524	0.897
c_e	0.368	0.127
b_i	2.837	0.809
c_i	2.396	0.745
v	0.144	0.037
ρ_e	− 0.184	0.063
P_e	6.637	0.402
ρ_i	− 1.198	0.372
P_i	2.713	0.236

Equation	R^2	MSE	Autocorr.
Fixed investment	0.712	16.387	− 0.088
Fixed capital	0.927	8.974	− 0.057
Production	0.752	22.620	− 0.168
Inventories	0.573	6.724	0.089
Invent. investment	0.635	8.817	− 0.171

The R^2 values are of the same order of magnitude as previously. The values of 0.712 for equipment investment, 0.752 for production, and 0.635 for inventory investment are satisfactory. The values for production and inventories are not as good as in Section 4.2, because here the complete model is used with endogenous I_e. The error of the inventory investment equation is now determined not only by the error of production, but also by the error of equipment investment.

More information is contained in Figs. 4.6–4.8. The fit for fixed investment is seen to be excellent. For production also, the movements, especially of the long cycle, are modelled correctly. The modelling of the short cycle can be

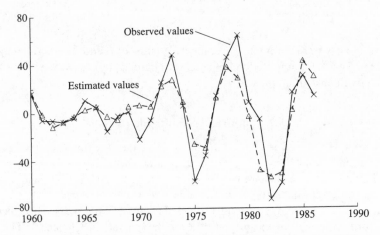

FIG. 4.6. Deviations from trend in private net fixed capital formation, USA: two-parameter model (1980 £ billions)

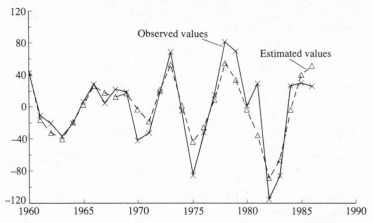

FIG. 4.7.   Deviations from trend in GDP, USA: two-parameter model (1980 $ billions)

judged by Figure 4.8. Most of the turning points are predicted correctly, but the amplitude of the movement is sometimes underestimated, probably because the estimate of the damping rate is too high.

For comparison, the estimates for the single-parameter version are given in Table 4.10. The table shows that the performance of the equipment model did not deteriorate much, and, contrary to that for the United Kingdom, the production model explains a significant part of inventory investment behaviour. This can be seen from Fig. 4.9: the amplitude of the short fluctuations is not underestimated any more—sometimes it is even overestimated; the turning points are identified correctly in most cases. The negative R^2 of inventories results mainly from some outliers.

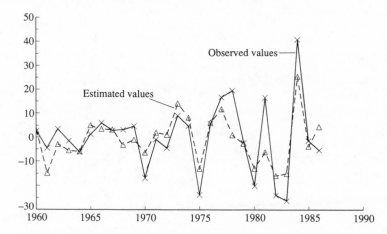

FIG. 4.8.   Deviations from trend in inventory investment, USA: two-parameter model (1980 $ billions)

TABLE 4.10 Parameter estimates for the USA: one-parameter model

Variable	Estimated value	Standard error	
a_e	0.926	0.098	
a_i	6.984	0.483	
v	0.123	0.025	
P_e	6.531	0.345	
P_i	2.378	0.082	
Equation	R^2	MSE	Autocorr.
Fixed investment	0.691	17.000	− 0.024
Fixed capital	0.923	9.234	− 0.213
Production	0.783	21.191	− 0.092
Inventories	− 0.052	10.830	− 0.004
Invent. investment	0.485	10.423	− 0.083

The stability over time of both models is shown by Table 4.11. For fixed investment a two-parameter version could not be fitted. This is probably because, taking the data from 1960 to 1980, fixed investment appears to have an exploding cycle, whereas the two-parameter model always implies a damped cycle. The values for the two-parameter model for 1960–80 in Table 4.11 were computed using a model including a one-parameter version for fixed investment and a two-parameter version for production. For the one-parameter model slightly shorter cycles are estimated. For the two-parameter model there are bigger differences: whereas the estimated cycle period does not change much, the damping rate is now considerably higher. This indicates that, similar to the case of the United Kingdom, there remain some problems with the two-parameter model of production behaviour.

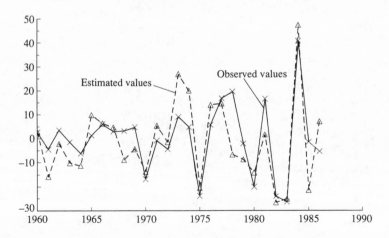

FIG. 4.9.   Deviations from trend in inventory investment, USA: one-parameter
model (1980 $ billions)

TABLE 4.11 Parameter estimates for the USA: comparison of sample periods

Variable	Estimated value for the period	
	1960–86	1960–80
Two-parameter model		
b_e	2.524	
c_e	0.368	
b_i	2.837	1.894
c_i	2.396	4.810
v	0.144	0.169
ρ_e	− 0.184	
P_e	6.637	
ρ_i	− 1.198	− 2.405
P_i	2.713	3.445
One-parameter model		
a_e	0.926	1.114
a_i	6.984	7.514
v	0.123	0.117
Cycle periods (1)	6.531	5.953
(2)	2.378	2.292

Table 4.12 compares the predictive performance of both models. Based on the MSE criterion, the forecasts of the one-parameter model are not very good. Figures 4.10–4.12 give more insight. The forecast for fixed investment predicts the turning points quite well; it misses the trough for one year and hits the peaks exactly. But the predicted amplitude is higher than the actual one, which is natural, given the data up to 1980. The one-parameter version predicts for inventory investment short movements with too high an amplitude, but hits some turning points. The two-parameter version predicts only a longer fluctuation; short fluctuations disappear because of the strong dampening. So the simpler version seems to match the characteristics of inventory fluctuations better, despite the higher MSE of forecasts. From this evidence it is hard to decide between the two models. Clearly the two-parameter version of production has some problems.

TABLE 4.12 Predictive performance of models: USA

Equation	MSE of the prediction, 1981–6	
	Two-parameter model	One-parameter model
Fixed investment		21.166
Fixed capital		25.592
Production		32.816
Inventories	5.192	13.561
Invent. investment	6.662	24.309

To sum up, the SOA explains the cyclical behaviour of equipment investment very well. For inventories the fit is not so good, according to standard

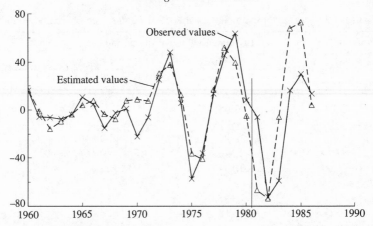

FIG. 4.10.   Deviations from trend in private net fixed capital formation, USA: one-parameter model, forecasts 1981–1986 (1980 $ billions)

criteria such as R^2; nevertheless, the cyclical pattern is modelled adequately. The results for the USA confirm the findings for other countries made in the previous sections.

6. Conclusions

In the previous sections it was shown that SOA models explain successfully the cyclical features of fixed investment, production, and inventory investment. The main results can be stated as follows.

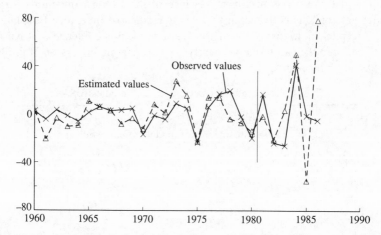

FIG. 4.11.   Deviations from trend in inventory investment, USA: one-parameter model, forecasts 1981–1986 (1980 $ billions)

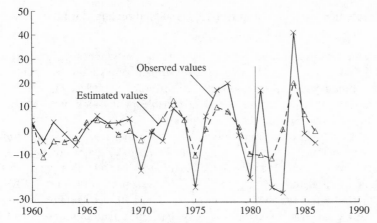

FIG. 4.12. Deviations from trend in inventory investment, USA: two-parameter model, forecasts 1981–1986 (1980 $ billions)

1. Fixed investment is dominated by a cycle of period 6.5–8 years. This cycle is only very weakly damped, indicating strong inertia of investment because of the high costs of changing investment levels.
2. The shorter cycle of 2.5–3.5 years originating from production dynamics is strongly damped.

This second result poses some problems. It contradicts the findings of the data analysis. Furthermore, a simulation of time series using the estimated parameter values did not show such a marked short cycle. This indicates that there is something wrong with the model. This is perhaps not surprising, because other researchers, using similar inventory equations, also came up with unsatisfactory results, which led to a lively discussion in the recent literature on production-smoothing (cf. Kahn 1987; Miron and Zeldes 1988 and references therein). The discussion was initiated by the rediscovery of the insight of Abramovitz (1950) that production fluctuates more than sales, a fact hardly reconcilable with the spirit of the production-smoothing model. Several proposals have been made to solve the problem. To us, the following aspects seem the most promising:

1. West (1988), using data for some two-digit industries, finds that production is smoother than demand when demand is measured by new orders rather than by sales. Net inventories, i.e. physical inventories minus backlogs, buffer production.
2. The procedure of this chapter (and of other researchers) does not take measurement errors into account. It is well known that data of inventory investment contain large measurement errors, and their impact on a dynamical system is very different from that of errors in the equations. The results of Reiter (1992) suggest that the inventory cycle is quite regular, but is obscured by measurement errors. Estimates of a model allowing for

measurement errors yield satisfactory results. It remains for future research to explore this aspect further.

The other estimated parameter values are in the range suggested by the stylized facts. It is remarkable that the estimates are quite stable between different time periods as well as between different countries. Therefore it is not surprising that the model yields reasonable predictions, with MSE not much higher than those of normal estimates.

These results are very promising and invite further research along similar lines. One obviously desirable step would be to make major components of residual demand endogenous. Secondly, although considerable work on the simultaneous modelling of growth and cycles was done in the past at SEME-CON, this work regrettably did not progress as far in the explanation of growth as in the explanation of cycles: it is to be hoped that this defect can be remedied in the future.

7. Econometric Issues

In this chapter we have had to use some methods that are not standard in econometrics, because the models to be estimated are formulated in continuous, not discrete, time. The special problems arising from this are discussed in subsections 7.1–7.3. Subsection 7.4 describes the formulas for the estimator and the statistics used.

7.1. Problems of Estimating a Continuous-Time Dynamic Model

There is a long tradition of authors favouring the use of continuous-time models in economics and econometrics. One of the earliest was Koopmans (1950); more recently, Strotz (1960), Bergstrom (1967), Gandolfo (1981), and Gandolfo and Padoan (1984) have strongly advocated this view. Many authors contributed to the solution of the estimation problems for these models. (Chapters on this topic are collected in Bergstrom 1976.) Today, continuous-time models can be estimated as satisfactorily as models in discrete time. Theoretical as well as pragmatical considerations may influence the choice. Among the reasons to formulate the structural equations of an economic model in continuous time we stress only one point, which is of particular importance in our case[7]: adjustment processes cannot be modelled in a plausible way in discrete time. Let us take as a simple example the SOA-equation introduced in Section 4.1:

$$DQ(t) = a_i [vZ(t) - K_i(t)]. \qquad (4.31)$$

[7] Other arguments are given in the literature cited above.

This explains production Q as serving the adjustment process of inventories K_i towards its desired level, which is proportional to final demand Z. For (4.31) there are two straightforward discrete analogues:

$$Q_t - Q_{t-1} = a_i (vZ_{t-1} - K_{i_{t-1}})$$ (4.32)

or

$$Q_t - Q_{t-1} = a_i (vZ_t - K_{i_{t-1}}),$$ (4.33)

where $K_{i_{t-1}}$ denotes the capital stock at the end of period $t-1$. Both formulations have serious deficiencies. Equation (4.32) implies that the demand of the current period does not influence production at all, which is the less plausible the longer the observation period is. Equation (4.33) presupposes that entrepreneurs know the demand of the whole period at the beginning of the period, which also is implausible. A further problem is that the flow Q changes the stock K_i during the period, which in turn will change the flow Q. Neither of the discrete formulations takes this into account.

Therefore, continuous-time models are clearly preferable in our case. When estimating such a model, there arise two problems. First, data are available only for discrete points or periods of time, so the model must be transformed into discrete time. If this is done in a crude way, as in (4.32) and (4.33), the advantages of continuous-time modelling are lost in the empirical application. Therefore, one has to find an *exact discrete analogue* (Section 7.2 below).

Secondly, the model contains flow variables such as production or investment as well as instantaneous variables such as capital stocks. In a differential equation system all variables are defined at a point of time, but flow variables can be measured only for a certain time *period*. Bergstrom (1983, 1985, 1986) and Harvey and Stock (1985) developed methods to obtain exact maximum-likelihood (ML) (or Gaussian) estimates for systems that include point as well as flow variables. These methods avoid the problems dealt with in Sections 7.1–7.3 below, but are very complicated. This chapter uses a simpler technique, for which it is necessary, in order to establish an exact correspondence between model and data, to convert all variables and data to either point or period form. For this purpose, several different methods are discussed in the literature, of which the most prominent is the following, containing two steps:

1. The model is integrated to express relationships between period variables.
2. The data of the instantaneous variables are converted into period form by numerical integration. Flow variables are observed as period integrals and need no further adjustment.

The transformations of the model are explained in detail in the next subsection.

Converting data from point to period form is quite simple. To obtain estimates of the integral of a variable K, e.g. capital stock, its time path during the period in question must be estimated, which is done by interpolation formulas. The simplest one is the trapezoidal rule, which interpolates a straight line between two data points and computes the integral, given by

$$\int_t^{t+1} K(\tau)\, d\tau = \frac{1}{2}\,(K_t + K_{t+1}) \tag{4.34}$$

A more exact approximation can be achieved by quadratic interpolation, fitting a second-order polynomial to every three successive data points and integrating the polynomial. For any two inner data points this can be done by using the right-hand or left-hand observation as third point. Actually, we computed it in both ways and took the arithmetic mean, which leads to the four-point formula

$$\int_t^{t+1} K(\tau)\, d\tau = \frac{1}{24}\,(-K_{t-1} + 13K_t + 13K_{t+1} - K_{t+2}). \tag{4.35}$$

In our case, where the time path of the variables is assumed to consist of cosine waves with a period length of about three observations or more, this approximation works very well.

7.2. Transformation of the Model

All the models of this chapter can be written in the form

$$Dx(t) = Ax(t) + Bz(t) + u(t) \tag{4.36}$$

where $x(t)$ denotes the vector of endogenous variables, z the exogenous variables, and $u(t)$ a vector of disturbances. (When there are identities in the model, their error may be thought of having a zero variance.) All the variables must be understood as quantities at a point of time, which are not measurable in the case of flow variables. To get a relationship between measurable quantities, (4.36) must be integrated over the observation period, which is one year in our case[8]:

$$\int_t^{t+1} Dx(\tau)\, d\tau = A \int_t^{t+1} x(\tau)\, d\tau + B \int_t^{t+1} z(\tau)\, d\tau + \int_t^{t+1} u(\tau)\, d\tau. \tag{4.37}$$

Over closed intervals, integration and differentiation may be exchanged, so

$$D \int_t^{t+1} x(\tau)\, d\tau = A \int_t^{t+1} x(\tau)\, d\tau + B \int_t^{t+1} z(\tau)\, d\tau + \int_t^{t+1} u(\tau)\, d\tau \tag{4.38}$$

or

[8] Some remarks are made in the following subsection about integration of a stochastic process.

$$Dx^o(t) = Ax^o(t) + Bz^o(t) + \int_t^{t+1} u(\tau)\, d\tau, \tag{4.39}$$

where $x^o(t)$ and $z^o(t)$ are defined as the vectors of period integrals of the variables. In the case of flow variables, these period integrals can be measured, and data of instantaneous variables can be converted to period integrals by the manipulation explained in the previous subsection. Equation (4.39) shows that the same relationship holds for the integrated variables as for the point variables, formulated in continuous time, except for the difference in the disturbance term.

The next step is to calculate the exact discrete analogue. For that we need the explicit solution of (4.39). Generally, the solution of a system

$$Dx(t) = Ax(t) + z(t) \tag{4.40}$$

with known functions $z(t)$ is given by

$$x(t) = e^{At} x(0) + \int_0^t e^{A(t-\tau)} z(\tau)\, d\tau, \tag{4.41}$$

where e^B with a square matrix B is defined as

$$e^B = I + \sum_{i=1}^{\infty} \frac{B^i}{i!} \tag{4.42}$$

(see e.g. Bellman 1960 : 169). Applying this to (4.39) yields

$$x^o(t) = e^{At} x^o(0) + \int_0^t e^{A(t-\tau)} Bz^o(\tau)\, d\tau + \int_0^t e^{A(t-\tau)} \int_\tau^{\tau+1} u(s)\, ds\, d\tau. \tag{4.43}$$

Writing (4.43) analogously for $x^o(t-1)$, we have

$$x^o(t-1) = e^{A(t-1)} x^o(0) + \int_0^{t-1} e^{A(t-1-\tau)} Bz^o(\tau)\, d\tau$$

$$+ \int_0^{t-1} e^{A(t-1-\tau)} \int_\tau^{\tau+1} u(s)\, ds\, d\tau \tag{4.44}$$

Multiplying (4.44) by e^A and subtracting from (4.43) yields

$$x^o(t) - e^A x^o(t-1) = \int_{t-1}^t e^{A(t-\tau)} Bz^o(\tau)\, d\tau + \int_{t-1}^t \int_\tau^{\tau+1} e^{A(t-\tau)} u(s)\, ds\, d\tau, \tag{4.45}$$

and, by the substitutions $r = t - \tau$ and $w = t - s$,

$$x^o(t) - e^A x^o(t-1) = \int_0^1 e^{Ar} B z^o(t-r)\, dr + \int_0^1 \int_{r-1}^r e^{Ar} u(t-w)\, dw\, dr. \quad (4.46)$$

This difference equation system can be written in the form

$$x_t^o + e^A x_{t-1}^o + \int_0^1 e^{Ar} B z^o(t-r)\, dr + v_t \qquad (4.47)$$

with

$$v_t = \int_0^1 \int_{r-1}^r e^{Ar} u(t-w)\, dw\, dr \qquad (4.48)$$

Equation (4.47) is the exact discrete analogue to (4.36). That means a stochastic difference equation system, which is equivalent to the stochastic differential equation system in the following sense: any set of equispaced points of a stochastic process generated by the differential equation system follows exactly the difference equation system.

For estimation, the integral

$$\int_0^1 e^{Ar} B z^o(t-r)\, dr \qquad (4.49)$$

must be evaluated approximately. This is done by approximating $z^o(t)$ by a quadratic function. For a detailed exposition of the procedure, see Gandolfo (1981 : 77 ff.).

7.3. Specification of Errors

Equation (4.48) reveals three important features about the distribution of the v_t:

1. Even if the disturbances $u(t)$ are uncorrelated (in the way explained below: see (4.50)), the v_t are serially correlated,[9] because the period of u entering into the double integral is two years long, so these periods for v_t and for v_{t-1} overlap.
2. The components of v_t, i.e. the errors of the different equations, are correlated, because they are all integrals of a weighted sum of all of the components of u.
3. For the same reason, the errors of the equations that were identities in the economic model have a nonzero variance.

---

[9] For a mathematical proof, see Bergstrom (1984).

The exact properties of v_t can be derived when the following strong assumptions are made about the distribution of $u(t)$:[10]

$$E\left(\int_{t_1}^{t_2} u(\tau)\, d\tau\right) = 0, \qquad ; t_1, t_2$$

$$E\left(\int_{t_1}^{t_2} u(\tau)\, d\tau\right)^2 = (t_2 - t_1)\, \Sigma, \qquad ; t_1, t_2 \tag{4.50}$$

$$E\left(\int_{t_1}^{t_2} u(\tau)\, d\tau\right)\left(\int_{t_3}^{t_4} u(\tau)\, d\tau\right) = 0, \qquad ; t_1 < t_2 \leq t_3 < t_4,$$

where Σ is a covariance matrix. It can be shown that (4.50), together with (4.48), implies that v_t follows a vector MA(1) process (Bergstrom 1984 : 1186). One can therefore give a transformation of the model (4.47) with uncorrelated errors. Bergstrom proposes the following simple transformation (Bergstrom 1984 : 1191), which approximately would remove the autocorrelation of the errors. Equation (4.47) is replaced by

$$x_t^* = e^A x_{t-1}^* + \int_0^1 e^{A\tau} B z^*(t-r)\, dr + v_t^*, \tag{4.51}$$

where all the variables and the error term are transformed by

$$y_t^* = y_t^o + \sum_{i=1}^{t-1} (-\alpha)^i y_{t-i}^o, \tag{4.52}$$

where $\alpha = 0.268$.

This transformation proved useful and was employed in all estimates reported in the previous sections, but there remained some autocorrelation of errors, which shows that (4.50) does not hold in our case, a fact that is not surprising. In particular, the last assumption in (4.50) (uncorrelated increments) is critical. Intuitively, it says that the disturbances of any two distinct time periods (meaning the integrals of $u(t)$ over these time periods) are uncorrelated. For example, the disturbances of May and June of the same year have to be uncorrelated. This is clearly unrealistic, because in this type of model the errors are to represent all influences on the variables not captured by the model, and certainly many of these influences will prevail for a longer period.

---

[10] It is best to describe $u(t)$ only by specifying the properties of its integral. The explanation here is only heuristic and is not explicit about how the integration of stochastic processes must be defined properly. A detailed analysis is given by Bergstrom (1984).

7.4. Estimation Formula

For the estimation of the models, the function

$$L = \frac{T}{2} \ln \left[\prod_{j=1}^{n} \left(\sum_{t=1}^{T} v_{tj}^{*2} \right) \right] \qquad (4.53)$$

was maximized, where v^* denotes the error defined by (4.48) and (4.51). The subscript t indicates the time period, the subscript j the jth equation of (4.51). Equation (4.53) can be interpreted as an ML estimation for the model, when the errors are specified as

$$v_t^* \propto N(0, \Sigma)$$

$$Ev_t^* v_s^{*T} = 0, \qquad t \neq s, \qquad (4.54)$$

where v_t^* is the vector of errors of time t and Σ is an unknown diagonal covariance matrix. Expressions (4.54) imply that the errors of different periods and the errors of the same period but of different equations (because of the diagonality of Σ) are uncorrelated. For errors of different periods, this should be approximately the case after the transformation of the model described in the last subsection, although for different equations it contradicts the assertion made there under item 2. But taking this form of correlation into account leads to more complicated estimation functions which, in preliminary estimates, sometimes produced unreasonable results. We decided, after testing different estimators, to rely on the simpler but probably more robust estimator (4.53), even if it lacks theoretical optimality. When discussing the empirical results, the standard errors of the parameter estimates are reported, calculated by the formula (Bard 1974 : 176 ff.)

$$v\hat{a}r\,(\hat{\theta}) = \left(-\frac{\partial^2 L}{\partial \theta^2} \right)^{-1}, \qquad (4.55)$$

where θ is the vector of the parameters, L is the function given by (4.53), and the second derivative is taken at $\theta = \hat{\theta}$. Estimated standard errors of nonlinear functions of $\hat{\theta}$ (the cycle periods in our case) can be obtained by linearizing around $\hat{\theta}$ and using the standard formula

$$\text{var}\,(Ax) = A\,\text{var}\,(x)A^T \qquad (4.56)$$

for any constant matrix A and random vector x.

As descriptive statistics for the single equations, the MSE, the R^2 according to the formula

$$R^2 = 1 - \frac{\text{variance of estimated errors}}{\text{variance of data}}, \qquad (4.57)$$

and the autocorrelation ρ of the errors are listed, using

$$\rho_j = \frac{T}{T-1}\left(\sum_{t=2}^{T} v_{tj}^* v_{t-1,j}^* \bigg/ \sum_{t=1}^{T} v_{tj}^* \right) \tag{4.58}$$

The Durbin–Watson statistic for a test of autocorrelation is not given, because it is well known that in the case of a model with lagged endogenous variables this statistic is strongly biased towards non-correlation (Nerlove and Wallis 1966).

Appendix: Sources of the Data

Germany: Statistisches Bundesamt, Volkswirtschaftliche Gesamtrechnungen.

United Kingdom: OECD, National Accounts. The stock series was obtained by summing up the increase in stocks. The absolute value of stocks is irrelevant because only detrended data are used.

USA: Fixed private capital was published by Survey of Current Business, 10/1988. Net fixed capital formation is the increase in capital. Other series are taken from OECD, National Accounts. Stocks were obtained as in the case of United Kingdom.

Only data at constant prices are used.

References

Abramovitz, M. (1950), *Inventories and Business Cycles*, National Bureau for Economic Research, New York.

Bard, Y. (1974), *Nonlinear Parameter Estimation*, Academic Press, Orlando.

Bellman, R. (1960), *Introduction to Matrix Analysis,* McGraw-Hill, New York.

Bergstrom, A. R. (1967), *The Construction and Use of Economic Models*, English Universities Press, London.

—— (ed.) (1976), *Statistical Inference in Continuous Time Economic Models*, North-Holland, Amsterdam.

—— (1983), 'Gaussian estimation of structural parameters in higher order continuous time dynamic models', *Econometrica*, 51 : 117–52.

—— (1984), 'Continuous time stochastic models and issues of aggregation over time', in Z. Grilliches and M. D. Intriligator (eds.), *Handbook of Econometrics*, II, North-Holland, Amsterdam.

—— (1985), 'The estimation of parameters in nonstationary higher-order continuous-time dynamic models', *Econometric Theory*, 1 : 369–85.

—— (1986), 'The estimation of open higher-order continuous-time dynamic models with mixed stock and flow data', *Econometric Theory*, 2 : 350–73.

Gandolfo, G. (1981), *Qualitative Analysis and Econometric Estimation of Continuous Time Dynamic Models*, North-Holland, Amsterdam.

—— and Padoan, P. C. (1984), *A Disequilibrium Model of Real and Financial Accumulation in an Open Economy*, Springer, Berlin.

Harvey, A. C., and Stock, J. H. (1985), 'The estimation of higher order continuous time autoregressive models', *Econometric Theory*, 1 : 97–112.

Hillinger, C. (1987), 'Business cycle stylized facts and explanatory models', *Journal of Economic Dynamics and Control*, 11 : 257–63.

—— and Schueler, K. W. (1977), 'Makroökonomische Modelle des Wachstumszyklus', in H. Albach, E. Helmstaedter, and R. Henn (eds.), *Quantitative Wirtschaftsforschung*, Mohr, Tübingen.

—— —— (1978), 'Cyclical fluctuations of the German economy : a continuous time econometric model', *Social Science Review* (Munich), 2 : 75–88.

Kahn, J. A. (1987), 'Inventories and the volatility of production', *American Economic Review*, 77 (4) : 667–79.

Koopmans, T. C. (1950), 'Models involving a continuous time variable', in T. C. Koopmans (ed.), *Statistical Inference in Dynamic Economic Models*, John Wiley, New York.

Miron, J. A., and Zeldes, St. P. (1988), 'Seasonality, cost shocks, and the production smoothing model of inventories', *Econometrica*, 56(4) : 877–908.

Nerlove, M. and Wallis, K. F. (1966), 'Use of the Durbin–Watson statistic in inappropriate situations', *Econometrica*, 34 : 235–8.

Reiter, M. (1988), 'Second-order accelerator models of cyclical growth : an econometric analysis', SEMECON Working Paper.

—— (1992), 'Observation errors and inventory cycles', *International Journal of Production Economics*, 26 : 99–105.

Strotz, R. (1960), 'Interdependence as a specification error', *Econometrica*, 28 : 428–42.

West, K. D. (1988), 'Order backlogs and production smoothing', in A. Chikan and M. C. Lovell (eds.), *The Economics of Inventory Management*, Elsevier, Amsterdam.

PART III

Economic Fluctuations in Planned Economies

5

Inventory Cycles in Hungary

Attila Chikan

1. Introduction

Inventories in any economy serve as an important signalling system for the operation of the whole economy. Two characteristics of inventories must be considered when judging their behaviour: their level, and the fluctuation of inventory investment. These play an important role in understanding and explaining general economic phenomena.

Inventory fluctuations are especially significant in the analysis of economic cycles. As the fastest changing component of GDP, inventory investment is the first to react to changes in the state of the economy; this makes it possible to recognize the current phase of the cycle and its change.

Beyond these general statements, there is still much to be done in the field of inventory cycles, both in market economies and to an even greater extent in planned economies. Neither traditional socialist economic theory (which emphasized the continuous unbroken development of the economic indicators) nor the early history of the socialist countries (which showed a rather fast and steady increase of the main economic parameters) stimulated cycle research. However, recent developments both in theory and in the actual socialist economies have made it necessary to study the fluctuating character of economic phenomena, including inventory investments.[1]

This chapter deals with the description and explanation of inventory fluctuations in Hungary. It will be shown that the fluctuations can be considered cycles and that these cycles can be explained in terms of the changes in the general state of the Hungarian economy. The inventory cycles in Hungary will be compared with those in market economies.

Inventory investments in postwar Hungary were always at a rather high level; they represented a relatively large part of the use of GDP compared with non-East European countries at the same level of development. However, in an international comparison, it is strikingly clear that all East European countries have the same or even higher inventory investment–GDP ratios. It was therefore a quite natural first step in the study of inventory behaviour in Hungary to attempt to explain this difference between the two types of economies.

---

[1] For a discussion of the literature on economic fluctuations and socialism see Nuti (1987) and Chapter 1 (Section 10) above.

In Chikan (1981a) and Chikan *et al.* (1986) it was argued that the reasons behind the high ratio of inventory investments can be found in basic characteristics of the planned economies. One reason is the general over-demand, which gives the suppliers a dominant position relative to the buyers, who have to hold large input stocks to protect themselves against uncertain deliveries and repeated shortages. Another reason is that firms have little incentive to economize the cost of holding inventories. While the ratio of aggregate stocks to aggregate quarterly output is about 1 : 1 in the West European countries, it is about 6 : 1 in Hungary.

Once we have an explanation for the high inventory investment, our attention must turn to the fluctuation of inventories, as we strive to obtain a further explanation for the inventory situation and its connections with other economic phenomena. In my first paper on the subject (Chikan 1984a) I presented the basic questions and outlined some of the explanations. In the following, a more detailed and elaborated analysis is given.

2. Inventory fluctuations in Hungary

In our analysis we consider the following data of inventory investment:

- inventory investment
- change of inventory investment
- growth rate of inventory investment
- chain index of change of inventory investment
- inventory investment/GDP
- chain index of inventory investment/GDP
- change of inventory investment/change of GDP

These data show very similar patterns year by year, and the analysis of any of them leads to similar conclusions. The data used in this paper are in the form of first differences.

In Chikan (1984a) I concluded that the inventory fluctuations experienced in the Hungarian economy can be considered *cycles*, because they satisfy the criteria of periodically repeating the same pattern as a consequence of the same basic reasons. My recent studies and inventory formation in Hungary in the past few years have tended to support this earlier conclusion.

In the following section the basic inventory cycle will be described and explanatioñs given. The analysis covers the period 1960–84. The following time series will be used to support the argument: GDP, final consumption, gross fixed capital investment, inventory investment, and the foreign trade balance. These data are given in Fig. 5.1. It is evident that, while both GDP and final consumption show rather smooth growth (their standard deviations are 59 and 61 per cent, respectively), fixed capital investment fluctuates more (107 per cent), while

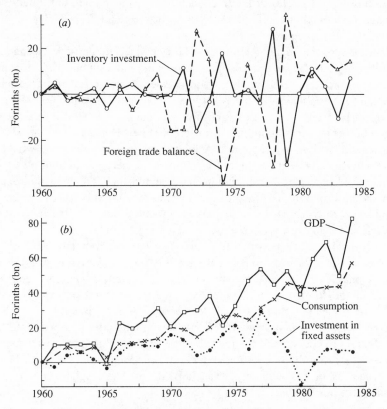

FIG. 5.1. Changes of distribution of GDP: first differences in current prices

the foreign trade balance and inventory investment both exhibit tremendous fluctuations (standard deviations of 1293 and 2215 per cent, respectively). These fluctuations might seem uncontrolled (or uncontrollable) unless we can perceive the regularities and causal relationships within the processes. One can see a fluctuation, behind which there seems to be a regularity, because peaks and troughs repeat every three to four years. It can also be seen that there is a deeper trough every seventh year (1965, 1972, and 1979) which always follows a relatively high inventory investment in the previous year.

In an effort to understand the inventory cycle, it is quite natural to turn first to an examination of the connection between production and inventory formation, since traditional theories of inventory cycles are mostly based on this relationship. However, the Hungarian inventory cycle shows a different character. Because the Hungarian economy, like other socialist economies, is in a state of chronic excess demand, capacity is always fully utilized and the growth of output takes place smoothly. This type of growth has also been encouraged by government policy. The inventory formation can be connected much more to the cycles of the fixed capital investment and the foreign trade balance, both of which definitely show a cyclic character, as is evident in parts (*a*) and (*b*) of the figure.

There is a strong negative correlation between the foreign trade balance and inventory investment (see part (*a*)): larger inventory investment is accompanied by a deterioration of the foreign trade balance. (The correlation coefficient between the variables is − 0.5702, between their first differences − 0.7558.)

It must be accepted that this is not a trivial connection. Both variables can play a buffer role in smoothing the differences between the aggregate supply and demand within any economy. A joint formulation in this case would be more natural: if the demand is overestimated and therefore there is an excess supply, then both inventories should increase and the larger potential export also should improve the foreign trade balance. On the other hand, shortages should lead to a decrease of inventories and greater imports. However, these rules do not apply for our economy.

The causal linkage between the variables derives from the fact that the internal tensions of the economy, the disturbances in the equilibrium of the internal market of both the investments and the current production, are transferred to the foreign trade balance, which thus becomes a very important indicator of the operation of the whole economy. At the same time (or perhaps directly because of that), the efficiency of economic policy is measured to a great extent by the state of the foreign trade balance. If this reaches a dangerous level, it certainly induces state intervention and regulation which influence all processes of the economy, especially the material sphere and, among others, inventories.

3. Government policy and the dynamics of the inventory cycle

In those years in which both inventory investment and the foreign trade deficit are at a maximum (1964, 1967–8, 1971, 1974, 1978, 1982), the government moves to impose restrictive measures. The two principal central restrictions are those that decrease investment in fixed capital (and thus the demand for investment goods) and those that constrain imports—both of which will decrease inventory investment.

In addition to placing restrictions on imports, there is a strong stimulation to increase exports. The success of the export-oriented policy depends to a great extent on factors beyond the control of policy-makers in Hungary. Therefore more time is required to realize a policy of export stimulations than one of import restrictions. In the 1970s the relatively fast adjustment of the economy was at least partly a consequence of the high demand of external markets, while among the reasons of the present long-lasting depression there can be found important external factors as well.

The decrease in investment demand, restrictions on imports, and the stimulation of exports together cause a decrease in inventory investment. The measures taken to decrease investment demand will first of all, through various channels, constrain the financial resources available for investments both in fixed capital and in inventories. Less new production capacity is put into operation, and this also means less demand for inventory build-up. The decrease of production in this period in companies producing investment goods will also decrease inventories. These measures in turn have an inventory-increasing effect inasmuch as the decrease of demand causes a build-up of unsaleable finished goods, but this effect is much weaker than those mentioned above.

Restrictions on imports will decrease inventories through the reduction of inventories of import origin and through the import-replacement campaign that usually follows the government's restrictive measures. (On the other hand, failing production plans, because of lack of imports, lead to a build-up in inventories of unfinished goods—but again, this is a weaker effect.)

Increased exports will lead to a decrease in the inventories of export goods. They also help to solve the capacity utilization problems caused by the reduction of internal demand and to reduce the inventories of raw material and parts. If the expected increase in exports does not occur, this causes an increase in the inventories of finished goods produced for export and in import inventories held for this production.

As mentioned, these measures are not directed mainly at decreasing inventory build-up, but are aimed, first, at regaining the normal status of the foreign trade balance and, second, at restoring equilibrium in the internal market. The restrictive measures of the government are basically oriented to cut back the internal use of the GDP, but they do not affect all components the same way. Restraining investments in new capacity is always the focus, but restrictions on inventory investment and consumption do not occur in each cycle, partly because of the lack of controllability and partly for political reasons. A strong constraint on inventory investment was introduced in those years when the fast restoration of a proper foreign trade balance was not attained by the cutback of other elements of the GDP and—mainly—by the increase in exports. In those years (1965, 1972–3, 1979) a radical decrease in inventory investment was imposed to help to decrease internal use of GDP. (It is important to note here that even in these years the change in inventories was positive: they increased, but at a much lower rate than usual.)

However, although this smaller inventory build-up has contributed to easing the disequilibrium of the foreign trade balance, it also produced other, internal, tensions—shortages in production, disturbances in inter-industry relations, inflationary tendencies, etc. The transformation of external tensions into internal ones causes the repetition of the cycle, since an improvement in the foreign trade balance makes it possible and necessary to turn again to internal problems. From all sides (companies, consumers, even politicians) pressure is put on the government to allow the increase of investment (both in fixed capital and inventories), and the expansion starts. The expansion leads to a larger inventory investment in many ways (inflow of imports, increase in production, inventory demand at new production capacities, more liberal financial conditions, etc.). Thus, the inventory investment is increasing and will accelerate even further when companies feel the signs of the oncoming restriction. This completes the cycle.

4. Conclusion

In general, it is my view that the inventory fluctuations in Hungary have a definite cyclical character. These cycles, however, are in many respects different from those in market economies. The basic difference is that, while in the market economies inventory cycles are direct consequences of processes in the market and as such are of primary character, in our economy inventory cycles are only indirectly influenced by the market. Market tensions do not really decrease company aspirations—they arise mostly when the government takes measures to improve the overall state of the economy, the main indicator of which is the foreign trade balance; therefore, inventory cycles in our economy are secondary, induced, features. This main difference leads to many consequences in the actual process of the cycles. Some of these are described above, but many more are yet to be discovered.

References

Chikan, A. (1981*a*), 'Market disequilibrium and the volume of stocks', in Chikan (1981*b*), pp. 73–87.

—— (ed.), (1981*b*), *The Economics and Management of Inventories*, Elsevier, Amsterdam, and Akademia Kiado, Budapest.

—— (1984*a*), 'Inventory fluctuations (cycles?) in the Hungarian economy', in Chikan (1984*b*), pp. 57–72.

—— (ed.), (1984*b*), *New Results in Inventory Research*, Elsevier, Amsterdam, and Akademia Kiado, Budapest.

—— (ed.), (1986), *Inventories in Theory and Practice*, Elsevier, Amsterdam, and Akademia Kiado, Budapest.

—— Kalotay, K., and Paprika, Z. (1986), 'Macroeconomic factors influencing inventory investments: an international analysis', in Chikan (1986), pp. 55–72.

Nuti, D. M. (1987), 'Cycles in socialist economies', in J. Eatwell, M. Milgate, and P. Newman (eds.), *The New Palgrave: A Dictionary of Economics*, Macmillan, London.

6

Gestation Lags and the Explanation of Investment Cycles in Socialist Economies

Andras Bródy

1. Introduction

Since the path-breaking publication of Goldman (1964), it has been widely recognized that the economies of socialist countries are also subject to characteristic fluctuations. These manifest themselves most clearly in the form of periodic movements in investment activity. This first recognition was followed by further research (Bajt 1969, 1971; Horvat 1972). An international conference on the subject of business cycles in capitalist and socialist economies was organized in order to obtain a clearer picture of similarities and differences, resulting in a book edited by Bronfenbrenner (1969). Somewhat later, Bauer (1978, 1982) published the most extensive analysis of cycles in socialist economies. Reviews of the literature on cycles in planned economies are given by Nuti (1987) and in Chapter 1 above, Section 10.

The literature cited compares the cycles of planned and market economies and the structures that are causally relevant in generating them. The most important similarities and differences are summarized below in order to motivate the subsequent formal model. The discussion is limited to cycles in fixed investment which are also the theme of the cited literature. Chikan, in Chapter 5 above, focuses on the similarities and differences of the shorter cycles in the two types of economy.

The most striking similarity is that both kinds of economy experience seven- to ten-year cycles in fixed investment. This corresponds to the cycle first identified for capitalist economies by Juglar in the nineteenth century.

A fundamental difference is that in market economies investment is related to profitability in general and more particularly to the capital–output ratio as exemplified by the flexible accelerator model of investment. In the socialist economies the situation is fundamentally different. These countries are characterized by chronic capital shortages and excess demand. Firms always try to obtain more funds for investment from the central authorities and to invest all of the funds they can obtain.

In capitalist economies the cycle is associated with a variable capacity utilization, the rate of utilization being a principal determinant of the willingness of the firms to invest. In socialist economies, capacity is always fully utilized.

The cycles of socialist economies exhibit characteristic changes in the ratio of new to continuation investment. Times during which many new investment projects are started alternate with times during which available funds may be insufficient to continue all of the projects started in the past. In such times there are few or no investment starts.

The preceding distinction regarding new and continuation investment points to the importance in socialist economies of *multi-period gestation lags* between the initiation and completion of investment projects. It should be emphasized that the gestation lag is a quite different concept from that involved in the distinction between investment *decisions* and *realizations* made by Kalecki (1935) and the *distributed investment* analysed by Hicks (1950: App. to Ch. 5). Kalecki's investment decision involves no actual expenditure or allocation of resources, whereas the investments considered by both authors (whether distributed or not) are always independent additions to the stock of productive capital. In the case of the gestation lag, resources must be devoted to investment in every subperiod, but only the investment of the final subperiod completes the project and leads to an expansion of productive capacity.

The reason for the greater prominence of gestation lags in the socialist economies is that socialist enterprises have an incentive systematically to underestimate the entire cost of a project when they apply for investment funds. In this way they get a foot in the door and hope that subsequently the greater funds required for project completion will be forthcoming (cf. Bauer 1978). The capitalist firm has no comparable incentive to fool itself, or its creditors, regarding the cost of a major project.

In the following sections an attempt is made to model the stylized facts of socialist investment cycles. Certain empirically important aspects, such as the financing of investments through foreign loans and the depreciation of capital, have been omitted from consideration in order to keep the model as simple as possible.

Characteristic phenomena relating to gestation lags arise when a lag of at least two periods is considered. Projects are started in the first and completed in the second period. The period need not correspond to a calender year, but may be defined as half of the total gestation lag.

For expository purposes, a model with single-period gestation lag is constructed in the next section and compared with the standard Harrod–Domar model. The two-period gestation lag is introduced in Section 3. The resulting model retains the equilibrium growth path of the simple model and in addition allows fluctuations around that path.

2. The Single-Period Gestation Lag and the Harrod–Domar Model

A good starting point for our discussion is the Harrod–Domar growth model in the two distinct interpretations that are usually associated with the two authors.

In the Harrod version, investment demand is given by the *backward* accelerator equation,

$$I_t = v(Y_t - Y_{t-1}). \tag{6.1}$$

Investment takes place so that

$$K_t = vY_t, \tag{6.2}$$

where K_t is the *end-of-period* capital stock.

The Domar model can be interpreted as requiring

$$K_{t-1} = vY_t. \tag{6.3}$$

The capital available at the beginning of the period determines the maximum output that can be produced during the period. Investment is therefore given by the *forward* accelerator equation,

$$K_t - K_{t-1} = I_t = v\,(Y_{t+1} - Y_t) \tag{6.4}$$

Assuming

$$I_t = S_t = sY_t. \tag{6.5}$$

the Domar model reduces to

$$Y_{t+1} = \left(1 + \frac{s}{v}\right)Y_t \tag{6.6}$$

which has the root

$$h = 1 + \frac{s}{v} \tag{6.7}$$

and the growth rate

$$g = \frac{s}{v} \tag{6.8}$$

For the Harrod model, we obtain

$$Y_t = \left(1 + \frac{s}{v - s}\right)Y_{t-1}, \tag{6.9}$$

implying the growth rate

$$g' = \frac{s}{v-s}. \tag{6.10}$$

In the Harrod version, v must be interpreted as an equilibrium ratio; production with less capital is possible and actually takes place. This explains why $g' > g$. (In the usual Harrod formulation it is assumed that $I_t = sY_{t-1}$, so that investment is reduced correspondingly and the growth rate is also g.)

The Domar model can be interpreted as involving a one-period gestation lag. Investment during the period increases productive capacity only at the end of the period. This is the viewpoint that will be generalized in the next section.

Rough orders of magnitude for the parameters for the socialist countries, for the period 1950–70, are $s = 0.3$, $v = 3$, and consequently a value of $g = 0.1$. While the 10 per cent growth rate is higher than what was actually experienced, it will be convenient to retain these parameter values as benchmarks against which the model with the two-period gestation lag can be compared.

3. A Model of Growth and Fluctuations with a Two-Period Gestation Lag

It will now be assumed that the gestation lag extends over two years, and that a fixed proportion a of the total investment must be made in the first year, leaving the proportion $1 - a$ for the second year.

Total investment,

$$I_t = s Y_t, \tag{6.11}$$

must be allocated according to the requirement that all projects started in the previous period must be finished. Full capacity utilization implies that investment completions are given by

$$I_t^c = (1 - a) v (Y_{t+1} - Y_t). \tag{6.12}$$

The remaining investment funds are used to start new projects which will add to productive capacity two years later. These investment starts are

$$I_t^s = a v (Y_{t+2} - Y_{t+1}). \tag{6.13}$$

Total investment must satisfy the equation

$$I_t^c + I_t^s = I_t, \tag{6.14}$$

or, equivalently,

$$a v (Y_{t+2} - Y_{t+1}) + (1 - a) v (Y_{t+1} - Y_t) = s Y_t. \tag{6.15}$$

Some simple algebra leads from (6.15) to

$$Y_{t+2} + \left(\frac{1}{a} - 2\right)Y_{t+1} + \left(1 - \frac{1}{a} - \frac{s}{av}\right)Y_t = 0. \tag{6.16}$$

The roots of this difference equation are

$$h_{1,2} = 1 - \frac{1}{2a} \pm \left(\frac{1}{4a^2} + \frac{s}{av}\right)^{\frac{1}{2}} \tag{6.17}$$

Since the discriminant is positive for $0 < a < 1$, there are two real roots. From the inequality

$$\left(\frac{1}{4a^2} + \frac{s}{av}\right)^{\frac{1}{2}} > \frac{1}{2}a, \tag{6.18}$$

it follows that the roots satisfy

$$h_1 > 1, \qquad h_2 < 0. \tag{6.19}$$

Furthermore, to a linear approximation around zero in the variable $g = s/v$, it is found that

$$h_1 = 1 + g, \qquad h_2 = 1 - \frac{1}{a} - g. \tag{6.20}$$

The model is seen to have an equilibrium growth path which is approximately the same as that of the Harrod–Domar model.

TABLE 6.1[a]

	a	h_1	h_2
1	0.1	1.099	− 9.099
2	0.2	1.098	− 4.098
3	0.3	1.096	− 2.430
4	0.4	1.096	− 1.596
5	0.5	1.095	− 1.095
6	0.6	1.095	− 0.761
7	0.7	1.094	− 0.522
8	0.8	1.093	− 0.343
9	0.9	1.092	− 0.204
10	1	1.092	− 0.092

[a] Assumed parameter values
are $s = 0.3$, $v = 3$, $g = 0.1$

Economic logic suggests that $h_1 < h$ where h is the root of the Harrod–Domar model since a two-period gestation lag must be less efficient than one-period lag. By similar reasoning, h_1 should be a declining function of a. These properties are illustrated in Table 6.1, where the values of s and v are the same as those used earlier in connection with the Harrod–Domar model. As can be seen from the analytical solution, and as is illustrated in the table, h_2 becomes unstable as a decreases. For $a = 0.5$, the two roots are equal in absolute value. For $a < 0.5$, the alternation increases more rapidly than the equilibrium growth rate. This means that the system is headed for a collapse at a point where the requirements for investment completions exceed savings.

Consider the ratio

$$r_t = \frac{I_t^s}{I_t^c} \tag{6.21}$$

The equilibrium path of output is characterized by

$$Y_t^* = h_1^t\, Y_0^* \tag{6.22}$$

From (6.12), (6.13), and (6.22), it follows that the equilibrium value of the ratio, r^*, is given by

$$r^* = \frac{a}{1-a}\, h_1 \tag{6.23}$$

To understand the disequilibrium behaviour of the system, consider an initial time period, $t = 0$, with $r_0 > r^*$. As the share of starts has been relatively high in period 0, the share of completions will be relatively high in period 1. The value of r will thus also alternate around its equilibrium value. For $a < 0.5$, these alternations will be explosive and will lead to a situation in which at some point the total required for completion of investment projects will be greater than the total available for all investment purposes. At this point the system as described collapses and the equations of the model become inoperative.

The crises predicted by the model are realistic descriptions of crises that have repeatedly occurred in socialist economies. The actual resolution of the crises has typically involved a postponement in the completion of investment projects. When these projects have been completed, however, a situation will be reached where there are few started projects in the pipeline, and therefore a massive increase in new investments is possible. This is a time of optimism in which many new projects are being started. We are thus at the beginning of the next cycle.

4. Conclusion

A very simple model has been presented to account for the stylized facts of investment cycles of socialist economies. The model has a Harrod–Domar type equilibrium growth solution. In addition, it can exhibit fluctuations around the growth path. These take the form of two-period alternations; i.e., they have the same duration as the gestation lag. In the plausible case in which more than half of the total investment has to be made in the second period, the fluctuation explodes at a rate exceeding the growth rate. A 'crisis' such as has occurred periodically in the histories of the socialist countries is then inevitable.

The original version of this paper was written in 1972, long before the current crisis of the socialist economies came into view. The current proposals for the reform of these economies have focused on the introduction of free markets for goods and services. The analysis of this chapter suggests that a functioning capital market is no less important if the socialist economies are to avoid violent gyrations in their future development.

References

Bajt, A. (1969), 'Fluctuations and trends in growth rates in socialist countries', *Ekonomsky Analiza*, 3(3–4) : 206–17.

—— (1971), 'Investment cycles in European socialist economies', *Journal of Economic Literature*, 9(1) : 53–63.

Bauer, T. (1978), 'Investment cycles in planned economies', *Acta Oeconomica*, 21(3) : 243–60.

—— (1982), *Terveyes, Beruchayas, Ciklusok*, KJK, Budapest.

Bronfenbrenner, M. (ed.) (1969), *Is the Business Cycle Obsolete?* John Wiley, New York.

Goldman, J. (1964), 'Fluctuations and trends in the rate of economic growth in some socialist countries', *Economics of Planning*, 4(2) : 88–98.

Hicks, J. R. (1950), *A Contribution to the Theory of the Trade Cycle*, Clarendon Press, Oxford.

Horvat, B. (1972), *Business Cycles in Yugoslavia*, International Art and Sciences Press, New York.

Kalecki, M. (1935), 'A macrodynamic theory of the business cycle', *Econometrica*, 3 : 327–44.

Nuti, D. M. (1987), 'Cycles in socialist economies', in J. Eatwell, M. Milgate, and P. Newman (eds.), *The New Palgrave: A Dictionary of Economics*, Macmillan, London.

7

Macroeconomic Fluctuations Based on Gestation Lags: A Formal Analysis

Tamas G. Tarjan

1. Introduction

A model of cycles in fixed investment of socialist economies, based on a two-period gestation lag, was presented by Bródy (1972; see also Chapter 6 above). The model revealed a conflict between the goal of *efficiency*, as reflected in a high growth rate, and the goal of *stability*. The more investment takes place in the second rather than in the first period of the gestation lag, the larger the growth rate, but the greater also the instability. If more than half of the investment is in the second period, the fluctuation becomes unstable.

The purpose of this paper is to generalize Bródy's model to a gestation lag with an arbitrary number of periods. It turns out that in such a generalized model a result analogous to that of Bródy can be proven.

2. The Generalized Model of Bródy

In order to construct a formal model, the following assumptions are made:

1. The economy consists of one sector; its total production of the period t is the GNP, y_t.
2. The only input is the capital stock K_t (more precisely, production capacity).
3. The GNP is divided into consumption C_t and investment I_t.
4. The economy is closed (no foreign trade).
5. The accelerator coefficient $v = K_t/Y_t$ is constant.
6. The accomplishment of investment projects requires a gestation time of T periods (years). The total investment is distributed over the gestation period in fixed proportions a_j ($j = 1, \ldots, T$) corresponding to the period numbers j, with

$$\sum_{j=1}^{T} a_j = 1. \tag{7.1}$$

7. There is no depreciation.
8. The rate of savings $s = I_t/Y_t$ is constant for all t.

From these assumptions, a difference equation describing the system dynamics can be derived.

It was supposed in assumption 6 that investments $a_j \Delta K$ for T years $(j = 1, \ldots, T)$ will lead to a growth of production capacity by ΔK in the Tth year and will therefore yield an increase of production by $\Delta Y = \Delta K / v$ one year later.

Hereafter, the total investment I_t of the period t consists of T contributions related to the increases of production capacity of the following T years:

$$I_t = a_T (K_{t+1} - K_t) + a_{T-1} (K_{t+2} - K_{t+1}) + \ldots$$

$$+ a_2 (K_{t+T-1} - K_{t+T-2}) + a_1 (K_{t+T} - K_{t+T-1}) \qquad (7.2)$$

$$= \sum_{j=1}^{T} a_{T-j+1} (K_{t+j} - K_{t+j-1}).$$

The first part contributes to investment projects that will be completed during the year t, the second part to those that will be finished one year later, etc. Therefore these investments $I_t = sY_t$ will be related to future increases of production according to

$$sY_t = \sum_{j=1}^{T} a_{T-j+1} v (Y_{t+j} - Y_{t+j-1}). \qquad (7.3)$$

Rearranging (7.3) and setting

$$a_0 = 0, \qquad a_{T+1} = -\frac{s}{v} \qquad (7.4)$$

yields

$$\sum_{j=0}^{T} (a_{j+1} - a_j) v Y_{t+T-j} = 0. \qquad (7.5)$$

This linear difference equation of Tth order determines the dynamic behaviour of the model. The dynamic properties of its solutions are given by the roots of the characteristic polynomial $h(z)$ of (7.5):

$$h(z) = \sum_{j=0}^{T} (a_{j+1} - a_j) z^{T-j}. \qquad (7.6)$$

This polynomial can be transformed into

$$h(z) = (z - 1) \sum_{j=1}^{T} a_j z^{T-j} - \frac{s}{v} \qquad (7.7)$$

in order to derive the following properties:

1. $h(z) < 0$, for $0 \leq z \leq 1$,
2. $h(z)$ is strictly increasing in $(1, \infty)$,
3. $h(z) \to \infty$ for $z \to \infty$.

From these three properties it can be concluded directly that $h(z)$ has exactly one real positive root λ. As λ is strictly greater than 1, the associated eigensolution is exponentially growing and may be regarded as the 'equilibrium growth path' $Y_t = Y_0 \lambda^t$ of the system. As a possible value for λ, we try

$$\lambda = 1 + g, \qquad g = \frac{s}{v} \tag{7.8}$$

where g is the Harrod–Domar growth rate. To a first-order approximation around $g = 0$, it is found that

$$h(1 + g) = 0 \tag{7.9}$$

The model thus approximates Harrod–Domar growth. As in the two-period case, $\lambda < 1 + g$, since it would be more advantageous to have capacity increase after one period than after many.

All other roots $z_2, \ldots, z_t$ are non-positive and correspond to oscillatory (periodic or alternating) solutions. These solutions will be dominated by the exponentially growing solution if λ has the greatest absolute value of all roots. Alternatively, if there is another root with absolute value greater than λ, the amplitude of the corresponding oscillation will increase faster than the exponential growth path.

The occurrence of such an unstable situation may be characterized under certain assumptions. For the special case of $s = 0$, a simple sufficient condition for stability can be given. From (7.7) it can be seen that the positive root of $h(z)$ is 1. The other roots are solutions of

$$\sum_{j=1}^{T} a_j z^{T-j} = 0 \tag{7.10}$$

or, after dividing by a_1 and rearranging,

$$\sum_{j=0}^{T-1} b_j z^j = 0, \qquad b_j = \frac{a_{T-j}}{a_1} \tag{7.11}$$

Because the b_j are all positive, the 'Generalized Kakeya theorem' (see Murata 1977 : 136 for a proof) says that

$$b_{T-1} = 1 > b_{T-2} \geq b_{T-3} \geq \ldots \geq b_0 > 0 \tag{7.12}$$

is a sufficient condition for all the roots of (7.11) having modulus less than unity, which implies stability. Equation (7.12) is obviously fulfilled if the a_j

form a monotonously decreasing sequence, $a_{j+1} < a_j$, for all j. These inequalities specify in the simplest possible manner that stability requires investments to be made early rather than late in the gestation lag period.

The properties of the cyclical movements and their stability depend on the distribution of the investment during the gestation time (given by the parameter set a_j ($j = 1, \ldots, T$)). This question has been studied by Bródy for the case $T = 2$. The statement above accords to Bródy's result for the two-period model that the system is stable if most (over half) of the investment is realized in the first period.

For the general case with s not necessarily equal to 0, the following theorem gives a *necessary stability condition*:

> THEOREM. Let $\lambda, z_2, \ldots, z_t$ denote the roots of $h(z)$ with $\lambda > 1$. If the system is stable, that is if $\lambda > |z_i|$ for $i = 2, \ldots, T$, then the following inequality holds:
>
> $$\sum_{j=1}^{T-1} (a_j - a_{j+1}) \lambda^{T-j-1} (T-j)j > 0. \tag{7.13}$$

Proof: see Appendix.

As is easily seen from (7.13), stability is violated if all the a_j are equal or if they form a monotonously increasing sequence, $a_{j+1} > a_j$ for all j. To give a plausible interpretation of (7.13) also for non-monotonous sequences, Tarjan (1985) has classified the investment distributions a_j ($j = 1, \ldots, T$) as 'stem-heavy' or 'stern-heavy' with a parameter c according to the following definition:

> DEFINITION. The coefficients a_j ($j = 1, \ldots, T$) form a *stem-heavy distribution with c* if
>
> $$\sum_{j=1}^{T} c^{T-j} a_j \left(\frac{T+1}{2} - j \right) > 0; \tag{7.14}$$

otherwise the distribution shall be called *stern-heavy with c*.

This definition may be illustrated by a physical analogy. Imagine a balance of the length $T - 1$ which is supported in the centre (position $(T + 1)/2$) and contains weights $a_j c^{T-j}$ at the positions $j = 1, \ldots, T$. This is illustrated in Fig. 7.1. In the case of a stem-heavy distribution (with c), the balance will decline on the side of the lower values of j, which implies higher weighted contributions in the earlier periods of the gestation time; otherwise the distribution will be stern-heavy (with c).

The following bound on the left-hand side of the necessary stability condition (7.13):

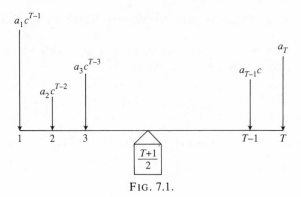

FIG. 7.1.

$$\sum_{j=1}^{T-1} (a_j - a_{j+1}) \lambda^{T-j-1} (T-j)j$$

$$\le \sum_{j=1}^{T} a_j \lambda^{T-j-1} [(T-j)j - \lambda(T-j+1)(j-1)] \quad (7.15)$$

$$\le 2 \sum_{j=1}^{T} a_j \lambda^{T-j} \left(\frac{T+1}{2} - j \right),$$

shows that the stability condition is violated if the distribution $a_j(j = 1, \ldots, T)$ is stern-heavy with the 'equilibrium root' λ. In this case the dynamics of Y_t is dominated by oscillatory behaviour. Of course, the last part of (7.15) is a weaker condition than (7.13), but gives an intuitive interpretation for stable sequences a_j, which need not be monotone.

3. Summary

Bródy's analysis of fixed investment cycles of socialist economies, based on gestation lags, is generalized in this chapter to an arbitrary number of lags.

As in the two-period case, the solution consists of a Harrod–Domar type growth path and a fluctuation around that path. Stability depends significantly on the distribution of investment over the gestation time. Higher contributions in the later part of the gestation time ('stern-heavy' distributions) lead necessarily to instabilities, whereas higher contributions at the beginning of the gestation period ('stem-heavy' distributions) may enable stable development. Specifically, the fluctuations are unstable if the distributional weights increase with time exponentially at a rate greater than the growth rate of the economy.

Appendix: Proof of the Necessary Stability Condition

It is to be shown that, if $\lambda, z_2, \ldots, z_T$ are the roots of $h(z)$ with $\lambda > 1$, and if $\lambda > |z_i|$ for $i = 2, \ldots, T$, then the following inequality holds:

$$\sum_{j=1}^{T-1} (a_j - a_{j+1}) \lambda^{T-j-1} (T-j) j > 0. \tag{7.13}$$

It was shown that λ is a single root of $h(z)$. Therefore the ratio

$$g(z) = \frac{h(z)}{z - \lambda} \tag{7.16}$$

is a polynomial of order $T - 1$ which is continuous at $z = \lambda$ with

$$g(\lambda) = h'(\lambda) = \sum_{j=1}^{T} a_j \lambda^{T-j-1} [(T-j+1)\lambda - (T-j)] > 0, \tag{7.17}$$

using l'Hospital's rule. If all roots $z_2, \ldots, z_T$ of $g(z)$ have absolute values less than λ, then all roots of the polynomial $g(\lambda z)$ have an absolute value less than 1.

$g(\lambda z)$ may be regarded as a characteristic polynomial of a difference equation. The associated differential equation (Jordan 1939) has the characteristic polynomial $G(w)$. With the notations

$$g(\lambda z) = \sum_{j=0}^{T} c_j z^{T-j}, \qquad G(w) = \sum_{j=0}^{T} d_j w^{T-j}, \tag{7.18}$$

the coefficients c_j and d_j are related by

$$d_j = \sum_{l=1}^{T} c_l \sum_{m=0}^{j-1} (-1)^m \binom{l-1}{m} \binom{T-l}{j-1-m}, \qquad 1 \le j \le T \tag{7.19}$$

(*proof:* see Jury 1964). Special cases are

$$d_1 = \sum_{j=1}^{T} c_j = g(1)$$

$$d_2 = \sum_{j=1}^{T} c_j(T - 2j + 1) = 2g'(1) - (T-1) g(1). \tag{7.20}$$

If all roots of $g(\lambda z)$ have absolute values less than 1, all solutions to the corresponding difference equation and the associated differential equation are damped. This requires that all roots of $G(w)$ have negative real parts, which is only possible if all coefficients d_j are positive.

Thus, equation (7.20) for d_2 implies the following inequality:

$$\lim_{z \to 1} 2 \frac{\partial g(\lambda z)}{\partial z} - (T-1) g(\lambda) > 0, \tag{7.21}$$

To evaluate the right-hand side of (7.21), note that

$$\lim_{z \to 1} \frac{\partial g(\lambda z)}{\partial z} = \lambda \lim_{z \to \lambda} \frac{\partial g(z)}{\partial z}, \tag{7.22}$$

and, from (7.16),

$$\frac{\partial g(z)}{\partial z} = \frac{h'(z)(z - \lambda) - h(z)}{(z - \lambda)^2} = \frac{h'(z) - g(z)}{z - \lambda}. \tag{7.23}$$

Therefore

$$\lim_{z \to \lambda} \frac{\partial g(z)}{\partial z} = h''(\lambda) - \lim_{z \to \lambda} \frac{\partial g(z)}{\partial z}, \tag{7.24}$$

using again l'Hospital's rule. Equation (7.24) implies

$$\lim_{z \to \lambda} \frac{\partial g(z)}{\partial z} = \frac{1}{2} h''(\lambda). \tag{7.25}$$

Equations (7.22) and (7.25) lead to

$$2 \lim_{z \to 1} \frac{\partial g(\lambda z)}{\partial z} = \sum_{j=1}^{T} a_j [\lambda^{T-j}(T-j+1)(T-j) - \lambda^{T-j-1}(T-j)(T-j-1)]. \tag{7.26}$$

Inserting (7.26) and $g(\lambda z)$ as given by (7.17) in (7.21) yields the necessary stability condition (7.13), after some rearrangements.

References

Bródy, A. (1972), 'Zur Feinstruktur der Investitionszyklen', manuscript of a lecture, Basle.

Jordan, C. (1939), *Calculus of Finite Differences*, Budapest.

Jury, E. D. (1964), *Theory and Application of the Z-transform Method*, John Wiley, New York.

Murata, Y. (1977), *Mathematics for Stability and Optimization of Economic Systems*, Academic Press, New York.

Tarjan, T. G. (1985), 'The stem-heavy and the stern-heavy investment distributions' (in Hungarian), *SZIGMA*, 18(3) : 137–47.

PART IV

Microeconomic Foundations

8

Micro Foundations of the Second-Order Accelerator and of Cyclical Behaviour

Claude Hillinger, Michael Reiter,
and Thilo Weser

1. Second-Order Accelerator of Investment and Production: An Intuitive Explanation

The *second-order accelerator* (SOA) is the basic mechanism of the models developed at SEMECON in order to explain the observed quasi-cycles in fixed investment, inventory investment, and production.

The SOA models were used at SEMECON because (1) their use allows the construction of very simple models which explain the observed stylized facts (cf. Chapters 1, 3, and 4) of macroeconomic fluctuations; and (2) strong plausibility arguments for the SOA can be given. This chapter provides a third type of justification, by deriving the SOA from intertemporal optimization of the firm in the presence of adjustment costs.

What is the SOA? It is best to begin the explanation with the standard flexible accelerator formulation for fixed investment. In continuous time it is given by

$$I = b(K^* - K), \tag{8.1}$$

where $I = DK$ is net investment,[1] K^*, K are the desired/actual stock of fixed capital, and b is the speed of adjustment. For the present discussion it is plausible to refer to (8.1) as the *first-order accelerator* (FOA), since it is a first-order differential equation in K.

The SOA results when I in (8.1) is interpreted as desired rather than actual investment,

$$I^+ = b(K^* - K), \tag{8.2}$$

and a new adjustment equation for actual investment is introduced:

$$DI = c(I^+ - I). \tag{8.3}$$

---

[1] In this simple formulation, replacement investment is assumed to have been subtracted from total investment to give net investment.

Inserting (8.2) in (8.3) yields

$$DI = c[b(K^* - K) - DK]$$ (8.4)

Since $DI = D^2K$, equation (8.4) is a second-order differential equation in K and this is the reason for the SOA terminology.

The basic thought behind the SOA is that there are adjustment costs involved in changing the level of investment, leading to a finite value of c and only a gradual adjustment of I towards I^+. We refer to this as the inertia of investment. As in physical systems, inertia potentially leads to overshooting and cyclical behaviour because $K^* = K$ does not imply $I = 0$, so that a positive or negative rate of net investment continues and K again departs from its equilibrium level.

We will use the term 'SOA' to refer to all formulations involving inertia of investment, even though they may differ from (8.3), (8.2) in detail. For example, transformations or ratios of the variables have been used. The SOA for fixed investment, as formulated here, bears close resemblance to models with a gestation lag such as those described in Chapters 6 and 7 above or referred to in Chapter 1, Section 5.2. If we employ a discrete model and interpret $K_t^* - K_t$ as the total investment commitment at time t, then this total would be distributed over several future periods. The principal difference is that in a gestation lag model the increment to the capital stock occurs only when the investment project is completed.

The SOA can also be used to model the inventory/output decision of a manufacturing firm or sector. We define K^*, K now as desired/actual stock of inventories, Q as output, Z as sales, and Z^* as the medium-term expectation of sales. The desired level of output is given by

$$Q^+ = Z^* + b(K^* - K).$$ (8.5)

Firms' desired output is such as to cover expected (i.e. normal) demand, excluding very short-run and often erratic fluctuations, and in addition to move the inventories on hand towards the desired level. Actual output is given by

$$DQ = c(Q^+ - Q).$$ (8.6)

Inserting (8.5) into (8.6) yields

$$DQ = bc(K^* - K) - c(Q - Z^*).$$ (8.7)

Equation (8.7) reflects the traditional assumptions that changing output involves adjustment costs and that there are also costs involved when inventory levels are too high or low. The variables are also linked by the basic identity

$$DK = Q - Z.$$ (8.8)

As shown in Section 3, equations (8.7) and (8.8) imply a second-order differential equation in Q or in K which is of the same form as that of the SOA for fixed investment. In the present instance, therefore, we speak of the SOA for the inventory/production decision.

The use of the SOA in macroeconomic modelling has a longer tradition for the output decision than for the fixed investment decision. This is probably because the former follows directly from the old and well-known idea that inventories serve to smooth production. The production SOA has from the beginning been used in all of the models of the DECG (cf. Chapter 1, Section 9).

The SOA for fixed investment appears in Hillinger (1976) and Hillinger and Schueler (1977). Subsequent publications (Hillinger 1986, 1987) employed both types of SOA in order to model the interaction of inventory and equipment cycles. The SOA for fixed investment was independently developed by Gandolfo, who employed both types of SOA (Gandolfo 1981; Gandolfo and Padoan 1984, 1987, 1990). Phillips (1961) already used a similar investment equation.

In the rest of this section we analyse the solution of the SOA equations. Because the homogeneous parts of (8.4) and (8.7) are completely analogous, it is sufficient to analyse (8.4). The characteristic polynomial $p(x)$ associated with the homogeneous part of (8.4),

$$p(x) = x^2 + cx + bc, \tag{8.9}$$

has the roots

$$x_{1,2} = \frac{1}{2}\left[-c \pm i\sqrt{4bc - c^2}\right]. \tag{8.10}$$

Therefore, the solution is periodic for $c < 4b$ and always stable. Under the assumption that changes of real investment are slow in comparison with desired changes in capital, that is

$$b \gg c, \tag{8.11}$$

the roots are purely imaginary, and (8.4) may be approximated by

$$D^2K = a(K^* - K), \quad a = bc. \tag{8.12}$$

The homogeneous part of this equation implies oscillations of constant amplitudes and the period $2\pi a^{-1/2}$. Corresponding to the idea of inertia, this implies that, the slower adjustment speeds, the longer the period of the cycle.

A similar argument leads to the approximation of (8.7) by

$$DQ = a(K^* - K) \tag{8.13}$$

The simplicity of this approach makes it very useful for theoretical and econometric applications. The essential property of the SOA equations is that they have *endogenous* cyclical solutions; i.e., their ability to describe investment cycles is independent from the specification of K^*. Another important feature is that, in contrast to other business cycle models, the approximate constancy of amplitude is obtained under weak assumptions.

The distinctive feature of SOA models is that cycles can be generated solely in the firm sector, which implies a minor role for consumption in the gener-ation of cyclical movements. This is in fundamental contrast to accelera-tor/multiplier models (Samuelson 1939), which assign an equally important role in the generation of cycles to the consumption sector.

In the following two sections, a model of intertemporal investment and production decisions under adjustment costs is analysed. The time path of desired capital and production is given exogenously by some price and de-mand expectations, and other influences are excluded.[2] The interest is focused on the question whether optimal solutions for the deviation between actual and desired capital and production may be cyclical: Can investment or production cycles be rational under adjustment costs?

At first glance this is counterintuitive, an impression strengthened by the fact that the FOA predicts that, in a stable environment, disequilibria decay exponentially.

A basic novelty of our approach, in the case of fixed investment, is that adjustment costs are assigned not only to changes of the capital stock, but also to changes of the level of investment. In the case of production, we assume costs of changing the level of production. Here the assumption is more tradi-tional and corresponds to production-smoothing.

Assuming costs of changing production is quite common in the literature. A detailed justification is given in Section 3. Adjustment costs related to changes in the level of investment have to our knowledge not been discussed in the earlier adjustment cost literature. Plausible arguments for the existence of this type of adjustment cost can be given. Investment processes are typically the result of past commitments, machines being typically ordered in advance and often constructed to specification. Contracts for new plants and associated equipment may have to be awarded some years in advance and cannot be cancelled without excessive costs. Recognition and decision lags also cause delayed adjustment. It requires time for an increase in the demand facing a firm to be recognized, more time for it to be classified as permanent rather than transitory, and still more time for the change to be reflected in long-range plans influencing the desired capital stock.

All of the factors causing such delays are collectively referred to as *inertia of investment*. The associated adjustment costs for short-term changes of in-vestment will turn out to be central in explaining *investment overshooting* and thus cyclical behaviour.

---

[2] In principle, it is possible to model simultaneously the determination of the equilibrium time path, dependent on technology and price expectations, and the deviations from equilibrium, which depend on adjustment costs. This has been done in the adjustment cost literature related to the FOA (cf. Lucas 1967; Gould 1968). We do not do so here, since we are interested in explaining the fluctuations away from equilibrium and want to keep the analysis as simple as possible.

The production decision is more short-term than the fixed investment decision. The basic reason is that it is easier, quicker, and less costly to change inventory levels in either direction than to change the stock of fixed capital. Another reason is that inventory levels fluctuate in the short run for reasons not under the control of the firm (fluctuations of sales), and short-run responses are required.

Our discussion here is similar to that of Keynes (1936: Chs. 5 and 12), who made a distinction between short-term and long-term expectations and stated that the former relate to the output, the latter to the investment decision. We need an even more differentiated view, because our analysis differs from that of Keynes in that we make an explicit distinction between the long-run equilibrium, the medium-term adjustments of fixed investment in disequilibrium, and the short-term adjustments of output in disequilibrium. The three-part distinction plays an important role particularly in Chapter 4, where long-, medium-, and short-term movements have to be separated empirically.

A basic feature of our approach is that adjustment costs are always viewed as applying to deviations from long-term (in the case of fixed capital) or medium-term (in the case of production) equilibrium. The costs (and revenues) of the equilibrium path itself are already fully accounted for in its determination. Consequently, the solution paths we calculate concern fluctuations around the equilibrium path. The reason why adjustment costs apply to deviations from long-term (medium-term) planning is that adjustment costs are especially severe if they concern changes that are unexpected in the sense that they have not been anticipated by a long-term (medium-term) plan.

For the mathematical analysis, we have found it convenient as well as appealing to use infinite-horizon models with discounting. A large discount factor implies that the more distant future has little influence on the current decision. It reflects high uncertainty about the future paths of the variables determining long-term planning. In case of perfect foresight, the discount factor is the rate of interest.[3] A significant but not surprising result is that significant cyclical behaviour arises if the future is discounted heavily.

The plan of this chapter is as follows. Section 2 derives the SOA of investment from a calculus of intertemporal cost minimization. Section 3 does the same for the SOA of production. Section 4 contains some concluding remarks.

2. Adjustment Cost Minimization for Fixed Investment

This section develops the adjustment cost model of equipment investment and derives the SOA of investment. The desired levels of the fixed capital stock K^* and its time derivatives are regarded as a result of long-term planning. In

---

[3] Reasons for treating uncertainty by a big discount factor, rather than using stochastic control theory, are discussed in Hillinger *et al.* (1991).

this model they are exogenously given, and the analysis is limited to the minimization of costs due to capital deficit and adjustment processes.

As has been explained above, all costs are formulated in terms of deviations k of the actual capital K from its desired value K^*; i.e., $k = K - K^*$, $Dk = D(K - K^*)$, etc. These costs may be expressed as a sum of contributions each quadratic in k, Dk, and D^2k. They can be explained as follows:

1. *Contribution due to* k: Idle equipment capital ($k > 0$) gives rise to costs because of inflexibility and enhanced depreciation; insufficient capital ($k > 0$) leads to missing production possibilities or too excessive capacity utilization (overtime). K^* is located at the optimum ($k = 0$) in between.
2. *Contribution due to* Dk: Changes of the equipment capital stock (net investment) may be costly in the case of imperfect substitutability with other production factors (e.g. labour). In this case changes of the capital stock imply either changes in or subefficient use of the other production factors and generate costs (e.g. training costs). These costs are particularly relevant if the net investment deviates from the long-term planning value DK^*. Therefore, it is appropriate to relate adjustment to Dk rather than DK.
3. *Contribution due to* D^2k: Equipment investment is usually based on long-term planning and contracts. The resulting *inertia of investment*, which is explained more explicitly above, implies adjustment costs for short-term changes of investment, i.e. non-vanishing D^2k.

Thus, the cost function $C(k, Dk, D^2k)$ takes the form

$$C(k, Dk, D^2k) = \alpha k^2 + \beta(Dk)^2 + \gamma(D^2k)^2. \tag{8.14}$$

Firms determine the time paths of their equipment capital in such a way that the present value of all future costs discounted with a constant rate ρ is minimized:

$$\min_{k(t)} \int_{t_0}^{\infty} [\alpha k^2 + \beta(Dk)^2 + \gamma(D^2k)^2] \, e^{\rho (t_0 - t)} \, dt. \tag{8.15}$$

As mentioned earlier, in case of perfect foresight the discount rate ρ has to be regarded as an interest rate, whereas in case of imperfect foresight higher values of ρ are appropriate.

The initial values for capital stock and investment, $K(t_0)$ and $I(t_0)$, are given. Relevant transversality conditions are:

$$\lim_{t \to \infty} Dk e^{\rho (t_0 - t)} = 0,$$

$$\lim_{t \to \infty} D^2k e^{\rho (t_0 - t)} = 0, \tag{8.16}$$

$$\lim_{t \to \infty} D^3k e^{\rho (t_0 - t)} = 0.$$

These conditions imply that investment and its time derivatives do not increase faster than firms discount the future.

The resulting Euler equation for $k(t)$ may be derived by means of standard techniques of variational analysis:[4]

$$\alpha k + \beta(\rho - D)Dk + \gamma(\rho - D)^2 D^2 k = 0. \tag{8.17}$$

The characteristic polynomial of this fourth-order differential equation,

$$P(x) = \alpha + \beta(\rho - x)x + \gamma(\rho - x)^2 x^2, \tag{8.18}$$

is quadratic in

$$y = (\rho - x)x. \tag{8.19}$$

In terms of y, the roots of $P(x)$ are

$$y_{1,2} = \frac{1}{2\gamma} \left(-\beta \pm \sqrt{\beta^2 - 4\alpha\gamma} \right), \tag{8.20}$$

and relating x with y via

$$x_{1,2} = \frac{\rho}{2} \pm \sqrt{\frac{\rho^2}{4} - y} \tag{8.21}$$

yields

$$x_{1,2,3,4} = \frac{\rho}{2} \pm \sqrt{\frac{\rho^2}{4} + \frac{1}{2\gamma} \left(\beta \pm \sqrt{\beta^2 - 4\alpha\gamma} \right)}. \tag{8.22}$$

The roots corresponding to '+' in the left $\pm$ sign have real parts greater than ρ. The associated explosive solutions do not satisfy the transversality conditions and are obviously not related to a cost minimum.

The remaining two roots may be transformed into

$$x_{1,2} = \frac{\rho}{2} \left[1 - \sqrt{1 + \frac{2}{\gamma\rho^2} \left(\beta \pm \sqrt{\beta^2 - 4\alpha\gamma} \right)} \right]. \tag{8.23}$$

They have negative real parts, which implies damped solutions, and are complex for

$$\beta^2 < 4\alpha\gamma. \tag{8.24}$$

---

[4] An introduction to variational analysis is given by Hadley and Kemp (1971).

This shows the relevance of the inertia of investment. The solutions are oscillatory for sufficiently great values of the cost parameter γ, which is associated with changes of investment. Another important finding is that the damping rate of oscillatory solutions depends crucially on the discount rate ρ, which can be related to the planner's foresight (cf. the explanations above).

In case of long-term foresight (small values of ρ), the leading contribution to the roots is

$$-\sqrt{\frac{1}{2\gamma}\left(\beta \pm \sqrt{\beta^2 - 4\alpha\gamma}\,\right)}. \tag{8.25}$$

In (8.25), the real parts are greater in absolute value than the imaginary parts, because it is the square root of a number with positive real part. This implies extremely high damping rates: within one period of the 'cycle' the amplitude decreases by at least $\exp(-2\pi)$, which is about $1/500$. In this case, significant oscillatory behaviour is excluded.

The contrary, and in the context of economic fluctuations more realistic, assumption is the case of short foresight (great values of ρ). In this case, (8.23) can be simplified using the approximation

$$\sqrt{1+h} \cong 1 + \frac{h}{2}. \tag{8.26}$$

The result,

$$x_{1,2} \cong \frac{1}{2\gamma\rho}\left(-\beta \pm \sqrt{\beta^2 - 4\alpha\gamma}\,\right), \tag{8.27}$$

shows that in this case the imaginary parts of the roots, i.e. the oscillatory character of the solution, may be dominating, whereas the above observed relation between foresight and attenuation of cyclical behaviour remains the same: lower discount rates (smaller values of ρ) imply stronger damping.

The values of $x_{1,2}$ given by (8.27) are the roots of the polynomial

$$\alpha + \beta\rho x + \gamma\rho^2 x^2, \tag{8.28}$$

which can be regarded as the characteristic polynomial of the differential equation

$$\alpha k + \beta\rho Dk + \gamma\rho^2 D^2 k = 0, \tag{8.29}$$

which is the SOA equation.

In the derivation of the common (first-order) flexible accelerator, changes of investment are cost-free. Setting $\gamma = 0$ in (8.29) results in

$$Dk = -\frac{\alpha}{\beta\rho}\,k. \tag{8.30}$$

Retransforming (8.30) into terms of K and K^* yields

$$DK = \frac{\alpha}{\beta\rho}(K^* - K) + DK^* \tag{8.31}$$

which corresponds to the equation for the first-order accelerator (8.1).[5]

According to the derivation of the SOA given in (8.2) and (8.3), equation (8.31) is interpreted as the equation for the desired level of investment I^+, and actual investment $I = DK$ is adjusted towards this level. Rewriting (8.29) in K and K^* shows this relation:

$$D^2K = DI = \frac{\alpha}{\gamma\rho^2}(K^* - K) + \frac{\beta}{\gamma\rho}(DK^* - DK) + D^2K^*$$

$$= \frac{\beta}{\gamma\rho}\left[\frac{\alpha}{\beta\rho}(K^* - K) + DK^* - DK\right] + D^2K^* \tag{8.32}$$

$$= \frac{\beta}{\gamma\rho}(I^+ - I) + D^2K^*.$$

This corresponds to (8.3) above.[6] The adjustment parameters b, c, and a of (8.2), (8.3), and (8.12) are related to the cost parameters α, β and γ via

$$b = \frac{\alpha}{\beta\rho}, \qquad c = \frac{\beta}{\gamma\rho}, \qquad a = \frac{\alpha}{\gamma\rho^2} \tag{8.33}$$

The assumption $b \gg c$ (8.11) leading to cycles of constant amplitude may be expressed in terms of cost parameters:

$$\alpha\gamma \gg \beta^2 \tag{8.34}$$

The period length of an investment cycle is often related to the technological inertia of the involved adjustment processes. This provides an intuitive explanation why inventory cycles are shorter than equipment cycles, which themselves are shorter than building cycles. In Section 1 it was shown that the period of a cycle is inversely related to the root of the accelerator coefficient a. Hence, (8.33) provides an explicit relation between the period length of cycles and the cost parameter γ: higher adjustment costs imply longer cycles.

Thereby, a microeconomic foundation of the SOA is provided.

3. Production Smoothing

This section derives a dynamic model for production behaviour, based on similar assumptions to those made in the derivation of the equipment investment equation. An outline of our assumptions is as follows:

[5] In a static environment such as commonly assumed, K^* is constant. In this case the contribution due to DK^* does not appear in the accelerator equation. We prefer the more general formulation including DK^* as it is compatible with equilibrium growth.

[6] The argument of the preceding footnote now extends to D^2K^*.

1. Firms have price and demand expectations, produce with a given convex technology, and hold inventories, which have a buffer function between sales and production. Firms decide directly about production and thereby control the inflows of the inventories, whereas the outflows are determined by sales.
2. Based on these price and demand expectations and the technology, some desired paths of inventory stock and production are predetermined. For reasons of unforeseeable fluctuations of demand, these paths cannot be realized precisely.
3. Quadratic costs are assigned to deviations of the inventory stock, production, and changes of production, respectively, from the predetermined desired paths.
4. The relevant planning horizon for adjustment processes is limited by the time horizon of a precise forecast of demand. This time span is typically short in comparison to an inventory cycle period of about three to five years.

Subsequently, these assumptions will be formalized and specified in greater detail.

Production Q may be split into sales Z and inventory investment DK:

$$Q = DK + Z. \tag{8.35}$$

For the purpose of this paper, price and demand expectations will be given exogenously. Assuming profit-maximizing behaviour and a strictly convex technology, they imply uniquely determined optimal values for future production Q^* and inventories K^* as well as sales expectations Z^*.

In what follows, the variables Z^*, Q^*, and K^* are regarded as predetermined. Furthermore, it is assumed that they are smooth and self-consistent; i.e.,

$$DK^* = Q^* - Z^*. \tag{8.36}$$

As K^* and Q^* are assumed to be derived from medium-term profit-maximizing, the subsequent analysis may be limited to the question of optimal control of the differences $k = (K - K^*)$ and $q = (Q - Q^*)$ in order to minimize the costs due to deviations from K^* and Q^*, depending on $z = (Z - Z^*)$.

These costs will be approximated by a sum of quadratic contributions in k, q, and Dq. This is explained as follows:

1. *Contribution due to k*: Idle inventory stock ($k > 0$) gives rise to unnecessary capital costs and enhanced depreciation; insufficient stock ($k < 0$) leads to missing sales possibilities (penalty costs). Therefore these costs may be assumed as approximately quadratic in k.
2. *Contribution due to q*: Given some production plan Q^*, suitable capacities (equipment capital) have to be provided. As these capacities may be as-

sumed to be optimal (i.e. cost-minimizing) to produce Q^*, Q^* is therefore the optimal production level once these capacities have been installed. This may be expressed in terms of costs that vanish for $Q = Q^*$ ($q = 0$) and are positive for both signs of $q = Q - Q^*$. They are approximated as quadratic in q.

3. *Contribution due to Dq*: This contribution corresponds to the well-known 'adjustment costs'. They appear as changes of production imply changing (or subefficient) use of factor inputs (e.g. training and lay-off costs for changes in labour input). In the common literature about adjustment costs they are formulated in terms of absolute changes of production (DQ). In this paper, however, we prefer to formulate them in terms of deviations (Dq) from DQ^*. The argument is that Q^* (and hence DQ^*) provides the basis for capacity planning and describes the firm's long-term expectations. It is therefore reasonable to assume that DQ^* does not include any rapid movements and generally takes small values. Moreover, as these changes are planned and therefore anticipated a longer time in advance, they are likely to cause only negligible adjustment costs. Significant adjustment costs, however, have to be expected for changes of production that are not anticipated by DQ^*, i.e. for changes given by Dq. Also, these costs will be assumed as quadratic.

Thus, the cost function C of this problem takes the form

$$C(k, q, Dq) = \alpha k^2 + \beta q^2 + \gamma(Dq)^2. \tag{8.37}$$

Firms determine their future production in such a way that expected future costs, given by the cost function $C(k, q, Dq)$ above, are minimized.

The relevant planning horizon for this question is limited by the time horizon of an exactly formulated forecast of sales.[7] This is obvious as z acts directly on k and it is only meaningful to optimize the adjustment process within a planning horizon for which the variables are known with sufficient accuracy. As was explained in Section 1, this is modelled by minimizing costs over an infinite horizon and using a high discount rate to reflect uncertainty.

These considerations may be formalized as follows. Firms are assumed to determine their future production in such a way that the present value of the expected future costs discounted with a constant rate ρ is minimized:

$$\min_{k(t),\, q(t)} \int_{t_0}^{\infty} C(k(t), q(t), Dq(t))e^{\rho\,(t_0 - t)}\, dt. \tag{8.38}$$

The initial values for inventory stock and production, $k(t_0)$ and $q(t_0)$, are given. Relevant transversality conditions are:

---

[7] In this context, the question whether these expectations are correct is of minor relevance.

$$\lim_{t \to \infty} q e^{\rho \, (t_0 - t)} = 0,$$

$$\lim_{t \to \infty} Dq e^{\rho \, (t_0 - t)} = 0, \tag{8.39}$$

$$\lim_{t \to \infty} D^2 q e^{\rho \, (t_0 - t)} = 0.$$

These conditions are weak and imply that changes of production and its time derivatives do not increase faster than firms discount the future.

In the following, we consider the dynamics of the deviations k and q of inventories and production from their desired values. Subtracting (8.36) from (8.35) yields the identity

$$Dk = q - z. \tag{8.40}$$

As firms can control production but not sales, (8.40) yields

$$\delta q = \delta(Dk) = D(\delta k), \tag{8.41}$$

which means that a variation of production induces a corresponding change of the inventory stock.

Using (8.41) and standard techniques of variational analysis, the Euler equation for $k(t)$ and $q(t)$ may be derived in the form

$$\alpha k + \beta(\rho - D)q + \gamma(\rho - D)^2 Dq = 0. \tag{8.42}$$

Differentiating (8.42) and remembering (8.40) yields

$$\alpha q + \beta(\rho - D)Dq + \gamma(\rho - D)^2 D^2 q = \alpha z. \tag{8.43}$$

This is a fourth-order differential equation for the decision variable q. Its homogeneous part is formally equivalent to (8.17). The analysis of the solution is therefore completely analogous to the analysis of Section 2.

In the case of great values of p, (8.43) may be simplified to

$$\alpha q + \beta \rho Dq + \gamma \rho^2 D^2 q = \alpha z. \tag{8.44}$$

The concept of the SOA can be derived from (8.44). Integrating (8.44) and using (8.40) yields

$$\alpha k + \beta \rho q + \gamma \rho^2 Dq = \text{const}, \tag{8.45}$$

where 'const' denotes a constant of integration. In the case of vanishing sales fluctuations ($z = 0$), the system approaches its equilibrium state, for which the left-hand side of (8.45) is equal to zero. Therefore, the value of 'const' has to vanish, and the final form of (8.45) is

$$\alpha k + \beta \rho q + \gamma \rho^2 D q = 0. \tag{8.46}$$

Equation (8.46) is equivalent to (8.7), except for terms in DQ^* and DK^*.[8] Thus, our model also provides a microeconomic foundation of the SOA of production.

Neglecting adjustment costs of production (i.e. setting $\gamma = 0$), (8.43) reduces to

$$q = -\frac{\alpha}{\beta \rho} k, \tag{8.47}$$

which is the FOA expressed in deviation form.

4. Summary

The idea of inertia of investment and production can be formalized in the concept of the SOA. Several authors have given plausibility arguments for the SOA and have successfully employed it in empirical studies. For the fixed-investment decision, adjustment costs apply to deviations from equilibrium of the capital stock, investment, and the rate of change of investment. For the output decision, adjustment costs apply to the deviation from equilibrium of inventory stock, the rate of production, and the change of the rate of production. The resulting models imply cycles of constant or decreasing amplitudes in equipment investment and capital stock.

In order to investigate the microeconomic foundations of this concept, we considered an intertemporal optimization approach. The major findings can be summarized as follows:

1. Both the FOA and the SOA can be derived from an intertemporal optimization approach under suitable restrictions.
2. Cyclical solutions may occur quite generally.
3. Cyclical behaviour is more pronounced if firms discount the future strongly (short foresight), whereas longer foresight attenuates cyclical behaviour.

References

Gandolfo, G. (1981), *Qualitative Analysis and Econometric Estimation of Continuous Time Dynamic Models*, North-Holland, Amsterdam.
—— (1984), 'Inventory cycles in a macrodynamic model of the Italian economy', in A. Chikan (ed.), *Proceedings of the Second International Symposium on Inventories, Budapest, 1982*, Akademiai Kiado, Budapest.

---

[8] As in the case of fixed investment, the intuitive derivation did not consider trend variations of the target variables.

Gandolfo, G., and Padoan, C. P. (1984), *A Disequilibrium Model of Real and Financial Accumulation in an Open Economy*, Springer, Berlin.

—— (1987), 'The mark V version of the Italian continuous time model', *Quaderni dell' Instituto di Economia dell' Universita di Siena*, 70.

—— (1990), 'The Italian continuous time model, theory and empirical results', *Economic Modelling*, 7(2) : 91–132.

Gould, J. P. (1968), 'Adjustment costs in the theory of investment of the firm', *Review of Economic Studies*, 35 : 47–55.

Hadley, G., and Kemp, M. C. (1971), *Variational Methods in Economic Analysis*, North-Holland, Amsterdam.

Hillinger, C. (1963), 'A theory of the inventory cycle', Ph.D. thesis, University of Chicago.

—— (1966), 'An econometric model of mild business cycles', *Manchester School of Economics and Social Studies*, 34 : 269–84.

—— (1976), 'Cyclical fluctuations in industrialized economies', paper presented at the Econometric Society Meeting, Atlantic City.

—— (1986), 'Inventory cycle and equipment cycle interaction', in A. Chikan (ed.), *Inventories in Theory and Practice*, Elsevier, Amsterdam.

—— (1987), 'Business cycle stylized facts and explanatory models', *Journal of Economic Dynamics and Control*, 11 : 257–63.

—— Schueler, K. (1977), 'Makroökonomisches Modell des Wachstumszyklus', in H. Albach and E. Helmstädter (eds.), *Quantitative Wirtschaftsforschung in Honour of W. Krelle*, Mohr, Tübingen.

—— Reiter, M., and Weser, T. (1991), 'Rational investment cycles and the modelling of uncertainty', *Münchner Wirtschaftswissenschaftliche Beiträge*, 91–115.

Keynes, J. M. (1936), *The General Theory of Employment, Interest and Money*, Macmillan, London.

Lucas, R. E. (1967), 'Optimal investment policy and the flexible accelerator', *International Economic Review*, 8 : 78–85.

Phillips, A. W. (1961), 'A simple model of employment, money and prices in a growing economy', *Economica*, 28 : 360–70.

Samuelson, P. A. (1939), 'Interaction between the multiplier analysis and the principle of acceleration', *Review of Economic Statistics*, 21(2) : 75–8.

9

The Aggregation Problem for Economic Cycles

Thilo Weser

1. Introduction

Theories of economic cycles have been formulated in terms of highly aggregated models. This approach involves an aggregation problem: what happens to the validity of theoretical implications if assumptions similar to those made at the aggregate level are instead postulated for the behaviour of disaggregated economic units? How can macroeconomic cycles be explained rigorously from the individual dynamics of different microeconomic subjects?[1]

Almost all theoretical models describe macroeconomic sectors using the concept of representative agents and/or commodities, postulating behavioural and technological relationships with representative parameter values. Based on such assumptions, commonly a set of dynamic equations is established to explain the behaviour of the aggregates. These models are investigated in order to identify restrictions on the parameters for which the system has oscillatory solutions and in order to characterize the properties of these solutions. Examples of this approach are the classical contributions of Samuelson (1939), Metzler (1941), and Hicks (1950) as well as Chapters 4, 6, and 7 above.

The purpose of this chapter is purely theoretical: to contribute to the understanding of stylized facts about macroeconomic cycles that have been established elsewhere. However, the suggested theory has some direct and concrete implications corresponding to empirical observations that are not too well established and will therefore be briefly noted in Section 2.

In Section 3, the aggregation problem will be considered more specifically in the context of the elementary cycle model, based on the second-order accelerator (SOA), which has already been discussed from the view of macroeconomic modelling (Chapter 4) and of intertemporal optimality on the firm level (Chapter 8). SOA models are essentially one-sectoral and can therefore be directly disaggregated. In this formulation the concrete difficulties of the aggregation problem become clear, and the known strong negative theorems for linear models can be illustrated.

---

[1] Up to now, the aggregation problem has been discussed almost exclusively in the context of static one-sector models, especially for production and consumption under individual maximization assumptions. For this situation satisfactory results have been achieved (see e.g. Green 1964; van Daal and Merkies 1984). Dynamic considerations of the aggregation problem have been given by Goodwin (1983), Schlicht (1985), Britton (1986).

The basic idea of this chapter is to abandon the assumption of parameter constancy and instead allow parameters to vary in the course of an economic cycle. This concept yields positive results on aggregation. The analysis will be performed in two steps. In Section 4 the parameter variation is assumed to be given exogenously. This approach provides not only a solution to the aggregation problem, but also an explanation to some stylized facts concerning intercycle relations. An endogenous modelling of the parameter variation will be presented in Section 5. This yields a closed solution to the aggregation problem.

2. Some Stylized Facts

Stylized facts (*SF*) regarding economic cycles which can be explained by an aggregative theory based on the SOA are discussed in Chapter 3 (*SF1–6*). Here additional stylized facts are listed, which can be explained by the disaggregated theory of the present chapter:

> *SF7.* The period lengths of different coexisting cycles often show harmonic relations. (Typically, the longer cycle has the double period of the short cycle.)
> *SF8.* Coexisting cycles with period relations of 2 : 1 show certain phase relations: the superposition yields typically shaped curves (M-shape, W-shape).
> *SF9.* There are individually different cycles on the firm level.

SF7 and *8* have already been mentioned by a number of authors. Although the phenomenon of harmonic relations was noticed a long time ago and may be found even in older standard textbooks (e.g. Samuelson 1973), no explanatory model is yet available. W- and M-shaped series have been reported for example by Hansen (1941).

Regarding *SF9*, Wilson's catalogue of cycles (1964) as well as preliminary studies performed at the SEMECON/Munich (see e.g. Hillinger and Weser 1988) give evidence that individual periodicity at the firm level can often be found.

In Chapter 3, *SF7* is discussed in relation to Table 3.7. A weak confirmation of the hypothesis is found there. The median inventory cycle is 3 years; the median equipment cycle 6.3 years. The variance of the observations is considerable. For German data it was possible to confirm the M-shape (Section 3.1).

3. A Disaggregated Model and the Aggregation Problem

The subsequent analysis is based on the SOA cycle models. Their mathematical simplicity makes them very useful for theoretical studies of the aggregation problem as they are essentially one-sectoral and therefore can be directly disaggregated. The models can be structured into multisectoral versions to explain the interaction of equipment, production, inventories, and demand, but the cycle-generating mechanisms are altered thereby only slightly, or, in the limiting cases, not at all.

The simplest version of the SOA equation for the equipment cycle (cf. equation (8.12) above) is

$$D^2 K_e = a_e(K_e^* - K_e). \tag{9.1}$$

Equation (9.1) describes the dynamics of equipment investment based on the single-parameter version of the SOA. When applied to a single firm, the homogeneous part of this equation generates autonomous cyclical behaviour, depending only on the individual adjustment parameter and the past history of the firm.

The more general two-parameter version of the SOA can generate only damped cycles which die out in the course of time. The two-parameter SOA is therefore not suitable for the deterministic analysis of this chapter. An additional justification is that it fits data reasonably well (cf. Chapter 4).

In a disaggregated context, the equipment investment sector is described by the equations

$$D^2 K_{e,n} = w_{e,n}^2 (K_{e,n}^* - K_{e,n}), \qquad w_{e,n}^2 = a_{e,n} \qquad (n = 1, \dots, U), \tag{9.2}$$

where n denotes the firm index. The total number U is not restricted: it is intended that the order of magnitude of U corresponds to real economies. The general solution to equation n of (9.2) consists of a particular solution depending on $K_{e,n}^*$ and the homogeneous solution

$$K_{e,n}(t) = A_{e,n} \cos (w_{e,n} t - S_{e,n}), \tag{9.3}$$

where $A_{e,n}$ and $S_{e,n}$ are determined by the specific initial conditions of the firm n.

The inventory cycle model based on the second-order accelerator of production may be reinterpreted analogously in a disaggregated formulation. The dynamic equation for production (equation (8.13) above) may be rewritten as

$$DQ_n = w_{i,n}^2 (K_{i,n}^* - K_{i,n}), \qquad n = 1, \dots, U, \tag{9.4}$$

where—as above—n denotes the firm index. These equations imply individually different production and inventory cycles on the firm level dependent on the generally different parameter values.

The subsequent analysis on the macroeconomic level is based on individual cyclical behaviour of equipment investment and production on the firm level. No specific assumptions about periods and phases are made. It is emphasized that there is no (explicit or implicit) requirement that all firms are alike (in the sense of the concept of a representative firm). For convenience, in the following all variables denote deviations from static or dynamic equilibrium solutions. They can therefore take negative as well as positive values.

The behaviour of the aggregates is given by summation over all individual contributions. The homogeneous parts of the equipment capital stocks $K_{e,n}$ for example yield the following aggregate K_e:

$$K_e(t) = \sum_{n=1}^{U} K_{e,n}(t) = \sum_{n=1}^{U} A_{e,n} \cos (w_{e,n} t - S_{e,n}). \qquad (9.5)$$

Equation (9.5) enables a concrete formulation of the aggregation problem: what is the result of such a summation? Is it compatible with the aggregated model? There would be no aggregation problem if the solution could be written (approximatively or exactly) in the form

$$K_e(t) = A_e \cos (w_e t - S_e), \qquad (9.6)$$

where A_e, w_e, and S_e would have suitable values obtained from the parameter distributions. However, such a representation is possible only under restrictive assumptions (e.g. equality of all $w_{e,n}$, $w_{e,n} = w_e$, $n = 1,\ldots, U$), but not in the general case. Even in the case of identical initial conditions, the behaviour of the individual firms will diverge in time and the firms will run out of phase. Therefore the model cannot explain a macroeconomic cycle with an approximatively constant amplitude.[2]

As an example, Fig. 9.1 shows such a situation for five firms. Their dynamic behaviour is described by an equation of the type (9.2), where the desired levels $K_{e,n}^{*}$ are set constant and the accelerator coefficients $a_{e,n}$ have different values (90, 95, 100, 105, and 110 per cent of their average). The individual firms show cycles of constant amplitudes with periods of about 95, 97.5, 100, 102.5, and 105 per cent of their medium length. The phases of the different cycles are initially synchronous and diverge in time. This leads to a decreasing amplitude of the aggregated cycle. Obviously, for the aggregate there is no representation in the form (9.1).[3]

The strength of the extinction effect is considerable. In the example of Fig. 9.1 the deviation of the periods from the average is about ± 5 per cent, which leads to a halving of the amplitudes within five periods. If the deviation of the periods from the average is doubled to about ± 10 per cent, the total amplitude decreases within 2.5 periods to about one-third of its initial value. (This can be seen in the first plot of Fig. 9.5.) Such a decreasing amplitude is not consistent with empirically observed macroeconomic cycles, although a period dispersion of about ± 10 per cent may be regarded as a modest assumption.

[2] There are strong general impossibility theorems about the aggregation problem for linear models (see. e.g. Theil 1965; Schlicht 1985). They apply to the problem under consideration here, but the more specific discussion given in this paper may illustrate the nature of the problem more concretely.
[3] Similar illustrative calculations have been performed by Britton (1986).

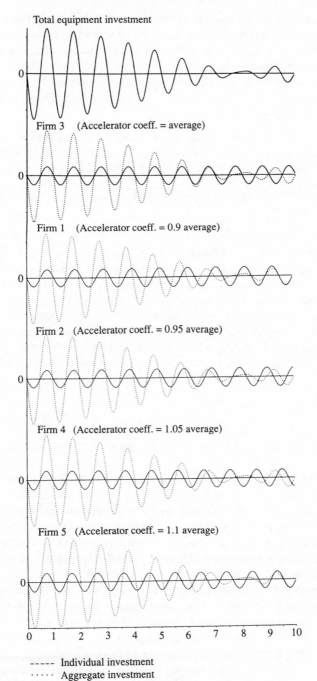

Total equipment investment

Firm 3   (Accelerator coeff. = average)

Firm 1   (Accelerator coeff. = 0.9 average)

Firm 2   (Accelerator coeff. = 0.95 average)

Firm 4   (Accelerator coeff. = 1.05 average)

Firm 5   (Accelerator coeff. = 1.1 average)

----- Individual investment
····· Aggregate investment

FIG. 9.1. · Disaggregated equipment cycle model: five firms with the same initial
phases and different accelerator coefficients

This example shows that the aggregated and disaggregated formulations of the same model may lead to contradicting conclusions (constant v. decreasing amplitudes). The importance of the extinction effect has already been emphasized by several authors.[4]

In the context of linear models with different eigenvalues, the extinction effect is universal; in the context of (one of his own) linear models, R. M. Goodwin remarks:

> The point about this linear . . . mechanism is that it is . . . equilibrium seeking (analogous to maximizing entropy) . . . Even though it may contain many constituent cycles, they are minor ripples, out of phase with one another, and rapidly dissipated amongst the sectors. What it does not do is to produce the generalized, alternating motions . . . , it is not an oscillator, a generator of cycles: for that we need other, nonlinear relations. (Goodwin 1983 : 68)

It follows from these considerations that macroeconomic cycles of roughly constant amplitudes remain unexplained: aggregated models based on typical representatives require implausibly restrictive assumptions; disaggregated (linear) models with individually different microcycles predict extinction effects and strongly decreasing amplitudes on the macro level.

A satisfactory solution to the aggregation problem requires a mechanism that on one hand admits individually different microcycles and on the other hand leads (despite extinction effects) to an aggregated cycle. This requirement can be met by synchronizing the cycles of certain firms with respect to their periods and phases. This is accomplished by the models of the following sections.

4. Aggregation by Exogenous Parameter Variation

In this section the investment behaviour of firms is studied under the assumption of exogenously given periodic variation of the accelerator coefficients. Thereby the aggregation problem will be solved partially (explanation of an aggregated longer cycle given an aggregated shorter cycle). Furthermore, the relations between different cycles (SF7 and 8) are derived. In Section 5 the variation of the accelerator coefficients is modelled endogenously, hence one obtains a closed solution to the aggregation problem.

The impact of an exogenous parameter variation is exemplified with respect to equipment investment. The dynamic investment equation on the firm level is given by equation (9.2) where n denotes the firm index. The basic novelty introduced in this section is the assumption that the accelerator coefficient

---

[4] Very often in the context of reinvestment cycles ('echo theory'): this theory explains investment cycles essentially by the idea that times of high equipment investment activity induce high reinvestments ('echos') after the technical lifetime of the equipment goods. The echo theory is one-sectoral and therefore may be directly disaggregated; the assumption of different lifetimes among the equipment goods leads to extinction effects (Matthews 1959; Bober 1968).

$w_{e,n}^2$ is time-dependent and varies periodically with the frequency v around its average $w_{0,e,n}^2$:

$$w_{e,n}^2 = w_{e,n}^2(t) = w_{0,e,n}^2[1 + h_{e,n} \cos(vt)]. \tag{9.7}$$

The relative strength $h_{e,n}$ of the variation is of the order of magnitude of some percentage points.

Such a variation of the accelerator coefficients of the equipment investment can be explained by the influence of an aggregated inventory cycle. If a firm has a deficit of equipment capital, and therefore increases its equipment investment according to the SOA, the capital adjustment is not performed instantaneously because of adjustment costs.[5] It is reasonable that the adjustment process is affected by the availability of resources, reflected in the level of aggregated inventory stocks. When inventories are above average, the delivery lags will be below average. Therefore, in the case of a deficit of equipment capital, when the firm wishes to invest positively, it can do so more quickly if the aggregate level of inventory is high. In the case of equipment capital stock that is excessive (in relation to demand facing the firm), one can expect that equipment investments tend to decrease faster if aggregated inventories are high, because there is a reduced opportunity to utilize the excessive capacity for building up stocks. Both considerations can be modelled by assuming that the accelerator coefficients of equipment investment depend positively on the level of aggregate inventories.

According to these considerations, it is plausible that the accelerator coefficients of equipment investment fluctuate depending on the level of aggregated inventories. Beside this mechanism, other sources of influence on the accelerator coefficients are possible, such as, for example, the macroeconomic cycles of other countries.

In the following (9.7) is regarded as given. The interest is focused on the dynamics of the homogeneous part of (9.2). For this part, one obtains

$$D^2 K_{e,n} + w_{0,e,n}^2[1 + h_{e,n} \cos(vt)] K_{e,n} = 0. \tag{9.8}$$

In the mathematic literature (9.8) is called *Mathieu equation*. An analytical treatment may be found in Bogoliubov and Mitropolsky (1961) or Minorsky (1962), among others. In this chapter I limit myself to stating some qualitative results.

For constant accelerator coefficients $(h_{e,n} = 0)$ the solutions to (9.8) are sinoidal oscillations with frequency $w_{0,e,n}$ and constant amplitudes. In general, these properties of the solutions remain essentially unchanged in the case of varying parameters $(h_{e,n} > 0)$. An exception occurs if the frequencies $w_{0,e,n}$ approximatively satisfy one of the following relations:

$$\frac{2w_{0,e,n}}{v} \cong N, \qquad N = 1, 2, 3, \dots \tag{9.9}$$

---

[5] A detailed discussion of the SOA with respect to adjustment costs is given in Chapter 8.

In such a situation the solutions are no longer bounded. For certain phases (in relation to the parameter variation) the amplitudes grow exponentially. This effect is called *parametric resonance*, and (9.9) is called the *resonance condition*. The strength of the growth effect decreases rapidly with increasing N, so that $N = 1$ is the only relevant case from a practical point of view.

This case is considered in greater detail. For $N = 1$, the resonance condition is

$$w_{0,e,n} \cong \frac{v}{2},$$ (9.10)

and the resonance effect has the following properties:

1. The strength of the resonance effect increases with the magnitude of the parameter variation, i.e. the value of $h_{e,n}$.
2. The strength of the effect decreases when the relative deviation of $w_{0,e,n}$ from $v/2$ increases. Outside of certain limits (depending on $h_{e,n}$), no resonance occurs.
3. The exponentially growing oscillating solution approaches a certain phase relative to the exogenous parameter variation: zero passages/extrema of $DK_{e,n}$ coincide with positively/negatively sloped zero passages of the parameter variation $\cos(vt)$.

The solution to the aggregation problem and the explanation of the stylized facts is based on these properties.

The index set of all firms is divided into two subsets C and IC such that a firm index $n \in C$ if $w_{0,e,n}$ fulfils the resonance condition (9.10) and $n \in IC$ otherwise. The aggregated equipment capital stock is obtained by summation over all individual contributions (cf. equation (9.5)). This sum may now be written as

$$K_e(t) = \sum_{n \in C} K_{e,n}(t) + \sum_{n \in IC} K_{e,n}(t).$$ (9.11)

All cycles of the first partial sum have approximatively the same frequency ($v/2$), approach the same phase (modulo $+/-$), and grow exponentially. Owing to these properties, the first contribution in (9.11) will be called the 'coherent' part.

The second partial sum contains all microcycles that do not fulfil the resonance condition and are therefore not influenced systematically. This partial sum may also contain all contributions of such firms that do not behave at all according to the model equation (9.8). This sum will therefore be called the 'incoherent' contribution. It contains no systematic contribution, and it may be assumed that the components cancel out statistically. Therefore the systematic dynamics of the aggregate is generated solely by the coherent part. The following conclusions can be drawn.

First, within the coherent part, two phases (contributions of opposite sign) are possible. If they are equally strong they cancel out completely; if one part is stronger, this part dominates the total sum and gives rise to an aggregated cycle.

It is seldom possible to give empirical evidence for two antiphase contributions within one aggregate, as the smaller one or, in case of equal size, both are cancelled out completely. However, a clear example is given by the data of the United Kingdom in the years 1870–1913 (see Fig. 9.2, taken from Matthews 1959). The following series are shown: net national income at factor cost; gross domestic capital formation; overseas balance of payment on current account (which can in good approximation be regarded as foreign investment); and the sum of the last two, which may represent total capital formation. As can be seen in part (*a*) of the figure, net national income and total investment fluctuate rather synchronously around their trends with period lengths of about 8–10 years. But as shown in part (*b*), the decomposition of total investment into its domestic and foreign contributions discloses enormous fluctuations in both series, each having the same periods (about 18–20

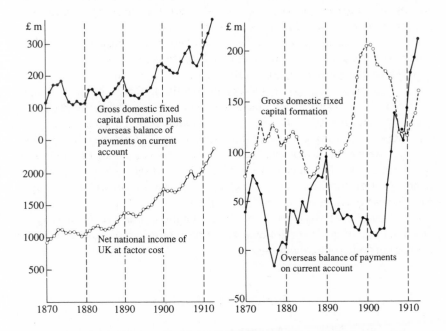

FIG. 9.2.   (*a*) National income and capital formation in the United Kingdom, 1870–1913. (*Source*: taken from Matthews 1959) (*b*) Home and overseas investment, United Kingdom, 1870–1913 (*Source*: taken from Matthews 1959)

years (2 : 1 relation!)) and amplitudes, but exactly contrary phases, and there-fore offsetting each other in the sum.

An aggregate cycle can be observed only if one of the two antiphase contributions is dominant. The following examples show how this can plaus-ibly occur as a result of initial conditions. After the Second World War the capital stocks of many countries were destroyed. In all these countries firms started to rebuild their equipment capital roughly at the same time. An example concerning inventories is discussed in Hillinger's (1966) study of the post-Korean War US inventory cycle: anticipation of rising prices and short-ages caused widespread synchronous hoarding on the part of households and firms.

Second, if the coherent part gives rise to a cycle in the aggregate, the resonance condition (9.10) implies that its frequency is $v/2$. This effect directly explains the 2 : 1 relation between the periods of different coexisting cycles (*SF7*).

To give a concrete example, if the accelerator coefficients of equipment investment vary under the influence of an aggregated four-year inventory cycle, the variation mechanism leads to an aggregated eight-year equipment cycle. The only assumptions concern the existence of some firms which be-have according to the accelerator equation (9.8), satisfy the resonance condi-tion (9.10), and have initial conditions that are (in total) asymmetric with respect to the two equivalent phases discussed above.

Third, there is a certain phase relation between the aggregated cycle and the parameter variation (cf. property 3 above). If the influence of the aggregated in-ventory cycle on the accelerator coefficients of equipment investment is speci-fied as argued above (cf. the text after equation (9.7)), that is, if the accelerator coefficients vary positively with the aggregated inventory stocks, the resonance effect distinguishes the following phase relation between both cycles. The negatively sloped zero passages of the inventory stocks (minima of the produc-tion cycle related to inventories) coincide with the extrema of the equipment investment cycle. The sum of the production/inventory cycle and the invest-ment cycle (together dominating the changes of total output) will be M-shaped (*SF8*). These relations are illustrated in Fig. 9.3.

The discussion above is based on the assumption of an exogenously given parameter variation. In the following section a fully endogenous solution to the aggregation problem is presented.

5. Endogenous Solution

To solve the aggregation problem endogenously, the interaction between dif-ferent firms has to be modelled. For the disaggregated models presented in Section 3 above, this interaction can be specified in two ways:

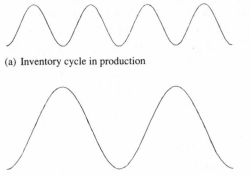

(a) Inventory cycle in production

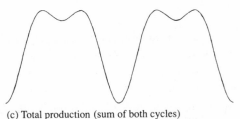

(b) Equipment investment (equipment cycle in production)

(c) Total production (sum of both cycles)

FIG. 9.3.   Phase relations

- *Indirectly*, by introducing a (homogeneous) demand sector which acts uniformly on the firms' desired capital stocks.
- *Directly*, by assuming a variability of the model parameters (accelerator coefficients) in a way that has to be specified.

The first possibility is economically meaningful, but in case of stable demand any influence on the individual firms vanishes again. Therefore this possibility is inadequate to the stylized fact that 'investment cycles can occur even in case of stable demand' and is too weak to serve as a basis for the solution to the aggregation problem.

The second possibility is stronger. As has been shown in the previous section, the assumption of varying accelerator coefficients not only provides a positive solution to the aggregation problem for investment cycles, but also implies exactly those relations between different macrocycles that correspond to the *SF7* and *8*.

In Section 3 it has been argued that a satisfying treatment of the aggregation problem requires an interaction model between different firms. In this sense the model presented in the previous section is incomplete as it is based on the assumption of another exogenously given aggregated cycle. With such a model it is possible to infer from a given (say, four-year) inventory cycle the existence of an aggregated (eight-year) equipment cycle of the double period, but the aggregation problem for the shorter cycle remains unsolved.

A very neat solution would be to start from the exogenous seasonal cycle and then go step-by-step up the 'ladder' of 2 : 1 relations, each time using the concept of parametric resonance. Indeed, there is evidence for other steps of a ladder of such harmonic relationships: corresponding to 8–10-year equipment cycles, 16–20-year building cycles have been observed (cf. for example Hansen 1941), and there is also some evidence for cycles of around two years which might provide the 'missing link' between the seasonal cycle and the four-year inventory cycle. However, the observed period lengths deviate too frequently from the strict scheme given by 1–2–4–8–16 years.

Therefore, the necessity remains to solve the aggregation problem endogenously on the basis of the interaction between different firms. Again using the concept of parametric resonance, such a model will be established for the inventory cycle.[6]

The dynamic behaviour of production and inventories on the firm level is given by the accelerator equation (cf. (9.4)):

$$DQ_n = w_{i,n}^2 (K_{i,n}^* - K_{i,n}), \qquad n = 1, 2, \ldots, U; \qquad (9.12)$$

that is: the firm n adjusts its production Q_n according to the deviation of its inventory stock $K_{i,n}$ from the desired level $K_{i,n}^*$.

A demand sector is introduced in order to close the model. For reasons of simplicity, the demand sector is regarded as homogeneous, and the desired level of inventories $K_{i,n}^*$ is assumed to be proportional to total demand Z_i:

$$K_{i,n}^* = k_{i,n} Z_i, \qquad n = 1, 2, \ldots, U, \qquad (9.13)$$

whereas demand itself changes according to the adjustment equation:

$$DZ_i = d_i(Z_i^* - Z_i). \qquad (9.14)$$

The desired level of demand Z_i^* is set equal to production:[7]

$$Z_i^* = Q = \sum_{n=1}^{U} Q_n \qquad (9.15)$$

Stability of demand implies small values of d_i; in the limit case $d_i = 0$ demand and all desired inventory levels are constant.

---

[6] The essential ideas could, *mutatis mutandis*, be applied also to the discussion of the equipment cycle.

[7] The model construction given here assumes zero savings and therefore a non-growing economy. However, this simplification is irrelevant with respect to the aggregation problem.

The main idea of the endogenous solution of the aggregation problem is as follows. The production behaviour of an individual firm n is influenced by the production of all other firms, and this influence is modelled as impact on the accelerator coefficient. The production of all other firms $Q - Q_n$ may be approximated by the aggregated production Q, and the influence depends on the actual state of the individual firm, characterized by its (positive or negative) inventory deficit $(K_{i,n}^* - K_{i,n})$.

The accelerator coefficient of the firm n is therefore given as

$$w_{i,n}^2 = w_{i,n}^2((K_{i,n}^* - K_{i,n}), Q). \tag{9.16}$$

Regarding this dependence, it may be assumed that the behaviour of the aggregate (i.e. total production) reflects general expectations. In a very simple formulation, high/low levels of production indicate optimistic/pessimistic expectations about future profits.[8] These expectations do not completely reverse the production plans of the individual firms, but they may reinforce (accelerate) or damp (retard) the realization of these plans. If a firm raises its production, because the actual inventory stock is smaller than the desired one, this rise will be greater/smaller if the level of total production is high/low. On the other hand, if the actual inventory stock exceeds the desired level and the firm reduces its production, the reduction will be greater/smaller in case of lower/higher level of total production.

TABLE 9.1   Influence of total production on the individual accelerator coefficients

	Variation of the accelerator coefficient [a]	Total production	
		$Q < 0$	$Q > 0$
Individual	$K_{i,n}^* - K_{i,n} < 0$	+	−
Firm n	$K_{i,n}^* - K_{i,n} > 0$	−	+

[a] All variables represent deviations from equilibrium.

A survey of these assumptions is shown in Table 9.1 The most elementary formal specification of these assumptions is given by

$$w_{i,n}^2(K_{i,n}^* - K_{i,n}, Q) = w_{0,i,n}^2 [1 + h_{i,n} \operatorname{sign}((K_{i,n}^* - K_{i,n})Q)], \tag{9.17}$$

where the function sign (.) is defined as follows:

$$\operatorname{sign}(x) = \begin{cases} -1 & \text{if } x < 0 \\ 0 & \text{if } x = 0 \\ 1 & \text{if } x > 0 \end{cases}. \tag{9.18}$$

[8] The importance of collective expectations as a psychological factor influencing economic cycles has been stressed by Spiethoff (1955).

Equation (9.18) implies that the actual value of the accelerator coefficient deviates from its mean $w^2_{0,i,n}$ by a certain percentage $h_{i,n}$ depending on the signs of the own inventory deficit and of total production. By this construction of the parameter variation, the essential one-sectoral character of the model remains unchanged as the accelerator coefficients are independent of the demand sector. Therefore the cycle-generating mechanism (which will be supposed to provide an endogenous solution to the aggregation problem) works independently of the question of the stability of demand.

An analytical treatment of large nonlinear systems such as given by (9.12)–(9.15) and (9.17) is hardly possible. Therefore, extensive numerical simulations have been performed in order to study the inherent properties. In what follows only a few examples are presented. In each case the results for varying parameters and constant parameters ($h_{i,n} = 0$) are compared graphically (solid and dashed lines, respectively); the plots of the firm cycles also include the related aggregates (dotted lines).

Figure 9.4 shows a system of five firms with the same accelerator coefficients but different initial phases. In the case of constant accelerator coefficients, the firms describe production cycles of constant amplitudes and keep their initial phase. The resulting aggregated cycles have constant amplitudes.

On the other hand, in the case of varying accelerator coefficients, the individual phases approach the phase of the aggregate (firms 1, 2, 4, and 5 in Fig. 9.4). Cycles having roughly the same phase as the aggregate show increasing amplitudes. Therefore, partly because of the synchronization effect, partly because of growing individual amplitudes, the amplitude of the aggregate cycle increases.

The example also contains a cyclical demand sector. The fluctuation of the demand is chosen to be small (parameter d_i) so that the influence of demand on the production sector may be neglected. In both cases (constant and varying accelerator coefficients) the demand cycle follows the production cycle with a phase difference of one-quarter of a period.

In the examples depicted in Fig. 9.5 and 9.6, a system of five firms with equal initial phases but different accelerator coefficients is considered. The accelerator coefficients deviate from their average by $0, \pm 10$ and ± 20 per cent and imply individually different cycles (periods about 90, 95, 100, 105, and 110 per cent of their average). In these examples the deviation of the frequencies is greater than in Fig. 9.1. Therefore, the extinction effect (for constant parameters) is stronger: the amplitude of the aggregated cycle decreases to about one-third of its initial value within less than three periods.

In the case of varying parameters the relatively slow cycles (firms 1 and 2) are accelerated and the relatively fast cycles (firms 4 and 5) are retarded. Moreover, the amplitudes of certain firms' cycles increase. The examples of Figs. 9.5 and 9.6 are different with respect to the strength of the interaction (parameter $H_{i,n} = 0.1$ and $H_{i,n} = 0.15$, respectively). In Fig. 9.5 the extinction effect is significantly smaller than in the case of constant parameters, but the

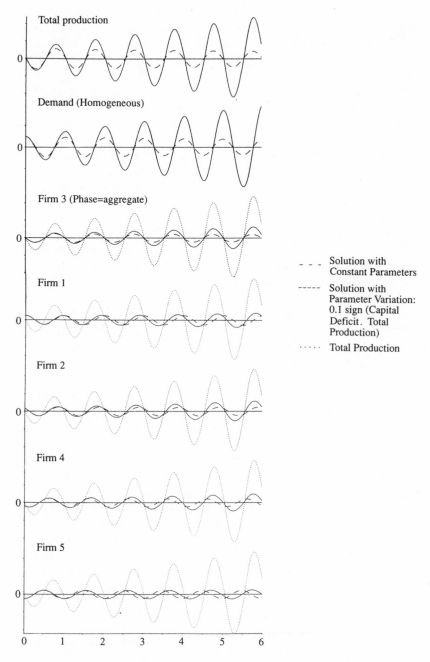

FIG. 9.4. Disaggregated inventory cycle model: five firms with the same accelerator coefficients and different initial phases

T. Weser

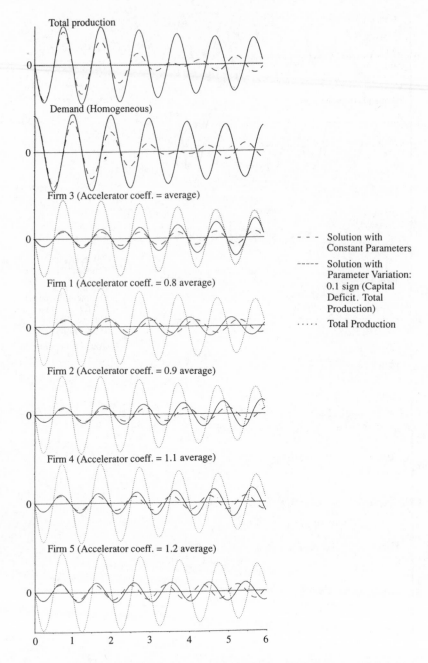

Total production

Demand (Homogeneous)

Firm 3 (Accelerator coeff. = average)

Firm 1 (Accelerator coeff. = 0.8 average)

Firm 2 (Accelerator coeff. = 0.9 average)

Firm 4 (Accelerator coeff. = 1.1 average)

Firm 5 (Accelerator coeff. = 1.2 average)

– – – Solution with Constant Parameters

----- Solution with Parameter Variation: 0.1 sign (Capital Deficit. Total Production)

····· Total Production

FIG. 9.5. Disaggregated inventory cycle model: five firms with the same initial phases and different accelerator coefficients

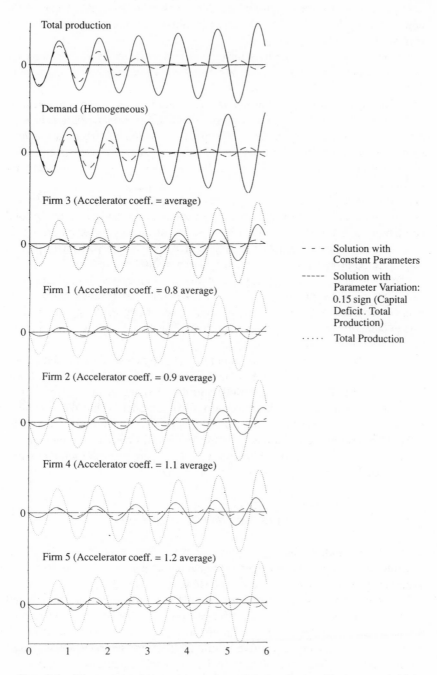

Fig. 9.6. Disaggregated inventory cycle model: five firms with the same initial phases and different accelerator coefficients

strength of the parameter variation is too weak to prevent the decay of the aggregated cycle. In Fig. 9.6 the mechanism is strong enough to enable an increase of the aggregated cycle.

Numerous further simulations have been performed in order to extend the investigation presented above (cf. Weser 1988). They may be summarized as follows:

1. The specification of the parameter variation as given by equation (9.17) has been replaced by a variety of other functional relationships. It was found that the most important features of the model (frequency adjustment, phase synchronization) are independent of the concrete specification of the parameter variation as long as the sign of the variation remains unchanged.

2. The concept of endogenous parameter variation has been transferred, *mutatis mutandis*, to a disaggregated equipment cycle model where the total equipment investment represents the influence of the aggregate on the single firm. The endogenous model of the aggregated equipment cycle thus obtained has the same properties as the inventory cycle model studied above.

The two alternative concepts (exogenous and endogenous parameter variation) for the equipment cycle can be combined as follows. Some firms behave according to one concept, the others according to the other concept. The explanationary value with respect to *SF 7* and *8* (cf. the discussion at the end of Section 4) remains unchanged.

3. The aggregated interaction model of both cycles (inventory and equipment cycle) presented in Chapter 4 has been studied in disaggregated form. The 2 : 1 relation of the cycle periods and the M-shape of production turned out as stable features. The basic novelty of this model is that the aggregate production, which determines the variation of certain accelerator coefficients, is M-shaped rather than sinoidal as in the simulations above. The aggregation mechanism is preserved, provided the sign of the parameter variation remains unchanged.

6. Summary and Conclusion

This chapter studied the aggregation problem for economic cycles. Is it possible to derive the existence of macroeconomic cycles rigorously from the dynamics of individual microeconomic subjects?

The traditional business cycle models are formulated on the aggregated level, and the economic literature does not provide a satisfactory solution to the aggregation problem. For linear models there are strong impossibility theorems. In this chapter a positive solution to the aggregation problem, based on elementary versions of Hillinger's economic cycle models of the SOA type, has been presented. These models are essentially one-sectoral and may be disaggregated directly.

The disaggregated reinterpretation of these models predicts cyclical behaviour on the firm level. In general, these cycles will be individually different and there is no simple argument for obtaining a macroeconomic cycle. If it is not postulated that all cycles have the same length and phase, it is necessary to provide an explicit aggregation mechanism.

Such a mechanism is suggested above. The basic idea consists in the concept of varying parameters and assumes that the accelerator coefficients of the individual firms fluctuate over the business cycle. The parameter variations may be modelled in two ways. If they are assumed to be exogenously given (for example as a result of an aggregated cycle which is not explained within the model), some individual cycles are stimulated resonantly and certain periods and phases are distinguished. The resulting aggregated cycle has the double period and a certain phase relation with respect to the existing cycle. Hence strong predictions about different coexisting cycles are obtained which correspond to empirical observations which have long been noted in the literature. For example, an (exogenous) four-year inventory cycle will give rise to an aggregated eight-year equipment cycle with a phase relation corresponding to a M-shaped movement of total production.

If the variation of the accelerator coefficients is endogenously formulated, a closed solution to the aggregation problem is obtained. The underlying assumptions are elementary. The firm behaviour that has been predicted by the models with constant parameters is slightly modified under the influence of general expectations, where these expectations are represented by a suitable aggregate (for example total production). Further investigations indicate that both exogenous and endogenous parameter variation can be combined without difficulty.

Both the formal problem of the aggregation of cycles and the mathematical method employed for solving it are to our knowledge novel in economics and may find applications in other contexts.

References

Bober, S. (1968), *The Economics of Cycles and Growth*, John Wiley, New York.

Bogoliubov, N. N., and Mitropolsky, Y. A. (1961), *Asymptotic Methods in the Theory of Non-linear Oscillations*, Gordon & Breach, New York.

Britton, A. (1986), *The Trade Cycle in Britain*, Cambridge University Press.

Goodwin, R. M. (1983), 'Disaggregating models of fluctuating growth', in R. M. Goodwin, M. Krüger, and A. Vercelli (eds.), *Nonlinear Models of Fluctuating Growth*, International Symposium, Siena. Reprinted in *Lecture Notes in Economics and Mathematical Systems*, no. 228, Springer, Berlin, 1984.

Green, H. A. J. (1964), *Aggregation in Economic Analysis*, Princeton University Press.

Hansen, A. H. (1941), *Fiscal Policy and Business Cycles*, W. W. Norton, New York.

Hicks, J. R. (1950), *A Contribution to the Theory of the Trade Cycle*, Oxford University Press.

Hillinger, C. (1966), 'An econometric model of mild business cycles', *Manchester School of Economics and Social Studies*, 34 : 269–84.

—— (1986), 'Inventory cycle and equipment cycle interaction', in A. Chikan (ed.), *Inventories in Theory and Practice: Proceedings of the 3rd International Symposium on Inventories, Budapest, 1984*, Elsevier, Amsterdam.

—— and Weser, T. (1988), 'Aggregation and parametric resonance in business cycle theory', in A. Chikan (ed.), *Proceedings of the 4th International Symposium on Inventories, Wesleyan University, 1987*, Elsevier, Amsterdam.

Matthews, R. C. O. (1959), *The Business Cycle*, University of Chicago Press.

Metzler, L. A. (1941), 'The nature and stability of inventory cycles', *Review of Economic Statistics*, 23(3) : 113–29.

Minorsky, N. (1962), *Non-linear Oscillations*, Van Nostrand, New York.

Samuelson, P. A. (1939), 'Interaction between the multiplier analysis and the principle of acceleration', *Review of Economic Statistics*, 21(2) : 75–8.

—— (1973), *Economics*, 8th edn., McGraw-Hill, New York.

Schlicht, E. (1985), *Isolation and Aggregation in Economics*, Springer, Berlin.

Spiethoff, A. (1955), *Die wirtschaftlichen Wechsellagen*, Mohr, Tübingen; see also A. Schweitzer, *Spiethoff's Theory of the Business Cycle*, University of Wyoming Publications, Laramie, 8 : 1–30 and references therein, 1941.

Theil, H. (1965), *Linear Aggregation of Economic Relations*, North-Holland, Amsterdam.

van Daal, J., and Merkies, A. H. Q. M. (1984), *Aggregation in Economic Research*, Reidel, Dordrecht.

Weser, T. (1988), 'Das Aggregationsproblem in der Konjunkturtheorie', Ph.D. thesis, University of Munich.

Wilson, L. L. (1964), *Catalogue of cycles*, i, Foundation for the Study of Cycles, Pittsburgh, Pa.

Index